PRAISE FOR *FDR'S FUNERAL TRAIN*

...ra revives a long-forgotten event with precision and pathos, allowing
...ers a coveted Pullman berth for a ride through three of this coun-
...darkest yet most formative days."
—Gay Talese, author of *A Writer's Life*

...ert Klara's *FDR's Funeral Train* is a well-written and vivid account of
...rica's greatest national mourning since Abraham Lincoln was shot.
E...ry page here is illuminating. At times Klara practically transports the
r...back to 1945. A major new contribution to U.S. history."
—Douglas Brinkley, author of *The Wilderness Warrior:
Theodore Roosevelt and the Crusade for America*

"...Funeral Train* is a fascinating tale well told. Hop aboard with the
ski... storyteller Robert Klara. You'll be glad you did."
—James Bradley, author of *Flags of our Fathers* and *Flyboys*

...e in 1945, friend or enemy, was unmoved by the death of Franklin
...sevelt, after his dozen critical years in the White House. *FDR's
...l Train* vividly recalls the nerve-racking week behind the head-
...when his family and his government rose above a trainload of per-
...problems to help the nation across the chasm left by his demise.
...citing addition to the Roosevelt bookshelf, Klara's book is over-
...ng with the stuff that every history reader craves—fresh, original
research."
—Julie Fenster, author of *The Case of Abraham
Lincoln* and *FDR's Shadow*

"With great skill and riveting detail, Robert Klara uses a three-day train
journey to provide readers with a fascinating glimpse into the inner
workings of the Washington elite in the d... f... FDR's death. This
fast-paced narrativ... ...plenty of intrigue.

It also manages to shed new light on a critical moment in our nation's history."

—Steve Gillon, author of *10 Days That Unexpectedly Changed America* and Resident Historian, The History Channel

"In the manner of Bob Greene's *Once Upon a Town* or Jody Rosen's *White Christmas*, similar, bite-sized slices of World War II—era home-front history, Klara charms as he informs. A little gem."

—*Kirkus Reviews* (starred review)

"An intriguing account of FDR's last journey and a must read for all those still caught up in the romance and mystery of rail travel."

—David B Woolner, Senior Fellow, Roosevelt Institute and Associate Professor of History, Marist College

"A riveting, sumptuously detailed look inside a luxurious, mysterious private train swaying from one presidency to another—the picture windows in its last car showcasing a bronze coffin to thousands of trackside mourners ignorant of the vivid tensions in the cars ahead."

—John Stilgoe, Robert and Lois Orchard Professor in the History of Landscape, Harvard University and author of *Outside Lies Magic: Discovering History and Inspiration in Ordinary Places*

"No fan of FDR and his presidency can afford to pass up this book. Klara takes you inside FDR's funeral train, and into the minds and hearts of those who made the president's last journey with him. Klara offers a unique, never-before-told perspective on the sudden transfer of power, the players who wanted to grab some of that power, and the widow whose grief was tinged with the bitter taste of betrayal. A remarkable story by a true storyteller."

—Lorraine Diehl, author of *The Late, Great Pennsylvania Station*

FDR's FUNERAL TRAIN

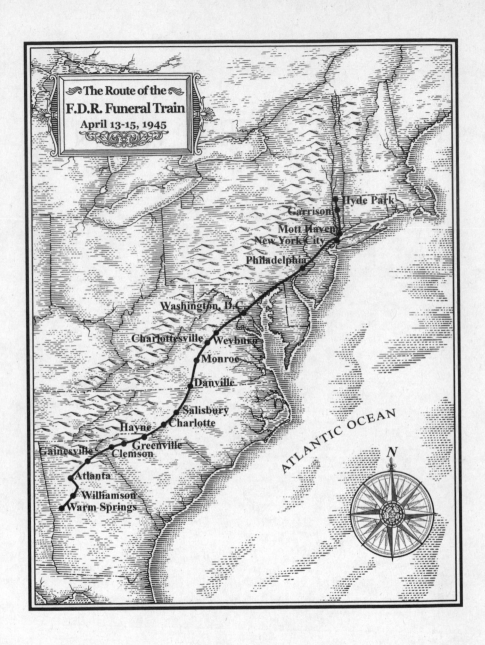

The Route of the
F.D.R. Funeral Train
April 13-15, 1945

Hyde Park
Garrison
Mott Haven
New York City
Philadelphia
Washington, D.C.
Charlottesville   Weyburn
Monroe
Danville
Salisbury
Hayne   Charlotte
Greenville
Gainesville   Clemson
Atlanta
Williamson
Warm Springs

ATLANTIC OCEAN

N

FDR's FUNERAL TRAIN

A BETRAYED WIDOW,
A SOVIET SPY, AND
A PRESIDENCY IN
THE BALANCE

ROBERT KLARA

The frontispiece map is created by Steven Noble and is reproduced by permission.

FDR's FUNERAL TRAIN
Copyright © Robert Klara, 2010.

First published in hardcover in 2010 by
PALGRAVE MACMILLAN®
in the United States—a division of St. Martin's Press LLC,
175 Fifth Avenue, New York, NY 10010.

Where this book is distributed in the UK, Europe and the rest of the world,
this is by Palgrave Macmillan, a division of Macmillan Publishers Limited,
registered in England, company number 785998, of Houndmills,
Basingstoke, Hampshire RG21 6XS.

Palgrave Macmillan is the global academic imprint of the above companies
and has companies and representatives throughout the world.

Palgrave® and Macmillan® are registered trademarks in the United States,
the United Kingdom, Europe and other countries.

ISBN: 978–0–230–10803–5

Library of Congress Cataloging-in-Publication Data

Klara, Robert.
    FDR's funeral train : a betrayed widow, a Soviet spy, and a presidency
in the balance / Robert Klara.
        p. cm.
    ISBN 978–0–230–61914–2 (hardback)
    (paperback ISBN: 978–0–230–10803–5)
    1. Roosevelt, Franklin D. (Franklin Delano), 1882–1945—Death and
burial. 2. Funeral rites and ceremonies—United States—History—20th
century. 3. Railroad travel—United States—History—20th century.
4. Roosevelt, Eleanor, 1884–1962. 5. Spies—Soviet Union—Biography
6. Truman, Harry S., 1884–1972. 7. United States—Politics and
government—1933–1945. 8. World War, 1939–1945—United States.
I. Title.

E807.K56 2010
973.917092—dc22   2009047755

A catalogue record of the book is available from the British Library.

Design by Newgen Imaging Systems (P) Ltd., Chennai, India.

First PALGRAVE MACMILLAN paperback edition: July 2011

10 9 8 7 6 5 4 3 2 1

Printed in the United States of America.

For my father

"There is something almost terrifying in the transition of a presidential train into a funeral train."
                    —Thomas F. Reynolds, *Chicago Sun*, April 14, 1945

CONTENTS

FOREWORD

*L*ate into the afternoon of Thursday, March 29, 1945, the warm, languid breezes blowing off the Tidal Basin carried with them the only promise that Washington, D.C., ever entirely keeps: a summer of voracious humidity. But spring still had a few weeks left; this afternoon's haze was slight. As the setting sun applied its amber brushstrokes to the limestone of the Bureau of Engraving and Printing, a motorcade turned off 14th Street and made a left onto D, slipping behind the Bureau's new Annex building. There it disappeared into a rusty fan of railroad tracks that branched from the main line as it curved eastward off the Potomac bridge. The cars' destination was a spur track and platform, used mostly for the offloading of ink barrels and bolts of the cotton-linen weave that, once they had been spooled into the presses upstairs, would slip away as sheets of United States currency.

The loading platform possessed a second purpose, however, a top-secret one[1]—one that became apparent as the limousines' engines settled down to an even purr beneath their long hoods and the Secret Service men stepped from the running boards, their hard-soled shoes and the sounds of slamming doors echoing down the concrete platform. Drawn up alongside the idling cluster of automobiles was a train, but this was no string of freight cars. Six coffee-green Pullmans, glistening from a recent bath in the yards, lined up in the shadows. Through the windows, uniformed men could be seen moving up and down the aisles. The preparation for this trip had been under way for several hours. Franklin Delano Roosevelt was leaving town.

The elaborate process of transporting the president began with a telephone call from the White House placed by a man named Dewey Long, a onetime Department of Agriculture employee whose mastery of detailed arrangements had landed him the job of coordinating Roosevelt's travels. After conferring with Mike Reilly, the White House chief of the Secret Service, Long had called the railroad.[2] As Roosevelt's train usually moved over more than one line, the carriers— the B&O, Southern, and Pennsylvania most commonly—had long ago suspended their usual competitiveness and worked in unison to get the president where he needed to go. Long usually directed his first call to Daniel Moorman, the B&O's general passenger agent in Washington. (With Moorman in charge, the presidential party could expect, as the staff often termed it, a "happy train" with an indulgent menu.[3]) For a trip anywhere south of D.C., the phone would also ring on the desk of Luther Thomas, assistant to the Southern's vice president, a dapper man with graying temples and a pocket kerchief, whose endless responsibilities included dispatching the railroad's own police force.[4] Dewey Long's receiver was hardly back in its hook when the Southern's men—maintenance crews, division superintendents, foremen, and trainmasters—began to mobilize. Within the hour, the railroad's police would begin taking up posts at overpasses and junctions. Plainclothesmen would appear at stations along the route, peering over broadsheets and watching for anyone who struck them as suspicious.[5] Track gangs would begin a slow, watchful trek by foot down every mile of track that the president's train would travel, checking for broken rails and locking switches as they went.[6] Soon dispatchers would be overriding the schedules for all passenger trains on the designated route, making sure that none preceded or followed the chief executive's train by at least thirty minutes. Finally, a pilot locomotive would prepare to depart, solo, a mile ahead of the president, a final and formidable bulwark against any trouble.[7]

There were times, not long ago, when yardmen had orders to assemble an entire decoy train and send it up the line, all in an effort to confuse and foil saboteurs.[8] The fears that led to maneuvering like this were not altogether absurd. It was wartime, and the memory of the December 7, 1941, surprise attack at Pearl Harbor still festered. There had been talk of spies in Washington, some even operating inside the White House itself. Allowing the presidential train to depart from nearby Union Station, one of the busiest railroad terminals in America, was to leave the commander in chief open to plain view. On this afternoon, the United States had been at war for 1,208 days. For that entire time, it had also been under the leadership of one man, the one whose six foot, three-inch frame Mike Reilly now lifted through the rear door of the presidential limousine (the president's favorite—a four-ton, blue Packard convertible[9]) and into a wooden wheelchair. With Reilly pushing, the rubberized wheels trundled toward a private Pullman car at the rear of the train. The car's name was *Ferdinand Magellan*.

Franklin Roosevelt had just turned sixty-three. An attack of poliomyelitis had left him paralyzed from the waist down for twenty-four of those years. Polio was part of the reason why Mike Reilly had chosen this secret train platform for the chief executive's departures—FDR's paralysis had been largely concealed from public view with the cooperation of a gentlemanly press corps. But polio was not responsible for the president's pallid skin and sagging shoulders as he rose to the *Magellan*'s open vestibule via a hydraulic lift anchored to the car's underframe. Nor was it—clinically, at least—the grueling "Big Three" meeting with Churchill and Stalin at Yalta, a round trip of 14,000 miles, from which Roosevelt recently returned looking haggard, frail, and bloodless.

The culprit was hypertensive heart disease. Under mounting pressure from FDR's daughter, Anna, FDR's personal physician, Admiral Ross McIntire, had reluctantly sent his charge for a workup with Dr. Howard G. Bruenn, a cardiologist at Bethesda Naval Hospital.[10] Bruenn's first examination of the president the previous March revealed the true nature of a problem that Dr. McIntire had been whitewashing with diagnoses including bronchitis, a head cold, and a need for sunshine.[11] When Bruenn removed the pressure cuff from Roosevelt's arm as recently as December 6, he'd tallied a reading of 260/150, and such stratospheric numbers, it had emerged, were hardly unusual for Roosevelt. Nor was the problem that faced every cardiologist of the time: No medications existed to reduce extreme blood pressure on the body's arterial walls. As Bruenn would later attest, about all the president could do was lose weight, sleep, and limit his stress. In the end, though, he had little to do but wait for what Bruenn termed a "pop," a neat but ghastly euphemism for a stroke or a vascular hemorrhage.[12]

Shortly before the president's motorcade had left the White House, butler Alonzo Fields had overheard fellow staffer John Mays do something rare for a doorman—voice his opinion. As Admiral McIntire passed, Mays had taken the doctor aside. "I know it is none of my business, sir," the doorman whispered. "But the President looks very bad to me. Don't you think you should have gone with him?"

"I don't think he'll need me," McIntire answered, not unkindly. "However, if it will make you feel any better, I have assigned the Navy's top man [Dr. Bruenn] to go with him." McIntire paused, then said of the president: "I am sure he will come back a different man."[13]

With the exception of Dr. Bruenn and Anna Roosevelt, none of the presidential entourage assembled on the platform beneath the Bureau of Engraving and Printing on this fading afternoon knew about the president's specific condition. What they did know was what they could see, and that was that their chief needed a rest, desperately. Those who later would write about this trip would recall a shared feeling of hope—albeit a taut, nervous hope—that it would return the old FDR to them, the one whose jaunty manner and sparkling smile had recently disappeared beneath a drawn face and hands that shook so badly he could hardly get a lit match to the tip of his cigarette. The chief's all-too-apparent exhaustion was why, in a few more minutes, once the cooks had finished stocking the dining car's pantries and the conductor had given his pocket watch a final glimpse before stepping aboard, this train would be heading south.

The train was bound for a hamlet outside Atlanta known as Warm Springs, a sleepy, rural resort that drew thousands of polio patients to thermal pools whose warmth and high mineral content were known to add buoyancy to atrophied legs. It was also, aside from his boyhood home in Hyde Park, New York, the president's favorite place in the world. On the hilly, secluded grounds of Warm Springs, a man accustomed to silk bow ties and walnut-paneled libraries lived in a simple plank cottage built on a foundation of fieldstones. The press called the place "the Little White House."[14]

Integral to the small miracle of coordination and secrecy required to prepare the presidential train, even for a short trip like this one, were code words. "U.S. 1" was the name that the Secret Service preferred over *Ferdinand Magellan*, whose name didn't appear anywhere on the car's ⅝-inch-thick steel skin. There was "The Informer," the name coined for FDR's Scottie dog, Fala, who accompanied the chief everywhere he went and could be counted on to blow his cover.[15] Finally, there was the code word for the train itself: POTUS. The clunky and undignified ring to the acronym couldn't have been more at variance with the consequence of its namesake: President of the United States. On a superintendent's lips or on a brass-pounder's key, a single mention of POTUS could bring a railroad's entire system to a halt, diverting every eye, ear, and hand to the safe conduction of the president over the high iron.

Roosevelt's staffers climbed out of the motorcade and made their way to the ten-car train, toting along all the materials required to conduct the presidency some 720 miles away from Pennsylvania Avenue. Grace Tully, Roosevelt's trusted secretary, recalled taking a "tremendous stack of letters and bills" in addition to "the usual leisure-time paraphernalia, [FDR's] stamp collection, catalogue and equipment."[16] Someone hoisted aboard a huge wooden box stuffed with books, which the president intended to sort and autograph. Although Tully would not think much of it at the time, she recalled later that Roosevelt twice referred to the wooden box of books as a "coffin."[17] Tully's typist, Dorothy Brady, accompanied her. Presidential assistant and trusted letter writer William Hassett, functioning as press secretary in place of Steve Early, who would be staying behind, walked toward the train along with his secretary, Alice Winegar. Louise Hackmeister—"Hacky," as everyone knew her—went along to handle the telephone switchboard once the train reached Georgia.

Also along for this trip were two passengers who had no official titles or duties but upon whom the weary president had become as dependent as he was on Dr. Bruenn: Laura "Polly" Delano and Margaret "Daisy" Suckley, two Roosevelt cousins who had recently come down from Hyde Park for no other purpose than to keep the president company. With First Lady Eleanor Roosevelt so often away, delivering lectures and doing the sort of domestic glad-handing that FDR often could not do himself, that duty had of late been taken up full time by Anna Roosevelt. But she, too, would be staying behind for this trip. Her six-year-old son, Johnny, was at Walter Reed Army Medical Center with a voracious glandular infection. The doctors were giving the boy penicillin, a potent and experimental new drug used only in serious cases.[18]

Dewey Long grabbed the handrails and trotted up into one of the Pullmans, as did Lieutenant Commander George Fox, who sometimes gave rubdowns to the president. Leighton McCarthy, the Canadian ambassador who had somehow also found the time to be a trustee of Warm Springs, was along for the trip, too, as was Toinette "Toi" Bachelder, who had once been a patient of the Springs until FDR hired her as an assistant on his White House staff. Three seasoned reporters (dubbed the "Three Musketeers") would be riding with POTUS, as they usually did: Harold Oliver of the Associated Press, Robert Nixon from the International News Service, and Merriman Smith from the United Press. For the newsmen, duty on the chief's train wasn't just a plum assignment, it was mostly downtime; little important news broke while the president was at Warm Springs.

"It was a smaller party than usual," as Tully recalled, but it was still a considerable group.[19] Representatives from the Southern Railway and from the Pullman Company—along to attend to such details as FDR's preference for pheasant and terrapin on the menu and his insistence that the train's speed stay below 30 miles per hour, allowing him to wheel himself around without having to anchor his wheelchair[20]— dropped their suitcases in the carpeted aisles of the sleeper *Imperator*. The Secret Service detail made its way down to its own Pullman, the sleeper/lounge *Conneaut*. The *Conneaut* was always coupled one up from the *Ferdinand Magellan* with its lounge section facing aft so the agents could keep an eye on FDR's car, a task aided considerably by the lounge car's large observation windows.

The non–Secret Service passengers found compartments—or, if they were of a loftier rank, staterooms—aboard the Pullmans *Glen Doll* and *Wordsworth*. But the enviable quarters were aboard the *Hillcrest Club*, which, in addition to its eight spacious rooms, harbored a lounge at one end with soft, low chairs perfect for reading in and wooden tables just big enough for a game of cards. Coupled one up from the *Conneaut*, Southern Railway dining car No. 3155 served everybody on its linen-draped tables except, of course, for the president, who was served his meals in the *Ferdinand Magellan*'s dining room on the presidential china, kept in four cabinets with felt-lined drawers.[21]

A thin, distinguished-looking black man named Fred Fair did the serving, and just about everything else aboard the *Magellan*. Attired in his white Pullman jacket, Fair was the one man who never left the president's car, even when it idled between trips in the forgotten corners of railroad yards for weeks at a time. Born in 1898, Fair knew the *Magellan* and its countless quirky features: the cigar holders in the bathrooms, the fact that the car's rear door opened only from the inside. Fair had once saved a Secret Service agent trapped out on the vestibule from asphyxiating just as POTUS entered a smoke-filled tunnel.[22] A repository of countless overheard secrets, Fred Fair still remembered how embarrassed FDR had been the day the two had first met, years before, when "the Boss"—as most everyone called FDR, including those who did not work for him—had fished in this pockets for change but found them empty. "I want to tip these people," FDR had whispered to an aide.[23] The leader of the free world who was concerned about tipping a Pullman porter—that was the president that Fred Fair knew.

While the trusted porter darted around the car, making final preparations, the Army's communications men were warming up the equipment inside B&O car No. 1401, a rolling nerve center tucked up near the locomotives. Converted from an ordinary baggage car by the White House Signal Detachment in 1942, the No. 1401 had more rivets in its skin than a suspension bridge. Stuffing its insides were two Federal BC-339 transmitters, several 50-watt FM transmitters, cipher machines, and a gaggle of telephone and teletype equipment, all ready to keep the Boss connected to any office, embassy, or house of state the world over.[24]

Suddenly the sound of scraping metal split the air as men slid massive ramps down from the deck of B&O baggage car No. 748. One by one, the limousines dropped into gear and rumbled up the ramps into the cavernous darkness of the railroad car. The maneuver required both planning and fancy clutch work, but after a few minutes four of the cars—including at least one of the Secret Service's 1938 Cadillacs, rolling arsenals stuffed with pistols and ammunition boxes—rested inside the railroad car, their chrome bumpers just inches apart. No. 748 was an end-loader; once its heavy doors were closed and latched, the pair of locomotives could back down and couple to the train.[25]

Though she would be staying in Washington to be with her sick boy, Anna had come to see her father, and his train, off. But first, she took Grace Tully aside to speak to her in private. "Grace," she said, "I wish you would try to have Father work a little bit each day on his mail. If he doesn't, he will get terribly behind and I think it is good to keep him busy."[26]

It was a strange request. Tully had pinned her hopes on this trip rejuvenating the president as Warm Springs had done so many times in the past. The retreat was an opportunity for less work, not more of it. But Anna, like everyone else who'd grown worried about the president's increasingly haggard appearance, had been groping for a solution, the magic blend of the rest FDR needed and the complexities of his office that he'd once thrived on, to somehow rekindle her father's effervescence and kinetic charm. Anna had watched her father's inexorable decline, perceived Bruenn's helplessness to halt it, and was desperate.

As the Magellan's elevator reached the deck of the car, someone—probably FDR's longtime valet, a refrigerator-size black man named Arthur Prettyman—threw his weight into pulling open the rear door. A welcome, air-conditioned breeze rushed through the gap. FDR must have smiled; immobile legs he could handle, but the heat of Washington—in evidence even on this March day—was known to wither the president's spirits. The door closed as heavily as it had opened; it weighed 1,500 pounds.[27]

Everything on the *Ferdinand Magellan* weighed too much, but that had been the idea. Three years earlier, during the dark, first days of the war, Steve Early and Mike Reilly had decided that it would not do to have the president of the United States traveling around in an ordinary Pullman. At the time, seven Pullmans, all built in 1929 as part of the same lot, had formed the presidential railroad fleet. Early and Reilly chose the *Ferdinand Magellan* to be sent to Pullman's Calumet shops outside Chicago for a special overhaul.

Workers stripped the *Magellan* down to its ribs, reinforced its frame, and added armor plating and three-inch-thick bulletproof glass. It was said that the *Magellan* was strong enough to withstand a fall of over a hundred feet from a railroad trestle without telescoping.[28] If anyone aboard happened to survive such a plummet, roof hatchways offered an escape (though not, ironically, for a paralyzed president). The *Ferdinand Magellan* tipped the scales at over 142 tons; other Pullman cars of its vintage weighed only 80. It was a boulder, or more like an entire mountain; it was a literal rolling fortress with a president inside. One locomotive engineer said that the *Magellan* "drag[ged] like a brick bat on the tail of a kite."[29] Because of the car's weight, trainmen usually were forced to add an extra locomotive up front to make sure that POTUS could make it over the steep grades.

While the *Magellan*'s interior was spare compared to the lavish Victorian clutter that ran riot within the White House, the Pullman was plenty fancy. Entering through the vestibule's heavy door, the visitor stepped into an observation lounge packed with stuffed, velvety armchairs in shades of rust, green, and blue. Draperies hung from each of the room's eight windows. Gleaming deco ashtrays sprouted like chrome fountains from the carpeted floor.

A settee stood against the bulkhead that gave onto a two-foot-wide corridor on the port side that stretched past four staterooms, each with a wooden door—"A" through "D" as one walked forward. Of all the rooms, "C" was the biggest. It was the president's room. Fitted with a highboy dresser, chair, telephone, and eagle-print bedspread, it wore a coat of baby blue paint, cheered further by cream-white curtains. The corridor's opposite end opened onto a large meeting room that doubled as a dining area. This room was, in both spirit and intent, a rolling Oval Office and, except for its rectangular shape, it looked the part. Panels of richly carved limed oak covered the walls below an ivory-colored ceiling accented in gold. An American flag on a freestanding pole graced one corner. Dominating the room was a mahogany table large enough to fit eight chairs, each upholstered in a satin damask of gold and green stripes. At night, light spilling from the gold wall sconces suffused the space in an amber glow.[30]

As the populist president knew well, his Pullman was far nicer than the spaces most Americans called home, and he treasured the car accordingly, never seeming to lose the boyish thrill he felt each time he rode in it. The *Magellan* belonged, technically, to the Association of American Railroads, but it was never presumed to be anything other than the Boss's car.

He'd christened the Pullman himself a few days shy of Christmas 1942. Half-sunk destroyers still jutted from oil slicks at Pearl Harbor, and FDR—secreted to the basement platform in the bowels of the Engraving and Printing building—had hardly grown used to the mania over his safety. Hassett had been aboard that night and later wrote that "immediately upon coming aboard, the President inspected the car from end to end and gave it his approval."[31] Daisy Suckley related to her diary: "Great excitement over the new car. Decoration is grey-blue & tan—Very nice. Fala tried all the chairs & decided he liked the one with the arms upholstered."[32]

Now, on this fading March afternoon in 1945, Roosevelt had boarded his beloved Pullman once more. Like everyone else aboard, Fred Fair noticed that FDR looked tired, but he didn't appear as troubled by the president's appearance as the others. The porter's opinion was based largely on Admiral McIntire—specifically, his absence. If Mr. Roosevelt's own doctor wasn't coming, Fair reasoned, how bad could things be?[33] Still, there were obvious signs of trouble that did not require a Navy physician to notice. In earlier, easier times, the president would have stayed in the *Ferdinand Magellan's* observation lounge to play cards and mix his favorite cocktail (Old Fashioneds—good and strong) as he, Fala, and their guests sank into the armchairs. But the familiar sound of ice dropping into tumblers would not be heard on this trip. Wheeled down the narrow corridor, FDR stopped at the door to bedroom "C," where, between the cool cotton sheets, he promptly went to sleep.[34]

It was time to go. The porters dropped and locked the vestibule hatchways as the first, tentative tugs of the engines coaxed a rusty protest from the train's wheel trucks. The brakes relinquished their grip and POTUS snaked out onto the Maryland Avenue main line, following the bend to the southwest that took the train onto the Potomac River bridge. As the engines turned their noses toward the setting sun, gold light danced along the string of windows and across the wide planks of riveted steel that wore a dignified coat of Pullman green. Inside, communications men donned headphones, journalists unpacked typewriters, dining-car cooks prepared to start serving dinner, and a lone black Scottie whose silver collar tag read "I belong to the President"[35] made himself comfortable in the *Magellan's* lounge.

The evening of Thursday, March 29, 1945, would be the last time POTUS carried a living Franklin Delano Roosevelt. Upon its return two weeks later—to the same city, via the same tracks, made up of the same cars—it would carry the thirty-second president's mortal remains. In the newspapers, it would no longer be POTUS, or "Roosevelt's train" or "the Presidential Special." It would be, simply, "the funeral train."

This is the story of that train.

ONE

PINE MOUNTAIN

On the afternoon of March 30, following the overnight trip from Washington, POTUS had rounded the tight bend at Warm Springs, eighty-four miles south of Atlanta. The town perched along a branch line so insignificant it resembled a piece of lint on the Southern Railway's sprawling route map. Long before the clang of the locomotive's brass bell could be heard, a distant plume of smoke over the treetops announced the train's approach. POTUS's engineer touched the throttle gently to summon the steam needed to nudge the over-weight *Magellan* up the slight grade by the depot.[1] The ten cars rumbled through, slowing up until the train's tail was even with the road crossing. Then the brakes gripped the wheels tight. A mighty hiss followed as the reservoirs spat their pressurized air into the dirt. FDR had arrived in the sleepy Georgia hamlet for the forty-first time.[2] It was Good Friday.

Here, in the yard beside the station, there was plenty of room for bystanders. For locals, the president's arrival was always a special occasion, familiar as it had become. Helped to his Pullman's vestibule, FDR would never fail to doff his fedora and smile at his assembled "neighbors," a term Roosevelt essentially applied to everyone inside the Georgia state line. But today it would be different. It was a ghost's face that appeared in the shadow of the *Magellan*'s open doorway. Regulars in the crowd could tell right away that something was wrong.[3]

Pushed in his wheelchair toward the waiting automobiles, Roosevelt joggled like a rag doll, and as Mike Reilly lifted him into the car, he landed as though he were a wet sandbag.[4] The Secret Service chief, who'd grown accustomed to the president's summoning the tremendous strength he had built up in his shoulders to literally vault from wheelchair to auto-mobile, was disturbed.[5]

Reilly deposited the president into the car's seat—not the passenger one, but the driver's. Roosevelt kept his royal-blue 1938 Ford coupe permanently garaged down in Warm Springs (its Georgia plates read "F.D.R.1"[6]). FDR soaked the carburetor with gasoline and the little car took off, roaring up the road lined with wild violets and dogwoods, the Secret Service phaeton hot on his tail. Watching him fly up the hill, some in the crowd felt a sense of relief. The president had looked frail, but he was the same road demon he'd always been.[7]

"When I'm worn out," Roosevelt had told his doctors in 1928, "I'll come back to Warm Springs. In a few days I'll be like new again."[8] FDR had uttered those words when his bid for the New York governor's mansion signaled the start of his political career and the end of his efforts to rehabilitate his legs. Yet Roosevelt had called it right: Warm Springs—a gone-to-seed Victorian resort he'd discovered in 1924 and purchased outright two years later—did somehow always make him new again.

Though Roosevelt's first dip in the property's thermal waters had imbued only a fleeting sense of buoyancy to his shrunken legs, some-thing about the place with its pine-scented air possessed the power to restore the rest of him. His Wall Street friends scoffed when Roosevelt parted with two-thirds of his personal fortune to incorporate Warm Springs as a foundation and open it as a treatment center for polio vic-tims.[9] They didn't understand that the dividends FDR had in mind would not be paid in cash.

After buying the land, Roosevelt selected a hilltop near Georgia Hall, the property's old hotel, and raised a simple cottage of white clapboard. Hanging from a chain over the cottage's front door was a ship's lantern, lit only when the president was in residence. FDR had insisted on a simple, rustic décor of hook rugs and knotty-pine furniture. Measuring fifty-four feet at its widest point, the cabin was shorter than the Pullman car that would bring him there. Roosevelt adored the place.

Just prior to the president's arrival from Washington on that spring Friday of 1945, Daisy Bonner, a local cook who had prepared each and every meal for FDR when he was in Georgia,[10] had climbed up to the empty cottage to stock the kitchen and air the rooms out. As Bonner stepped inside, she gasped at the sudden sound of wings beating over her head. A tiny, snow-white bird was fluttering around up at the ceiling. Bonner had no idea how the creature had gotten in. It was, she'd say later, a sign.[11]

Elizabeth Shoumatoff, Russian-born portraitist of America's aristocracy, saw the president seated in the back of his parked limousine outside a corner drugstore in Greenville, Georgia, and her heart sank. The ebullient man she'd painted at the White House in the spring of 1943 could not possibly be the pale, diminished one before her now, the evening of April 9, eleven days into his vacation in Georgia. Though the night air was warm, Roosevelt had wrapped himself in his heavy Navy cape. He was sipping a Coca-Cola, doing his best to smile. The Russian gazed at the president she had just traveled hundreds of miles to paint a second time. "How," Shoumatoff thought, "can I make a portrait of such a sick man?"[12] Lucy Rutherfurd had been responsible for setting up the whole thing, but if Shoumatoff blamed her longtime friend for her predicament, she also knew the importance of Lucy's being here—of their *both* being here. "He is thin and frail," Rutherfurd had warned, weeks earlier. "But there is something about his face that shows more the way he looked when he was young."[13]

No woman would have known better. The youthful, handsome countenance of Franklin Roosevelt had been etched into the mind of Lucy Mercer Rutherfurd from their first meeting, when he was the newly minted assistant secretary of the U.S. Navy and his wife needed an appointments secretary.

During the winter of 1914, the Roosevelts were new to Washington and overwhelmed by the social demands that went with Franklin's title, so they were grateful for the young, polished, and well-connected Lucy Mercer. Her easy laugh and statuesque beauty charmed the Roosevelt children—but charmed their father even more. It is not certain exactly when the romantic affair began, but by September 1918, it had met its abrupt end. With World War I winding down in Europe, Franklin had returned home, ill with pneumonia, from an inspection tour of the front lines in France. Unpacking his trunks, Eleanor discovered a hidden cache of love letters from Lucy. Though she had suspected her husband's duplicity for some time, Eleanor was devastated by the evidence that proved it. She later wrote that at that moment, "the bottom dropped out of my own particular world."[14]

Divorce—viewed in those days with nearly as much disdain as adultery—was the remedy Eleanor had initially demanded. But the social shame of marital dissolution would not only have meant the end of FDR's burgeoning political career, it would have cost him his inheritance, as his mother, Sara Delano, had made icily clear.[15] So from 1918 onward, Franklin and Eleanor Roosevelt remained husband and wife on paper and for the sake of press photographers. The secret terms that permitted FDR to keep both his public career and his solvency included his agreeing never to see Lucy Mercer again.

Mercer went on to marry the rich but elderly Winthrop Rutherfurd, and Franklin, whose intimate relations with his wife ended as abruptly as her trust in him,[16] had gone on to attain the White House. But Mrs. Rutherfurd and the president had never quite gotten around to severing their ties. There were limousines that mysteriously arrived to bring Lucy to Roosevelt's inaugurals, phone calls discreetly routed through the White House switchboard.[17]

Shoumatoff had first met Lucy Rutherfurd in 1937, after one of the Rutherfurd children hired her to paint their mother, and an enduring friendship had grown out of that sitting. From the first, Lucy admired Shoumatoff's ability to capture not only a face, but also a soul with little more than her studied glance and the silver box of watercolors she carried around in her purse. "You should really paint the President," Lucy suggested one afternoon in the spring of 1943.[18] At first, Shoumatoff doubted she could arrange it. By the following morning, Lucy had done just that.

Two weeks later, inside the Oval Office, Shoumatoff managed to capture FDR's pensive depths as well as his handsome face on a tiny square of canvas. Delighted, Roosevelt immediately resolved to sit for the Russian again, this time for a larger, more official portrait. But the war had intervened, robbing the president of both the time to be painted and the physical strength and striking features that were worth painting. By the time FDR raised the long-deferred sitting with Rutherfurd again, it was the spring of 1945. He was no longer well, and Rutherfurd—whose furtive meetings with FDR had made her a witness to his alarming decline—sensed intuitively that there was not much time left. "If the portrait is to be painted," she told Shoumatoff, "it should not be postponed."[19]

Rutherfurd had made sure that it was not. And so, on April 7, Shoumatoff set off from her home in the Long Island suburb of Locust Valley, detoured into Manhattan to fetch her assistant Nicholas Robbins, and then began the long drive down to Aiken, South Carolina, where Rutherfurd waited for them to pick her up. When the three finally rendezvoused with FDR in Greenville—a tiny town nine miles from Warm Springs—Shoumatoff had been driving for three days. She had helmed her big white Cadillac convertible, its fuel tank topped off despite the strict gasoline rationing. (This, too, was apparently some of Lucy's alchemy at work.)[20]

That night of April 9, FDR settled Shoumatoff and Rutherfurd in one of the intimate guest cottages near his own. Shoumatoff would begin her first sketches of the president the next morning. The 1943 Oval Office sitting had been shoehorned into the frenetic affairs of state, but at Warm Springs, the painter would have more time. Although Roosevelt did some work during the day at his retreat, his schedule had consisted mainly of late risings, early bedtimes, and long afternoon drives in the big, open Packard that the train had hauled down from Washington. In all, Shoumatoff would have three days to stare over her easel at the face of Franklin D. Roosevelt.

On that first night of her stay, as Roosevelt mixed his beloved cocktails, Shoumatoff was struck by the figure of Laura "Polly" Delano, FDR's unmarried cousin who lived alone with her championship dachshunds in a Tudor-style mansion in Hyde Park. With her silk pajamas, jingling bracelets, and "bright blue hair" the 59-year-old spinster strutted about the room like an exotic water fowl. The painter was not exaggerating. FDR's son Elliott described his aunt as "a sprite no more than four feet nine inches tall with parchment skin and purple hair . . . her fingers heavy with rings."[21]

Polly—the family's grande dame and gadfly—approved of everything about Franklin except for one thing: his wife. She had never considered Eleanor a suitable match for his sparkling personality and seldom failed to find ways of indicating as much. Polly's efforts to bedevil Eleanor took such forms as plying the grown Roosevelt boys with liquor while their mother watched uneasily. Polly's behavior had been heartless; she had to have known that Eleanor had lost both a father and a brother to alcoholism.[22]

On the morning of April 12, Roosevelt slept late and awakened with a headache but looked good to Dr. Bruenn, who decided to go for a swim with Mike Reilly, Toi Bachelder, and Grace Tully in the foundation's pool, two miles down the road. That left the president in the company of his cousins Daisy Suckley and Polly Delano, his correspondence secretary William Hassett, the painter Shoumatoff, her assistant Robbins, and, sitting nearby in quiet admiration, Lucy Mercer Rutherfurd.

FDR picked a spot near the French doors that opened onto the patio, where he sat in his favorite leather chair with a card table pulled up to it so he could work. As Shoumatoff set up her easel and began mixing colors, Hassett was laying around the room—on tables, chairs, even the couch—letters and documents to which the president had just put his name. FDR was a blotty signer, pressing hard on the fountain-pen nib and laying a thick trail of ink on the page. The tremor in his hands didn't help matters; the signatures needed time to dry. FDR joked that Hassett was setting out his "laundry."[23]

Within the next hour, Elizabeth Shoumatoff had already completed the handsome face of the president, his thoughtful eyes staring intently into the viewer's and yet somehow also deep into some unknowable distance within and beyond. Altering the facts in a way only painters can, Shoumatoff also removed at least ten years with her brush. Yet she agonized to replicate one detail of the man before her. A glorious ruddiness had spread over the president's face only minutes before, chasing away the pallor that had hollowed his cheeks. Such vigor in that color; Shoumatoff summoned all her talent to capture it. She never suspected that the rosy hues washing over president's face were in fact a sign that one of the blood vessels in his brain was about to break.[24]

It was 1:00 P.M. Down at Georgia Hall, a picnic in the president's honor was in the offing. A great kettle of Brunswick stew—Roosevelt's favorite—had been hoisted onto the coals. In the Little White House, Polly walked into the kitchen to put some water in a bowl of roses. Shoumatoff's brush pecked at the canvas. Suckley looked up from her crocheting.

The president seemed to be fumbling for something, his hands flitting about his head, as if waving away a moth that was not there.

Suckley rose and walked over to him. "Have you dropped your ciga-rette?" she asked.[25] Roosevelt turned and looked at her. His furrowed forehead was knitted with pain and yet he addressed her with a tired, apologetic smile. "I have," the president began, his hand reaching ten-tatively behind him, "a terrific pain in the back of my head."[26]

And then he slumped forward.

Though FDR would linger, unconscious, for another two and a half hours, it was all essentially over in that instant. Everything that fol-lowed—from camphor passed under the president's nose, to Dr. Bruenn's frantic injections of papaverine and amyl nitrate, to the summoning of Dr. James E. Paullin, a heart specialist who sped down from Atlanta just to plunge an adrenaline syringe into Roosevelt's heart—all of it would have no effect. Later, Dr. Bruenn likened the hemorrhage to "getting hit by a train."[27]

In the minutes before Roosevelt expired, a sense of helplessness, of inevitability, crept like a phantom through the rooms of the cabin. The rasping of FDR's incapacitated lungs made it clear to everyone that the end was upon him and that there would be no bargaining with it. Grace Tully abandoned herself to silent prayer; Hassett pointlessly studied his watch; the doctors around the bed stood still as oaks.[28] Yet at that moment, as Roosevelt lay *in extremis*, a purple cyanosis clawing its way across his skin, Polly Delano rose, dialed the White House, and calmly related to Eleanor that Franklin had suffered "a fainting spell" but that "there is no cause for you to upset yourself."[29]

It was an absurd understatement. Polly, the president's son Elliott later said, was playing for time—time to make sure that Lucy Rutherfurd was clear of the place, all evidence of her presence expunged, and everyone settled with sanitized recollections for the First Lady when she arrived.[30]

On Roosevelt's death certificate, file no. 7594 with the Georgia Department of Public Health, beneath the entry on line 10 for Usual Occupation—"President of the United States of America"—the cause of death appears as cerebral hemorrhage with a contributory cause of arteriosclerosis, duration two and one-half years. Line 23 lists the time of death as 3:35 P.M.[31]

When Hassett reached Steve Early at the White House with the news that FDR was gone, Early gave strict orders that no one was to be told until he could reach the First Lady—who'd left only a short time before for a fundraiser at the Sulgrave Club, a women's literary guild housed in a mansion off DuPont Circle. After taking Polly's call, Eleanor had not wanted to leave the White House, but Admiral McIntire had encouraged her to keep the afternoon's social appointments. As a physician who understood the severity of FDR's coronary picture, McIntire must have suspected that the president had suffered far more than a fainting spell. His blind devotion to FDR, Elliott Roosevelt later posited, was the only plausible explanation for his avoidance of the dark facts before him.[32]

Hassett repaired to his cottage, where he readied a brief announcement of the president's death for the reporters and then awaited Early's clearance to read it to them. Seated at the switchboard set up to route calls through the Little White House, operator Louise Hackmeister knew that in minutes she would be the conduit for a piece of news that would plunge the country into grief. It need only be released. A little after 4:30 P.M., she reached the United Press's Merriman Smith down at the picnic via a transmitter the Secret Service had set up inside an adjacent barn.[33] "Smitty?" Hacky said, trying to control the panic in her voice, "Mr. Hassett wants to see you. Find the other boys and get to his cottage as fast as you can."[34]

Smith was confused. Following a brief press conference a few days earlier, the three wiremen—Smith, the Associated Press's Harold Oliver, and Robert Nixon of the International News Service—had been told that "the lid" was on (meaning, no more news copy) for the trip.[35] Suddenly the three were in the big Lincoln with a Secret Service man at the wheel. The speedometer needle tickled 90 as the heavy convertible lunged up the road. Smith guessed that Hitler must have died. Bob Nixon thought the war was over. But when Smith stepped into the living room of Hassett's cottage and saw Grace Tully's swollen eyes, he knew she had not been crying about the end of the war, much less the end of Hitler. Hassett fumbled with some sheets of paper. "Gentlemen," he said quietly, "it is my sad duty to inform you that the President of the United States is dead."[36] The lid was off.

In Washington, where it was an hour ahead of Georgia time, at 5:45 P.M. one of the trunk-line wires at the Washington bureau of the International News Service indicated an incoming call. When one of the female typists answered, the voice on the other end demanded to speak to a chief editor. "This is the White House," he blurted. The managing editor had gone home for the day, but the cool-headed assistant called across the room to the daytime news editor. "Get on [line] 33 quick,"[37] she told him.

The editor picked up. "This is Steve Early," the voice on the phone said. "I have a flash for you. The President died suddenly this afternoon."[38] The minute hand of the clock on the INS newsroom wall stood midway between 5:47 and 5:48 as the men lunged for the wire machines. In seconds, the word would be out across the United States. FLASH: FDR DEAD. Seven letters. It was the shortest news flash in wire-service history.[39] Early, stranded hundreds of miles from Warm Springs, could only dispense the basic facts. "That's about all I have," he said, after fudging the exact time of death, which he appeared not to know. "You'll have to get the details from your reporters at Warm Springs."[40]

Hassett and Early had timed their briefings so that the wire services and the Warm Springs reporters would learn the news in unison. But Early's lack of details made it clear to the D.C. bureau chiefs that the entire story—at least until the train carrying the president's body reached Washington— rested on their men down in Georgia. Smith, Oliver, and Nixon didn't have to be told as much. Immediately, they began machine-gunning Hassett with questions: "What was the cause of death?" "Did you see him today?" "Was he ill then, or in good spirits?"[41]

Then, "Who was with him?" the reporters wanted to know. "Madame Shoumatoff was working on her portrait of him," Hassett said.[42] In the mayhem of a breaking story, the papers missed the name. Early accounts claimed that an "N. Robbins" (Shoumatoff's assistant) had been the painter.[43] But even after Steve Early corrected the record and Shoumatoff replaced Robbins in the newspapers, the name of Lucy Rutherfurd did not appear.[44]

After the reporters had dashed out the door to begin a night of hammering on typewriters, Hassett picked up the phone and called the Southern Railway's offices in Atlanta. He said simply that POTUS would be required at Warm Springs no later than 7:00 the next morning, then he hung up.[45]

Eleanor Roosevelt, who'd been called to the phone during the Sulgrave Club benefit, knew everything the instant she heard Steve Early's voice.

Come to the White House at once, he implored. "In my heart I knew what had happened," the First Lady said later. "But one does not actually formulate these terrible thoughts until they are spoken."[46] When she reached the White House, Eleanor went to her sitting room in the western corner of the second floor; Early and Admiral McIntire entered, and Early gave her the news. In the car on the way over, Eleanor had ridden with clenched fists but gave no other outward signs of her distress. Later, more than one observer would marvel at her stoicism. But Eleanor had been schooled from childhood in the Victorian propriety of concealing one's feelings in public. As she put it: "The amenities had to be observed."[47]

A few minutes after Eleanor had reached her sitting room, a White House usher opened the door and let Vice President Harry S. Truman inside. Mrs. Roosevelt rose and laid her hand on his shoulder. "Harry," she said, "the President is dead."[48] At first, Truman could not summon words to respond. When he did, he asked the First Lady if there was anything he could do for her. Eleanor Roosevelt paused, and in a slightly bemused voice she answered, "Is there anything we can do for you? For you are the one in trouble now."[49]

Truman hardly needed to be told. Indeed, the frailty of FDR's health had been haunting him for months. That FDR had persisted in carrying the burdens of his office despite his obvious physical exhaustion had even prompted his vice president to wonder if Roosevelt himself knew just how bad off he was.[50] Now, in the upholstered solitude of Eleanor's study, Truman felt the weight of world outside clamoring to climb onto his shoulders. But foremost he felt—and would never forget—the patient, gentle stare of Eleanor Roosevelt. "The greatness and the goodness of this remarkable lady showed even in that moment of sorrow," Truman would remember years afterward. "I was fighting off tears. The overwhelming fact that faced me was hard to grasp. I had been afraid for many weeks that something might happen to this great leader, but now that the worst had happened I was unprepared for it."[51]

No one else was quite prepared for it, either. As word of Roosevelt's death spread, most found the shock immobilizing, but the news caused some others to move quickly—some from a sense of duty; others, for personal motives.

Ferman White, a foreman for the Southern Railway, clocked off his shift at Atlanta's sprawling North Avenue Yards around 4:30 P.M. On his way home, White decided to stop and buy some groceries. It was in the store that he learned the news, and raced to the nearest phone. White had one thought on his mind as he called the roundhouse. It was a piece of knowledge that few men in Atlanta possessed and one that White guarded closely. On a layup track in the yards, a special train— the president's train—had been parked for two weeks. It would not, White knew, stay parked for long now. Charles Craft, another foreman, picked up the phone.

"Charley," White shouted into the receiver. "We'll need two light Pacific [engines]. What you got in sight?"

"The 1262 and 1337 are on the cinder pit," Craft answered.

"Get them going," White said.[52]

On the other side of Atlanta, a little after 7:30 P.M., another phone rang. This one was at the home of a man named Fred Patterson. Patterson, funeral director to Atlanta's elite, had spent the afternoon playing golf, and it was on the green that he'd learned about the president's death. Now, back at his house, Patterson was just about to light up a cigar and settle down with the newspaper when he heard the telephone.[53] The voice on the other end belonged to Dr. James Paullin, who was calling from Warm Springs. As the cardiologist spoke, it became clear to Patterson that he would not be reading the news that night; he would be playing a part in it. President Roosevelt had already been dead four hours. The funeral train would be leaving in the morning. Patterson was needed quickly.

Up in Spartanburg, South Carolina, James F. Byrnes was at home when he heard on the radio that Roosevelt had died. As the former director of war mobilization, Byrnes knew more U.S. diplomatic and military secrets than most anyone in the federal government. In the many years he had worked in Washington, "Jimmy" Byrnes had been so close to FDR that the newspapers had taken to calling him the assistant president, though of course no such official title existed.[54] Byrnes knew about a top-secret American project to build a bomb that exploded when atoms inside it were split—a project Harry S. Truman did not know about.

But Byrnes had quit Roosevelt's cabinet just a week before—angry, some said, over FDR's passing him over for the vice president's post in favor of the comparatively unknown Truman.[55] Whatever his reasons, Byrnes had returned home to Spartanburg, prepared for a long rest.

The shock of Roosevelt's death settled in as Byrnes got ready to go to bed. Then the phone rang. It was James V. Forrestal, Roosevelt's secretary of the Navy. Forrestal got to the point. An airplane was on its way down to Spartanburg, and Byrnes was to get on it.[56] Forrestal had reasoned that someone with Byrnes's experience might soon be needed around the Oval Office. He was right.

Democratic National Committee treasurer Edwin W. Pauley, whose primary occupation was in the oil business, was lunching at the Biltmore Hotel in Los Angeles when, a few minutes before 3:00 P.M. Pacific Time, the waiter told him an urgent phone call had come in from Washington. The caller was Robert Hannegan, DNC chairman, who broke the news as soon as Pauley picked up the line. Roosevelt was gone, and that meant one thing: Their mutual friend Harry Truman was about to become the most powerful man on the planet. Hannegan told Pauley to get to D.C. as fast as he could.[57] With a war on, there were of course no flights to be had for any price. Luckily for Pauley, his lunch companion that afternoon was the president of Trans Western Airlines; Pauley was airborne before nightfall.

Hours after Pauley's plane left Los Angeles, another airplane—this one an enormous B24 Liberator—lifted off the airstrip in Las Vegas and turned its nose toward D.C.[58] Aboard it was a greaser of political cogs named George E. Allen, a veteran from the old Kansas City Democratic machinery of ward boss Tom Pendergast, which had plucked a haberdasher named Harry Truman out of his bankrupt business and run him for a county judge's seat in 1921.[59] Allen had been on vacation in Vegas when he heard the news of FDR's death and sensed that Truman "would need help getting through the confusion of the next few weeks."[60] With every civilian flight booked solid, Allen had made some choice phone calls to get himself aboard the four-engine warbird bound for Washington. But George E. Allen was good at that sort of thing. "Fun-loving George," *Time* magazine later wrote, "knew everyone worth knowing in Washington."[61] He also knew how to write a hell of a speech.

Presidential aide Lauchlin Currie was in the capital when the news broke, as was John Maragon, a Baltimore & Ohio ticket agent who had gone to D.C. years before with dreams of being a political player. Currie likely presumed he would be getting a berth aboard the funeral train for its leg to Hyde Park, where FDR was to be interred. Maragon, on the other hand, could only hope he would. Yet Maragon counted among his friends Major General Harry Hawkins Vaughan who, in turn, counted among *his* friends Harry S. Truman. On the afternoon of April 12, John Maragon glimpsed a seam in the wall of power just wide enough to slip through.

Brigadier General Elliott Roosevelt was stationed in England, where it was near midnight when the news of his father's death reached him. As it happened, FDR's friend and advisor, the wealthy financier Bernard Baruch, was visiting London and offered the president's son a seat on his plane. They would lift off at noon the next day.

The three other Roosevelt boys were in the Pacific. There, on the afternoon that FDR died, it was already early morning the following day. John Roosevelt was aboard the aircraft carrier *Hornet*; FDR Jr. was on the destroyer escort *Ulvert M. Moore*; and James, a Marine, was stationed on the Philippine island of Leyte. The young enlistee who awakened James dropped a communiqué on his cot and ran away in tears.[62] "Father slept away," Eleanor had cabled each of her sons. "He would expect you to carry on and finish your jobs."[63]

Colonel James Roosevelt resolved to make it home in time for the funeral. His father would be buried in two days—8,000 miles away.

After Fred Patterson had finished his phone call with Paullin, he drove to the H. M. Patterson & Son funeral chapel in Atlanta's Spring Hill neighborhood. There was plenty to do. His first task was to call Hassett down at Warm Springs for as many details as he could obtain. Each presented a problem. Roosevelt's height—six feet three inches—severely narrowed the choices among Patterson's stock of coffins.[64] But the more pressing issue was metal. Wartime shortages had meant that steel and bronze coffins had been replaced by composites with names like Eternalite and Mineralite. Plastic and cloth-covered models had even begun appearing in funeral homes across the country.[65] But Patterson knew that no one would stand for the president of the United States to be buried in a container made of something called Permalith. Hassett had told him about a copper-lined mahogany casket that Roosevelt had picked out for his mother's funeral four years earlier and suggested that a similar model might be appropriate. Patterson had just purchased a mahogany coffin that was the right size, but of course it had no copper.

Then he remembered: He did have a National Seamless Copper Deposit model—solid copper, bronze finish, and an interior lined in velvet. It was an expensive and beautiful piece. (Also, critically, it measured six feet six inches.) If posterity was to matter—and to Roosevelt, it did—the copper casket was the only choice. But Patterson had sensed uncertainty in Hassett's voice during the phone call, and the mortician ultimately decided to take no chances.[66] Patterson picked up the phone again and summoned four of his men to the funeral home. He'd decided to drive two hearses to Warm Springs: the mahogany casket in the bay of one, the bronze-finished copper model in the other.[67]

Perhaps no single phone call had ever so thoroughly activated the bureaucratic machinery of the Southern Railway than the one Bill Hassett made in the early evening of April 12, when he requested the presidential train for what would be its final run with Roosevelt aboard. Because POTUS had not been scheduled to return FDR to Washington until April 18, its regular crewmen were off serving on other trains, some far from Atlanta. The Southern could have cobbled together a stopgap crew, but the brass was determined to reassemble the experienced hands. The eyes of America would be on this train; its run could be nothing less than flawless.

Up and down the main line, along the divisions the train would travel—Atlanta, Charlotte, Danville, Washington—phones rang. They were picked up by the manicured hands of officials and by the calloused hands of yard foremen. One superintendent located Claude E. Blackmon—a trusted engineer who'd pulled POTUS many times—and told him to stand by; he'd be taking over once the train reached Atlanta's Terminal Station.[68] In Atlanta, Pullman's assistant district superintendent called the D.C. office in a frantic search for POTUS's six regular porters and W. A. Brooks, the trusted conductor, who had presided over every run the train had made below the Mason-Dixon Line. The Pullman Company located Brooks on another train, returned him to Washington, and then routed him down to Greenville, South Carolina, where he would join the train. Pullman found POTUS's six regular porters, too, and would pluck them off the *Crescent Limited* when it steamed into Atlanta.[69]

Ferreting out the train's regular crew was a big enough problem, but the Southern had another: engines. Although there was enough time to rustle up four pairs of pristine locomotives for the mainline run to Washington, there were only two engines handy in Atlanta's North Avenue roundhouse for this night's duty. The locomotives would have to take the train down to Warm Springs to pick up the coffin and the presidential party, then haul it back up into Atlanta, where a pair of bigger engines would replace them. The two steamers in the roundhouse now—engines No. 1262 and No. 1337—were well past the point where locomotives were trusted to take charge of first-class passenger trains, let alone that of a president. No. 1337 itself had been blowing smoke for sixty-four years.[70] But the men had to work with what they had, and now, at nearly 6:00 P.M. on the day FDR died, they were determined to get the machines ready. White had returned to the roundhouse, where he watched his engineers inspect every rivet and seam of the pair of 80,000-pound machines.

Fortunately, the presidential train itself was nearly ready to run. POTUS had been holed up in the North Avenue Yards since dropping FDR off at Warm Springs. The string of handpicked Pullmans had been tucked onto a layup track, while ordinary trains cut screeching paths around it. The last crew had made sure to restock the cars with countless provisions—linen, ashtrays, matches, soap—so the train would be ready to leave within minutes of a phone call. Those were the rules.[71] Still, none of the yardmen had expected to have to turn the President's Special into a funeral train. In the fading daylight, the yardmen decoupled POTUS right behind B&O communications car No. 1401, backed in the sleeper *Clover Pasture*, and closed the whole thing back up.[72] An extra Pullman would be needed for the run up to D.C.

At 7:00, a switcher pulled the train—now eleven cars long—down onto Track 10 at the far western end of Terminal Station. With a slow and rhythmic exhalation of steam that some might call beautiful, engines No. 1262 and No. 1337 backed slowly down the track until the couplers locked in a rusty handshake. POTUS was ready.

As the daylight faded, the world of tracks and platforms that fanned out beneath the massive terminal turned to an eerie realm of deserted stairways and soot-covered signs. With time to wait until the running orders came through, the engine crews wandered down the track until they were out in the open, beneath the night sky, and sat down on the rails. There Engineers O. B. Wofford and H. E. Allgood and their men reminisced about Roosevelt, about all the times they had pulled him in the *Ferdinand Magellan*.[73] As the crewmen talked, the clang of crossing bells announced the arrival of other trains that crept past on nearby tracks. Their coach windows aglow, the trains would pause briefly to disembark passengers before chuffing off again. None of the people on the platform could have guessed that the long, empty string of sleepers waiting on Track 10 would soon become the funeral train of the president.[74]

Three hours would pass, until finally the crewmen looked up to see the trainmaster and the superintendent on their way down the stairs from the station. With them was Conductor Emmit Whittle, who clasped the running orders in his hand. At seven minutes after 10 P.M., with fresh, hot fires in their bellies, the locomotives lurched ahead, eclipsing the Mitchell Street Bridge with coal smoke as they passed beneath.[75]

Down in Warm Springs, thirty minutes shy of midnight, the cottage's door opened to a tall, slightly stooped woman with probing blue eyes. Eleanor Roosevelt had arrived. In what was probably his first official act as president—made before he'd even been sworn in—Harry Truman had ordered a Douglas C-47 Skytrain to fly the First Lady from Washington National Airport to Fort Benning, Georgia, gently dismissing her concern that the use of the plane might be seen as extravagant.[76]

Steve Early and Dr. McIntire, who'd flown down with her, stepped inside. Patterson's hearses had arrived at Warm Springs forty-five minutes earlier, but the men had been told to wait. The president's body lay on the simple pine-frame bed in his room off to the left but was not visible from the living room, which appeared as neat and informal as it always had. One of the president's ship models stood on the mantel of the fieldstone fireplace, flanked by shelves stuffed with his books. Below was a small couch arranged with cushions.

Eleanor kissed Grace Tully. Her arms even spread, briefly, around Polly Delano.[77] Then she walked over to the couch and sat down. The corner floor lamp cast a soft glow behind the First Lady, who had changed into a black dress before boarding the plane. Now, one by one, she asked Tully and the two Roosevelt cousins to tell her exactly what had happened. Each recounted what she had planned, previously and in private, to say.[78] The stories included the painter Shoumatoff but omitted Lucy Rutherfurd. The big secret had held.

Or had it? Later accounts disagreed about how and when Eleanor Roosevelt's inquisitive spade finally struck upon the stone of Lucy's presence, but one version suggests that she already knew much more than she was letting on. According to press secretary Jonathan Daniels, the first thing Early blurted to Hassett as he arrived from the airfield and stomped into the cottage was: "Bill, there's hell to pay. Mrs. Roosevelt knows that Mrs. Rutherfurd was here."[79]

The dusty heel of Elizabeth Shoumatoff's shoe rode cautiously on the accelerator of her white Cadillac. She'd been on the road since 2:30 that afternoon, gripping the steering wheel and determined to reach Aiken, South Carolina, before dark.[80] But getting pulled over for speeding by one of these southern troopers was, she knew, unthinkable. He would surely ask questions, and then all would be lost. Then again, in a way, all was lost already.

Beside the Russian painter in the passenger's seat sat Lucy. Though she would be fifty-four years old in another two weeks, Rutherfurd, with her trim figure and a hint of flame in her eyes, was still a strikingly beautiful woman. From time to time, she'd bring a handkerchief up to her face and dab her tears. The sound of the wind and the hot engine filled the convertible. Otherwise, the two women in the front seat and Nicholas Robbins, the lone man in the back, rode in silence. Their suitcases traveled with them—valises they'd stuffed with clothing so hastily there had hardly been time to fold anything. Earlier that afternoon, immediately after FDR had wilted before her eyes inside the Warm Springs cottage, Shoumatoff had screamed and called to Lucy that something had happened to the president.[81] The ensuing panic had been surreal; Shoumatoff heard Secret Service cars, heavy footfalls, the clicking of a telephone dial. Then, like a spirit, Lucy was suddenly at her shoulder. When her friend had whispered, "We must pack and go,"[82] it was clear what would happen if they did not.

As the car passed through the Georgia town of Macon, Shoumatoff noticed that the flags had been lowered to half-staff.[83] It was confirmation of news that the women, in their hearts, knew already. They had known it before the people of Macon did; they had known it before the people of the world did.

⊹═▶ ◀═⊹

United Press man Merriman Smith would recall the twelve hours beginning with Hassett's late-afternoon announcement of Roosevelt's death as a "nightmare, a horrible, discordant symphony of people shouting for telephones, automobiles racing along dusty clay roads, the clatter of telegraph instruments and typewriters."[84] Up in D.C., Steve Early had been clear that the Boss wouldn't have wanted the cottage swarming with reporters, so the entire world would hear a story told by only three men.

"Warm Springs, Ga., April 12—(UP)—Death today removed Franklin Delano Roosevelt from a war-torn world and left peace-expectant millions shocked and stunned," Smith's lead story would read. "Death gave the 63-year-old President of the United States short notice."[85] Smith wrote all night. He wrote, he said, until he swore another word could not issue from his typewriter.[86] And then, of course, he wrote some more.

Meanwhile, the newsmen not lucky enough to be among Steve Early's chosen three haunted the periphery of the compound. Having acted on the assumption that the First Lady would travel to Warm Springs by train, journalists besieged the little station. When word came, after midnight, that Mrs. Roosevelt would not be arriving by train but had in fact already touched down in a military plane and was ensconced in the Little White House, the reporters knew there would be no story until the morning when the train left.

The newsmen moved like the dispossessed toward Georgia Hall. Because the Secret Service men were often quartered at the hotel during the president's stays, perhaps some of them would be around and willing to talk. The troupe of reporters found the windows ablaze despite the hour. In one of the rooms, Dewey Long and Mike Reilly were working out the schedule of the train for two days hence,[87] when it would steam out of Washington to take the president's coffin north to Hyde Park—but the newsmen never discovered the work going on upstairs. Oblivious, they fanned out into the lobby instead.

Here were men accustomed to life on the underside of the clock; to the front seats of cars or the hard benches of police precincts serving as beds while they waited for announcements that might or might not be news; men for whom a candy bar produced from a back pocket often stood in for dinner. So it came as a particular surprise to enter a Victorian hotel and find a banquet laid out on white tablecloths—just for them.

The hotel's manager spoke over the din: "The President and his party were to have attended a barbecue here at 5 P.M.," he said. "We had the food all prepared. You may eat it if you are hungry, for it will only go to waste. It's on the house."[88] The newspaper, magazine, and radio men took plates and formed a buffet line, filing past mountains of lamb, pork, and beef and bowls of salads. Inside an enormous kettle was a batch of Georgia Brunswick stew.

Dave Snell of the *Atlanta Constitution* found a seat and set his plate before him. He looked around, listening to the conversations in earshot. Men of the ink trades tend to maintain exteriors of iron. The job demands it. To go soft is to cause your colleagues to lose respect for you. And yet, Snell was to write later of the talk at those tables, despite the "same jargon, the same outward irreverence, there is a mist in many eyes."[89] It was usual for newsmen on third watch to ease the boredom with drink. Tonight, not a drop of alcohol was in sight.

High up behind their locomotives' boilers, Engineers Allgood and Wofford choked off the steam as POTUS rolled into Williamson, 53.3 miles south of Atlanta. Pressurized air blew out of the release valves as the brake shoes squeezed down behind the flanges as the train eased to a stop. The night was warm and still, the air laced with honeysuckle. It took a few minutes to turn the two locomotives around. Williamson—a junction town—was the last place this could be done; the remaining 30.7 miles down into Warm Springs lay along a single, lonesome track. To run the funeral train out the next morning with the engines in front, the crew had no choice but to back the train in now.[90] The men opened up the throttles again. This time, though, they leaned out of their cab windows and looked at the dizzying spectacle of eleven railroad cars swaying ahead of them.

As the train crept backward through the night, R. K. McClain, assistant VP of the Southern, was at his desk at the railroad's offices with the hand-scribbled schedule POTUS would follow for its run to D.C. the next morning. When he finished, he awakened every division boss up and down the line and ordered them to scrutinize his work. It had taken several passes, but McClain had finally hammered it all out. POTUS would change engines and crews first at Atlanta, then at Greenville, South Carolina, and Salisbury, North Carolina, with the final swap out of men and equipment to come at Monroe, Virginia.

There would be some combination of coal and water for the locomotives and ice to fill the Pullmans' air-conditioning bunkers waiting at the Georgia hamlets of Williamson and Gainesville; at Hayne, South Carolina; and finally at the stops of Danville and Weyburn in Virginia. The vice president had determined that POTUS's slow speed would run afoul of two scheduled trains in Virginia, so he issued orders to let Train No. 30 pass at Applegate and stand aside again at Bealton to make way for the No. 48.[91]

A few minutes after 1:00 A.M., a headlamp set the silvery spine of the curving rails aglow in the darkness as POTUS creaked around the bend by the Warm Springs station. The arc belonged to a pilot locomotive that had been coupled to the back end for the final leg into town. Nos. 1262 and 1337 were doing the pushing.[92] In the morning, the pair of steamers would be in position at the head end, the way a proper train should look. And looks would matter a great deal. Tomorrow morning, POTUS would take on a new name. It would be, simply, the funeral train.

With the long-awaited train finally in his block, Station Agent C. A. Pless powered up his depot's floodlights. Then he blinked in surprise. People were everywhere. Drawn by the news on their radios, they'd walked to the station. Some were crying. Some stood in the nearby woods like phantoms. There were just so many of them. "It looked," Pless said, "like people just fell out of the sky."[93]

Toward the head end of the train, black laborers pulled open the heavy door of the baggage car and then slid out the two heavy tire ramps, fastening the top ends to the deck and dropping their opposites down to the weedy ground. One by one, the Secret Service men drove the presidential automobiles back onto the train. Last up the ramp was the Packard convertible. The clamor of the men loading the train (eighteen golf bags figured among the luggage) would drag on through the night, echoing down the train's corridors and into its compartments. The noise, however, would not stop Steve Early and Drs. McIntire and Bruenn from crawling into berths at 2:30 A.M. With no spare beds at the cottages, the train was the only place left for the men to sleep.[94]

As the hours limped past, no one could have blamed Fred Patterson had he wished he had never picked up the call that summoned him to the service of a dead president. His men were finally admitted to the Roosevelt's bedroom at 12:33 in the morning, local time. By then, FDR had been gone for nine hours; advanced rigor mortis and the president's blocked and hardened arteries would turn the task of embalming him into a five-hour ordeal.[95] Then, soon after the train arrived from Atlanta, Patterson shivered with another thought. Turning to a Secret Service man in the room he said quietly, "We need a carpenter."[96]

Within the hour, the foundation's maintenance manager, Douglas Shipp, carpenter Al Moody, and a gaggle of other men—most of them pulled out of bed by the Secret Service—formed a sullen quorum at the end of the train. For Shipp, grief and fatigue were mixed with the unlikely feeling of gratefulness: Many months before, he'd decided to set aside a choice pile of cut timber—Georgia pine, felled right on foundation property the previous year. "It was such good timber I had decided to save it for something special," he'd explain later. "Little did I realize . . . what that something special would be."[97] Now the men laid their rough hands on the boards and set to work building a loading ramp and a bier. Patterson had worked out the measurements himself.[98] Hammers flew beneath the station's lamps, high overhead.

The need for a ramp to load the coffin onto the train and a pedestal on which to set it down once aboard were not the only exigencies Fred Patterson had discerned. Apart from adding an extra sleeper, the Southern's yardmen in Atlanta had left POTUS's consist—the assemblage of the train—unchanged, sending the train down with the *Ferdinand Magellan* at the rear and the *Conneaut* next up. As he stood beside the parked train, Patterson could see the problem immediately.

The bronze-finished copper casket that Hassett had selected was a 600-pound monster, twenty-eight and a quarter inches wide and nearly twenty-five inches deep.[99] The *Magellan*'s vestibule door would never admit something so large, and its three-inch-thick windows were hardly an alternative. "It was impossible to use the President's armored car," Patterson would later explain.[100] His eyes wandered next to the stately *Conneaut*.

The Pullman car used by the Secret Service had been built back in 1911 as a sleeper/lounge car for the *20th Century Limited*. As part of that fabled train, the *Conneaut* had sprinted between New York and Chicago along the New York Central Railroad's "Water Level Route," laid atop the muddy shoulders of the Hudson River and, for a tiny slice of that, even passing along a strip of property in Hyde Park belonging to a family by the name of Roosevelt. FDR would not know the *Conneaut* until the car was commandeered for duty with the presidential train in 1942. Not long before it left regular passenger service, Pullman had hauled the car back into its Chicago shops to turn one of its eight compartments into a galley to serve light meals to passengers. The addition of the tiny kitchen had the effect of making *Conneaut* self-sufficient, which no doubt figured large in why the Secret Service agents had chosen the car to be their rolling headquarters.

The rear-facing lounge portion of the *Conneaut* featured a pair of oversize observation windows; Patterson chose the one nearest the end of the car. The rubber gasket would have to come off, of course, with the glass frame stowed somewhere during the loading. The Atlanta funeral director picked out a few men and walked them up to the window, explaining what would have to be done.[101]

Fired and ready, the locomotives coaxed POTUS up the track until the two rear cars rumbled over the nearest turnout. The railroaders decoupled the *Ferdinand Magellan* and the *Conneaut*, then switched them. As the train eased back to the platform edge at Warm Springs, the *Conneaut* was at the tail. Journalist Dave Snell, having finished his meal at Georgia Hall, was standing at the trackside when it did.

"A train is backing into the tiny station," he wrote. "There is a long chain of drawing room Pullmans, and near the end is a combination chair car and Pullman. You don't understand what makes you know it, but you are sure that this is the car that will carry the casket to the east."[102]

TWO

"RUN SLOW, RUN SILENT"

Sunrise spread over the foundation grounds as a cool breeze came in from the west. The sky was the color of topaz on the day the Boss would leave Warm Springs for good. More than a few residents noted how unfortunate it was that the day should be a Friday (and the thirteenth, no less); FDR was superstitious and had always done his best to avoid traveling on Fridays.[1] The air carried the intoxicating scents of brook water, weeds, and the red earth as the temperature climbed toward a comfortable 83 degrees. Inexplicably, as has happened so many times before and since, a great tragedy had been blessed with the backdrop of perfect weather.

Bill Hassett had crawled into his bed at 2:30 that morning and tried to sleep but with little success. Inside the parked train, Admiral McIntire and Dr. Bruenn had fared no better. Some, including Merriman Smith, had not even considered sleep possible, and didn't try. He and his typewriter had spent the night at the Little White House and its guest cottages, sponging up press secretary Early's announcements. "Steve gave us the funeral train plans as they developed," Smith recalled.[2] Shortly before dawn, the reporter hastened to Georgia Hall to check out of his room. He stuffed his clothes into bags, anyplace they would fit. Rummaging through his things, Smith discovered two bottles of bourbon he'd packed but forgotten about. He poured himself a drink straight up and managed to shiver half of it down.[3] As the reporter climbed down the stairs with his heavy luggage, the hotel's cook spotted him and tried to detour him into the kitchen, where she could warm up some leftovers. Smith refused, politely and wearily. "Food now would just make me sick," he told her.[4]

By 9:00 that morning, the population of Warm Springs—608 souls, according to the 1940 Census—had grown fivefold. Three thousand soldiers had arrived during the night. In number, they were sufficient to assemble a formal marching column for the cortege and still leave 2,000 paratroopers available to line both sides of the route all the way to the train station. The 99th Infantry Ground Forces and the 267th Army Ground Forces had both contributed musicians to the band that led the procession. Following them was a color guard assembled from the young men of Fort Benning's infantry school—28 miles down the road, near Columbus, Georgia—who'd come in full ceremonial dress, carrying streamers and Springfield rifles.[5] They waited for the signal to begin. Once it came, boots would crunch in the gravel. Boots would crunch all that morning, and the memory of the sound would stay with people always.[6]

The proceedings must have looked as rehearsed as if they had been planned for months. The truth was that FDR had died so unexpectedly and so far from Washington's apparatus of protocol that the Army brass simply improvised. Things went wrong. Someone misplaced the ceremonial flag, forcing Patterson to order the Stars and Stripes flying from a nearby flagpole pulled down and spread across the coffin's lid. The horse-drawn caisson that was to have taken the body to the train station never arrived, and here again Patterson stepped forward with a solution.[7]

Parked by the Little White House was the undertaker's Cadillac S&S limousine hearse.[8] The long black car glinted in the sunlight like a slab of buffed onyx. With its triple bands of fender chrome and green-curtained windows, it was a car befitting a president; in a wonder of coincidence, it even bore the coachbuilder's model name, "Statesman."[9]

The copper casket slid down the rollers in the back and the embalmers closed the car's heavy rear door behind it. One of Patterson's men got behind the Cadillac's steering wheel while another assistant slipped into the passenger's seat. The V-8 engine cleared its throat and turned over. The enormous hearse inched forward, falling in line behind the band and the color guard. Patterson and the other morticians drove ahead of the hearse in the lead car. Following the hearse came a sedan carrying Eleanor Roosevelt, Grace Tully, Laura Delano, and Daisy Suckley. Lying at the ladies' feet was Fala, "knowing that something was wrong," claimed the *New York Times*.[10]

In all his years of visiting Warm Springs, Roosevelt had never left without stopping at Georgia Hall first, where he could say goodbye to its hundred or more patients. Now, at Eleanor Roosevelt's behest, the hearse detoured into the circular drive,[11] pausing before the hall's white columns where scores of children, confined to wheelchairs and locked into leg braces, stared. One of them was Jay Fribourg, who could only clench his teeth to keep from sobbing as a reporter approached. "I loved him so much," Fribourg said. He was thirteen years old.[12]

The train was to have left at 10:00 A.M., but it was one minute past when the cars drew up at the station. The ramp that Douglas Shipp and his men had finished just hours before was a perfect hypotenuse of pine planks connecting the *Conneaut*'s sill with the ground. Shipp had spared nothing in terms of strength. Patterson had warned him: The coffin, once occupied, would weigh 760 pounds.[13]

Ten soldiers hoisted the coffin from the back of the hearse and tramped it slowly up the ramp. Pairs of ghostly hands appeared through the darkened opening in the back of the Pullman where the window had been taken out. In all, it took twenty men to navigate the president's casket through the frame. Eight would be chosen to stay aboard the car and stand at attention, four at a time, as an honor guard.

The *Conneaut*'s lounge had been stripped of all its furnishings except for a circular mirror that remained on the forward wall beside a coat hook. The bier stood on the floor in the center of the room, its unfinished Georgia pine covered by two green-brown Marine blankets. When the young men set the coffin down on it, Fred Patterson's foresight revealed itself in still another detail: He had specified the bier at twenty inches off the floor—high enough to make the coffin visible through the *Conneaut*'s windows.[14]

As one of the trainmen carefully resealed the window, Mrs. Roosevelt climbed up into the *Ferdinand Magellan*. During normal times, this would have been the golden moment when Franklin Roosevelt, though red and sweaty from his struggle up to the *Magellan*'s vestibule, would have said some words of farewell to the crowd and beamed his hundred-watt smile. But the president's wife said nothing, and she did not look back.[15]

With the coffin and First Lady aboard and the funeral train now nearly fifteen minutes late, things moved quickly. Stationmaster Pless, who had doffed his railroad cap when the hearse passed, stood fast with his lantern. The conductor planted his shoes in the dusty weeds a few cars ahead, looking up and down the curved track to watch both ends of his train. Then he gave the signal and stepped aboard. Engineer Allgood opened up his throttle.

Merriman Smith was still at the Warm Springs station, where a few hours before the telephone linemen from Southern Bell had installed a circuit for his exclusive use. Smith was calling in his last dateline from Warm Springs to the United Press's Washington bureau when he stopped in mid-sentence, watching in alarm as the conductor waved his arm toward the engine. A UP staff man named Fowler had come down from Atlanta to help with the reporting, and now Smith slapped the receiver into the man's palm and took off after the train. Whatever story Smith was phoning in, Fowler would have to finish it. Smith's foot landed on the tread board of one of the sleepers just as the train began to move.[16]

In a mechanical sense, POTUS had become the funeral train through little more than the coupling-on of the sleeper *Clover Pasture* in Atlanta and by shifting the *Conneaut* to the tail end. But by any name, it was a magnificent train—an eleven-car rail entourage whose trappings of luxury and raw functionality became, now that the president's remains were aboard, a consummate expression of dignity. First, behind the locomotives, came the auto and baggage carriers, followed by dormitory car *Imperator* and then the Signal Corps' B&O No. 1401, its copper transmission antennas bracketed in place along its length. Next was the Pullman cluster, the cars' names stenciled in gold onto their flanks— *Clover Pasture, Hillcrest Club, Glen Doll,* and *Wordsworth.* They were 80-ton rolling hotels from the 1920s whose compartments and drawing rooms boasted woolen blankets and silver-backed shaving mirrors. Southern dining car No. 3155 with its white-coated waiters and white table linen came next, and finally the specially built *Ferdinand Magellan* and *Conneaut.*[17] The latter's lack of an open vestibule gave the train something of a stub-ended appearance. The heavy canvas awning of the *Magellan*'s vestibule flapped strangely in the space between the last two cars. Yet the glow from the makeshift funeral car's blue- and red-glass running lanterns hanging on either side of the rear doorway was punctuation enough for this, the saddest and soon to be most famous train in the United States.

Smith picked his way ahead through the cars until he found his drawing room, where he collapsed onto the seat, relieved that he had had the sense to drop his bags aboard several hours before. The veteran reporter stared dazed out the window, unsure if the dispatch he'd just phoned in had made any sense. Smith had been "so choked with emotion," he wrote later, "that it was difficult to speak."[18]

Allgood coaxed the throttle open a little more, eyeing the track ahead as it straightened its back and aimed northward. Though the train was late, both he and Wofford, who was helming the locomotive behind him, were under strict orders not to push things. Shortly before they'd left, division superintendent W. F. Cooper had come to them with a request from Eleanor Roosevelt, channeled via Steve Early. "Mr. Cooper," Early had said, "the people down here were the President's very good friends and neighbors, and it is the request of Mrs. Roosevelt that you instruct your enginemen, wherever they see groups of people along the railroad, or at the crossings, to slow down sufficiently for them to have a last view of the casket. We have elevated it [in the last] car that this vision might be had."[19]

And so the engineers took it slow—even slower than the 30 mph FDR used to insist on. Back in the *Conneaut*, four young enlisted men, chests thrust forward and eyes fixed straight ahead, stood at the corners of Roosevelt's coffin, still draped with the flag that had flown over Georgia just hours before. The funeral train settled into a slow, steady rhythm—a kind of heartbeat that replaced the one that had ceased inside the little cabin. Washington, D.C., waited to the northeast, 721.5 miles up the main line.

No sooner had the train disappeared around the bend of the Warm Springs station than the crowd of townspeople inched forward toward the rough-pine ramp that led to where the *Conneaut* had been. Roosevelt would come no more, they knew, and in their collective sorrow and shock their hands went to work. In minutes, the ramp that had just borne the weight of FDR's casket lay in pieces.[20] One by one, the people selected a wooden fragment as a memento, turned, and then shuffled home.

The funeral train slowly picked up speed as engine No. 1262 led the way northward through the hot, verdant countryside. Aboard, Steve

Early decided to give his first en route press conference. These would have to be timed, he knew, to allow the reporters a chance to pound out their stories and file them at the next major stop—Atlanta, in this case, eighty-four miles up the line. Everyone was exhausted: Early, along with Admiral McIntire and Mrs. Roosevelt, had suffered a bone-jarring flight down from Washington less than twelve hours before, shaken by the angry engines of a Douglas C-47 on full throttle. Early, at least, had attempted a few hours' sleep aboard the parked train; the reporters had barely looked up from their portable typewriters.

Early handed the newsmen copies of FDR's Jefferson Day speech, the one he was to have delivered in Warm Springs that very night. The narrative's final line—a zigzagging trail of fountain-pen ink left by a trembling hand—had been the last words FDR had written on this earth: "Let us move forward with strong and active faith."[21] The sentiment was classic Roosevelt: inclusive, reassuring, fixed on the future. Now its optimism felt hollow and abandoned. But it was still a story. Everything was a story on this trip.

Inside communications car No. 1401, four cars behind the engines, the enlisted men sat hunched over their own machinery—teletype machines, decoders, and transmitter-receivers. But with no messages to send or receive, the radio boys had nothing to do. "The intricate Army Signal Corps radio mechanisms which had kept Roosevelt in constant touch with the affairs of the world," reported the *Philadelphia Record*, "were silent."[22]

Up in their locomotives, Engineers Allgood and Wofford were doing much the same. They had their orders—"run slow, run silent"[23]—and kept the iron horses under tight leash. The enormous driving rods cranked no faster than 25 mph. At this rate, it would take twenty-three hours to reach Union Station in Washington. Originally, the Southern Railway had been tempted to shotgun POTUS into D.C. in twelve hours,[24] which would have pushed the locomotives to just over 60 mph.

But as the crewmen looked down from the hot, windy cabs of their engines, it was plain that the First Lady, in requesting the speed restriction, had been prescient; highballing would have been thoughtless—and dangerous—with so many people along the tracks. Dazed and somber, they stood at the crossings; they stood in the little depots and on weedy sidings; they stood in the middle of nowhere. So long as the funeral train would pass them, people seemed satisfied with any spot. They were, Grace Tully later wrote, "unmindful of heat or chill, sunlight or darkness."[25] As the train approached, many dropped to their knees. "The people did not wave," *Life* magazine said. "They wept."[26]

"I never saw the like," remembered Timothy "Big Tim" Haulbrook, one of the roundhouse foremen who had decided to accompany his engines in case anything went wrong. "The stations were jammed with folks; at every crossing, where two soldiers stood at attention as we passed, were crowds that craned their necks to see over the ones in front."[27] Later on, it would be estimated that more Americans had stood along the tracks of the funeral train's route than had come to FDR's inaugurals—all four of them combined.[28] Harold Oliver of the AP would also note that in those enormous crowds forming in the heart of the Deep South, whites and blacks stood together.[29]

In the drawing room he shared with the AP's Harry Oliver, Merriman Smith—unfed, unwashed, and weakly buzzing from his shot of bourbon—sat slumped in his seat, too tired to write another word. But a few words written by another hand would not leave his head: "Some will never return. Embrace these, Father, and receive them. Thy heroic servants, into Thy kingdom."[30] It was Roosevelt's D-Day prayer, though the fallen soldier on Smith's mind now was not on a windy beach at Normandy but back within the Pullman *Conneaut*.

Inside the Magellan, Eleanor Roosevelt sat quietly as the leafy landscape of sassafras and honeysuckle slid past, distorted slightly by the thick bulletproof glass. About two hours under way, William Hassett stepped into the lounge and, finding the First Lady, "assured her I was standing by if I could be of service." She thanked him—particularly for all the arrangements he'd made with the undertakers—but said there was nothing she needed.[31]

Hassett lugged open the *Magellan*'s rear door and stepped out onto the vestibule between the cars. The summer air was warm and sweet. Maneuvering his feet over the gap between the bobbing cars, the secretary pushed his way through the door ahead of him and into the cool, sanctified air of the *Conneaut*. Hassett walked past the staff kitchen that the Secret Service agents used and passed into the corridor, where his stateroom door stood just feet from the rear lounge.[32] There, four servicemen—a soldier, a sailor, a Marine, and a Coast Guardsman—stood at attention at Roosevelt's casket. The flag draping it faced forward, its stripes pointing toward the locomotives.

Close as he had been to Roosevelt in life, Hassett could not have been overly pleased by his quarters so near to him in death. "Quietly devout" and "from tart Yankee Vermont beginnings," as press secretary Jonathan Daniels once described him,[33] the oft-uptight Hassett had been haunted for weeks by a premonition of FDR's demise. "He is slipping away from us," Hassett had confided to Dr. Bruenn two weeks before the president's death, "and no earthly power can keep him here."[34] Spiritual to the point of prudishness, Hassett would not go near Roosevelt's coffin once the undertakers in Warm Springs had finished.[35] Now he stepped into his compartment and closed the door. "By myself most of the time as the train coursed through the April countryside," Hassett wrote in the little journal he'd purchased at Hausler's stationery shop in Washington three years earlier.[36] Before closing the diary, he penned one more line as he stared out of his window, moved by the sight of women who held handkerchiefs to their eyes and men who doffed their hats and placed hands on their hearts as the train passed. "Everywhere grief and reverence,"[37] Hassett wrote.

Daisy Suckley and Laura Delano were given adjoining bedrooms aboard the *Conneaut*, near Hassett. "Dear little Fala knows something is wrong," Suckley penned in her own journal, which she updated faithfully every day. "He is depressed, he wanders around.—In the Pres.' car he feels at home, but he knows his master is not there."[38] For the duration of the funeral train's run, the little Scottie would refuse to set paw in Franklin Roosevelt's bedroom.[39]

FDR's little dog was, indeed, not the only creature aboard who was depressed. Few details escaped the attention of the press; the reporters could see plainly that the president's staff was in shock. "They stared vacantly at the landscape and the crowds," the *Philadelphia Record* would later print. "They couldn't adjust themselves to the feeling that 'The Boss' was gone."[40]

In the solitude of the *Magellan*, Eleanor Roosevelt would ask the car's porter, Fred Fair, to fetch her knitting basket from Bedroom "C."[41] For the First Lady, there was much to think about, and the 700 miles ahead of her would afford her plenty of opportunities, wanted or not, for that thinking. Foremost on her mind, though, was the one thing that could take the already grim loss of her husband and lead it firmly into the realm of the unbearable.

During William Hassett's initial press briefing at Warm Springs, attention had been focused, naturally enough, on the cause of the president's death and the immediate plans for the funeral. That an "artist" was sketching him seemed enough for the time. But now, as the funeral train made its way northward on this Friday morning, the reporters wanted clarifications. It was then that Steve Early said the artist was not a man, as had been assumed, but a woman with the last name of Shoumatoff, a naturalized Russian who made her home in Locust Valley, New York. The male "artist"—Robbins, whose name had appeared in some accounts[42]—turned out to be Shoumatoff's assistant.[43]

Even with the potentially sticky issue that Roosevelt had been with a Russian national at the time of his death, Hassett had not misled the press about Shoumatoff. He had mentioned the painter's name, but the newsmen had missed it.[44] Deliberately or not, however, Hassett had omitted any mention of Rutherfurd during his briefing.[45] Now, aboard the train—though he was purportedly clarifying these details—Early was about to do the same thing.

Everybody at the Little White House had known that Shoumatoff had arrived at Warm Springs in the company of Lucy Rutherfurd; indeed, it was Rutherfurd who had introduced her to the president in the first place. Hassett had known that Rutherfurd was the president's guest and, according to Jonathan Daniels's version of events, so had Early. But if Daniels was correct, Early's response to reporters' questions aboard the funeral train leaves troubling evidence that he was still advancing a sanitized version of the events to protect the president. Shortly after Early briefed the reporters, en route to Washington, about the presence of Shoumatoff, the Associated Press would run this bit of copy over the wires: "Secretary Stephen Early cleared the situation up on the train. He said Mme. Schoumatoff [sic] apparently was the only one in the room with Mr. Roosevelt when he was stricken."[46] Perhaps Early used "apparently"—that golden qualifier large enough to drive a train through—to lessen his concealment. Fortunately for him, the wolves from the press sniffed at the secret door, then ambled away.

Several Pullmans down from where the press corps had very nearly learned the truth, Eleanor Roosevelt, ensconced in upholstered seclusion of the *Magellan*'s lounge, was agonizing over it.

It probably will never be known for certain how the First Lady finally discovered that Lucy had been in the cottage when the president lost consciousness. Though many of FDR's intimates would publish Oval Office memoirs in the years to follow, when it came to the matter of Lucy and Warm Springs, Roosevelt's contemporaries chose either to sugarcoat the circumstances or, rather miraculously, forget them altogether. Grace Tully would write only that Rutherfurd was the woman who'd commissioned Shoumatoff to paint the president[47]; William Hassett, in the version of his journals he edited for publication, made no mention of Lucy at all.[48] In later years, even as the public wizened to the notion that the men they sent to the White House seldom behaved like altar boys, Lucy would still be described merely as FDR's "friend"[49] or, in Jonathan Daniels's vernacular, partner in a "great affection."[50]

If the First Lady did know of Lucy Rutherfurd's presence at the cottage before she herself arrived on the night of April 12, it probably was through sheer intuition alone. Yet even if Eleanor harbored suspicions on the flight down, she still had to confirm them once she arrived.

"Were you here, Grace?" Eleanor had asked Tully at the cottage, referring to the moment that Roosevelt had lost consciousness. Seated beside the First Lady on the couch that would serve as a kind of witness box, Tully recounted the events of the previous afternoon—truthfully, if incompletely.[51] Laura Delano managed a smooth delivery, of course, though a few accounts maintain that the wealthy spinster's jealousies got the better of her and she dumped the truth right then and there. Because Eleanor could never bring herself to write about the incident, the most plausible account belongs to her son Elliott. The middle Roosevelt boy was one of the few people in a position to question Eleanor about the delicate matter years later—and did.

Elliott believed that his mother broke the conspiratorial cover-up over Lucy the morning after FDR's death, shortly before the funeral train's departure, following a sleepless night during which she failed to reconcile all of the open ends of the various stories imparted to her. Eleanor had been part detective, part reporter, using skills she'd honed during FDR's first term, when the paralyzed president had dispatched her across the nation on fact-finding tours that he could not make himself.

"In the predawn hours of April 13, as she tried to compose herself for sleep," Elliott wrote years later in his published memoirs, his mother "could detect some inexplicable omissions in the account so far given of the events of the previous day." When the cottage guests awoke, hours before the funeral train steamed out of Warm Springs, "the information she was able to pry out," wrote Elliott, "made for a day which she described as 'long and heartbreaking.' She unearthed the story of Lucy's presence, and she pieced together what had occurred."[52]

What she pieced together, however, was more than just the presence of Lucy Mercer Rutherfurd in Warm Springs. The morning after FDR died, as the flimsy facades of the cover-up began to fall away beneath the blows of Eleanor's questioning, the First Lady learned that Lucy had in fact been back in her husband's life for quite some time. ("And was anything wrong with *that?*" spat Laura Delano, mean as a cat when Eleanor finally cornered her.[53]) But the cruelest revelation for the First Lady was that her only daughter, Anna, whom she loved and trusted thoroughly, had been among those in the know and had gone so far as to arrange Lucy's visits to the White House while Eleanor was out of town.[54] In sum, Elliott wrote, his mother "had been tricked, and she could not tell yet how many people had lied to her in the course of keeping Father's secret."[55]

It was this news—these realizations coaxed out of mouths and pieced together with the analytical glue of a sharpened mind—that preoccupied Eleanor Roosevelt as she sat in the *Magellan*'s lounge. What would have been a despairing train trip home turned into a day of emotional torture. For although Eleanor would receive many visitors and well-wishers in the *Magellan*, she would spend most of the twenty-three hours that the train would take to reach Washington completely by herself, turning the presidential Pullman into little more than a finely appointed, rolling prison. The questions of whether, in what manner, or to what degree the president had continued his romantic relationship with Rutherfurd could not supplant a knowledge just as terrible and far more elemental to Eleanor: Her husband had been deceiving her— again—for years, and his dying glances had not fallen upon his wife but upon the woman who had destroyed her marriage.

As Eleanor Roosevelt pondered the imponderable, the wheels of the funeral train rumbled northward past innumerable turnouts, cut-ins, and switches. She did not know that the cities up ahead—Atlanta, Greenville, Spartanburg, and Charlotte—were all junction points for tracks that led eastward, coiling and connecting their way into the leafy town of Aiken, South Carolina.[56] She did not know that the president had several times broken with his official schedule and routed the presidential train over lines such as these to reach that town.[57] On those occasions, the locomotive would gingerly ease the Pullmans onto the weeds on a rusty spur near the Rutherfurd estate, and Lucy would be waiting for him. While the two visited in the *Ferdinand Magellan*, the Secret Service men blocked off all the surrounding roads as the Signal Corps boys ran their phone lines into Lucy's big brick home to connect with the ground circuits. Inside the dining car or back in their compartments, the reporters sat down to endless games of cards. FDR's secret meetings were, after all, off the record.[58]

How many Roosevelt staffers had known about such meetings? How many railroad and security men did it take to route a presidential train off the main line and onto a lonely track in the woods? Scores of people had to have been in on the affair (and on similar unscheduled layovers that POTUS made near Rutherfurd's other home in Allamuchy, New Jersey).[59] And yet Eleanor Roosevelt—always speaking, lecturing, traveling—had known nothing. She still did not know everything. But what she'd discovered was sufficient, and it had to be contained, somehow, behind a facade that approximated dignity. About those hours on the funeral train Eleanor Roosevelt would write very little, and she would wait fifteen years to do it: "At a time like that, you don't really feel your own feelings. When you're in a position of being caught in a pageant, you become part of a world outside yourself and you act almost like an automaton. You recede as a person. You build a facade for everyone to see and you live separately inside the facade. Something comes to protect you."[60]

Whatever spirit did come to protect the First Lady during those hours of sitting alone with her knitting in a velvet wingback as the *Magellan* hissed along the Southern's tracks, it could not free her from the wanderings of her own mind. "There was no way," Elliott wrote, "in which she might suppress memories of Lucy Mercer."[61]

Three hours out of Warm Springs and running low on the water it had drunk at Williamson, the funeral train swept into the lower city limits of Atlanta, bound for the Southern Railway's base in the middle of downtown. Atlanta's Terminal Station, a magisterial castle of minarets and red-tile roofs, hadn't seen crowds like these since its 1905 opening. Affording the best perch over the tracks that passed beneath, the Mitchell Street Bridge was a mass of people who spilled onto all the nearby thoroughfares—anyplace with a view, however obstructed, of the yards below. The curious also took up posts along the tracks throughout the city, which had ground to a halt in expectation of the train's arrival. Theaters, jewelers, shoeshine stands—most every business had closed for the day.

At 1:32 local time, the crowd fell to a hush as engine No. 1262 hove into view. The locomotive's bell swung high, its clapper striking a steady clang. The train wound its way through the web of shadows cast by buildings and below the grid of streets, coming to a halt at Track 10 with a blast of air from the brake valves. Just as the train was pulling in, a municipal trolley had started over the Mitchell Street Bridge. The motorman stopped immediately so his passengers could watch.[62]

Some 20,000 Atlantans packed the terminal zone, but the soldiers trucked in from Camp Sibert allowed only about a hundred down the stairs and onto the platform.[63] They had come to provide security as much as pageantry: Each soldier clutched a bayonet in his white-gloved hands. Suffering the merciless Atlanta sun beneath steel helmets, the enlisted men—2,000 strong, many with overseas ribbons fluttering on their breasts—flanked the track like garden stakes.

A shrub-size wreath of red roses and white gladiola appeared over the platform's sea of fedoras. Arms passed it up to the *Conneaut*'s vestibule, and it was taken aboard. Steve Early stepped down to meet Mayor William B. Hartsfield, who presented the spray on behalf of the people of Atlanta. Then the men disappeared into the lounge car. Inside, Hartsfield positioned the flowers at the head of Roosevelt's casket.

It was a practice that would continue at every stop up the line, where local officials would arrive trainside with an elaborate spray of lilies and roses, carnations, ribbon, and fern—a kind of botanical admission ticket that allowed them into the rolling sanctum of the *Conneaut*. By the time the train reached Washington, flowers could be seen overflowing into the stately old Pullman's vestibule.

Presidential valet Arthur Prettyman, wearing his blue Navy dress uniform, saw his chance to give Fala some fresh air. It was warm and breezy in Atlanta that afternoon, and the little dog's nails sounded on the Pullman's metal trap stairs as the First Pet bounded down. But if

FDR's longtime aide—whose service as a chief petty officer had earned him the six gold stripes on his sleeves—hoped that the mayor and his floral tribute would keep the press distracted, he was wrong. Soon photographers' flashbulbs were popping as Fala sniffed his way through a forest of ankles. "Fala Strolls Station Platform" would join the headlines in the following day's *Atlanta Constitution*, which noted that the Scottie "wagged his tail in response to the sympathetic expressions of bystanders."[64]

Departing the *Conneaut*, Hartsfield made his way one car up to the *Ferdinand Magellan*. In his palm he secreted a single rosebud he'd pinched from the spray as a keepsake.[65] As Hartsfield and Early entered, Eleanor Roosevelt looked up. Grace Tully and her typist, Dorothy Brady, were seated alongside her. Otherwise, the car was empty and quiet, its curtains drawn tightly closed. Hartsfield stepped forward. "There are no words," said the mayor, "to express how we feel." The First Lady said graciously, "I understand."[66]

And she did. When reporters on the train asked Steve Early how the First Lady was bearing up, he said, "Wonderful. I have never met a braver woman. I have never seen a woman under similar circumstances so heroic, so calm, so courageous."[67]

The train would stay parked for forty minutes while yardmen re-iced the air-conditioning chests and Engineers Allgood and Wofford, having made the most important run of their careers, eased their steamers away. Now two Pacific-class locomotives—with Engineer Claude Blackmon in the lead—backed down to the open knuckle of baggage car No. 748 as men stood by to connect the hoses. By 2:10, everyone was back aboard, and the funeral train started again on its way. The Pullmans rumbled through the switches of the roundhouse yards, then briefly nosed toward Rockdale before making a long sweep to the north and out of the city. Some 638 miles stood between locomotive No. 1409's cowcatcher and the bumper posts of Washington's Union Station.

THREE

THE FISH ROOM

O n *the night* of April 12, 1945, the Thursday that America learned it had lost its president, the White House stood quiet and dark, the lights extinguished behind all but a few windows.[1] Most of FDR's key staffers had left aboard the presidential train for Warm Springs fifteen days before. Three of the notables who had not—Steve Early, Admiral McIntire, and the First Lady—had departed on the plane for Georgia almost immediately after word of Roosevelt's death had come. By sunset, the old mansion was virtually derelict.

Accompanied by one of the White House ushers, press secretary Jonathan Daniels stepped quietly into the Oval Office. Daniels was tired. From the moment the news of FDR's death had broken earlier that evening, he had worked nonstop—"a figure in a swarm," as he'd put it[2]—fielding the questions of a frantic press corps, then offering what advice he could as the protocol and Social Bureau people met to begin planning the funeral.[3] Now, late into the evening, Daniels knew he should be in bed. But he had an important task he wanted to complete before Truman's people would come and move everything around.

In the soft light of the wall sconces, the Oval Office looked as regal as it always had. But soon—very soon—its threadbare elegance would vanish. To be sure, some of the furnishings would stay—the green-velvet draperies emblazoned with gold eagle valences, the marble mantelpiece with its Ionic capitals—and it would take days before all of FDR's belongings could be cleared out. But tonight was, Daniels knew, the last time this office would look exactly as it did when Roosevelt ran the country from it.

Under FDR, the fabled, oblate room had become an apotheosis of clutter: Gilt-spined leatherbacks packed the bookcases; the grayish-green walls were hidden behind the profusion of portraits and sea-scapes that hung in heavy, carved frames. But few things bear better testimony to the personality of an important man than the appear-ance of his desk, and on this score, Franklin Roosevelt had no peer. The desk (originally Hoover's) was of lacquered Michigan maple, and FDR had covered every available inch of its top with a menagerie of trinkets, curios, and souvenirs. Some he'd collected; most had been sent to him as gifts. There was a tiny ship's wheel, a veined marble fountain pen set, a wood paperweight carved in the initials "FDR," and a statue of a donkey—the mascot of the Democratic party. The desk held so much bric-a-brac that the surface on which the president actually could work had shrunk down to a small rectangle above the center drawer.[4]

Daniels no doubt recalled how he had stood in this very spot just over a month ago, when FDR handed him the official commission to be the new press secretary, replacing Steve Early. The president's face had been bony and pale in the photos of that occasion—the last official ones ever taken of him[5]—but his smile was still inspiring; Roosevelt never lost that. He had known he was a sick man. He had even told friends, in 1944, that he'd wanted his third term to be his last. But the matter had never been simple. Tens of thousands of Americans could not imagine winning the war without the president who had led them through it thus far—even if that president was obviously ailing. "We know that you are weary," read a letter to the White House signed by 6,100 steel workers, "—yet we cannot afford to permit you to step down."[6] In time, FDR pledged that, while he would not volunteer himself for a fourth term, if he were to be nominated and elected, he would be a "good sol-dier" and serve.[7] As things turned out, he was nominated, was elected, and he had served—and, like a good soldier, he'd done his job until it killed him.

Carefully, sadly, Daniels and the usher began their work. The room's books, pictures, and larger pieces would have to wait; to-night there was only time to clear a few things off the old man's desk. One by one, the men picked up toy elephants, china dolls, and little sailing ships, then wrapped and nestled them into packing boxes. Later, staffers would each receive a trinket to remember the

Boss by.[8] Not that anyone who'd worked for FDR would need help doing that.

Earlier on that Thursday, immediately after hearing from Eleanor Roosevelt that FDR was gone, Harry S. Truman authorized the secretary of state to inform the cabinet and summon them to the White House immediately for the swearing in. With the power transfer smoothly in motion, news of the president's death could be released to the public.[9] As Truman left the First Lady's sitting room and made his way downstairs and into the West Wing, the terrible "We interrupt this program…" crackled across the radios of the country.[10] Trim in his gray suit and polka-dot bow tie, still looking every bit the haberdasher he'd once been, Truman strode into the cabinet room and waited. One by one, the appointees entered, until soon the chamber resounded with whispers and muffled sobs. Secretary of Commerce Henry Wallace—who was handsome and loquacious and too liberal to have been chosen as FDR's latest VP—stood still as a cigar-store Indian. Interior Secretary Harold Ickes swatted impatiently at reporters on his way into the meeting. In his rush to get to the White House, Chief Justice Harlan Stone had had no time to don his black robes, and arrived in an ordinary suit.[11] Everyone waited nervously as the usher darted around the adjacent rooms in search of a Bible. Finally, in the minute between 7:08 and 7:09 P.M.[12]—a little less than three hours after FDR had been pronounced dead—Harry S. Truman raised his right hand, recited the thirty-five words of the oath of office, and then stepped into the shoes of the greatest wartime president the country had known since Abraham Lincoln.

Immediately after Truman left her, Eleanor had started to pack for the flight to Warm Springs. At that point, it became clear to her social secretary, Edith Helm, that planning for the funeral could never wait until the First Lady's return. Rather than going home, Helm had dinner at the White House. Afterward, she sought out Anna Roosevelt and also Eleanor's personal secretary, Malvina Thompson. Anna had been living in the White House since January 1944, having moved in to be closer to her ailing father.[13] She would have followed him down to Warm Springs on this last trip, too, had it not been for her son Johnny, still bedridden at Walter Reed. No doubt, Anna had felt frustrated over having to stay behind, but it would all turn into a perverse blessing. Now that it was time to plan the funeral, Anna would be the sole Roosevelt present to represent the family until Eleanor's return.

First, Helm explained to the women, she needed their help in locating any records left from the funeral of the last president to die during his term.[14] That man had been Warren G. Harding, felled by apoplexy in an office that had overwhelmed him—"My God," he'd once said, "this is a hell of a job."[15] Though there was little that FDR would have wanted to imitate about Harding the Republican, death rites were another matter. State funerals set precedents—and FDR thought highly of following precedents. "It's important how things will appear in history," Roosevelt had once pronounced to his wife.[16] But Harding had died twenty-two years earlier, and the file was nowhere to be found. Helm gave up and decided to call a meeting.

In the West Hall, a cozy, second-floor nook dominated by a half-moon window overlooking the rose garden, a cluster of Roosevelt's intimates gathered in the glow of table lamps: Jonathan Daniels, Anna Roosevelt and Malvina Thompson, protocol chief George Summerlin, and Social Bureau officer A. B. Tolley (who was also White House Calligrapher). The meeting surely would have taken longer were it not for Summerlin, who had managed to locate the State Department's own file on the Harding funeral.[17]

With a byzantine task ahead, the committee immediately decided to borrow the same style and wording of the 1923 funeral invitation, simply replacing Harding's name with Roosevelt's. At 11:00 P.M., Tolley rose to take the order over to the Government Printing Office, just two blocks from Union Station on North Capitol Street. Inside the gargantuan brick building, the typesetters and pressmen prioritized the ticket; all of the cards were printed, cut, boxed, and ready by 9:00 the next morning.[18]

Running off invitations was one thing; whom to send them to was another matter. Within hours of the announcement of FDR's death, requests to attend the funeral had been crackling over the White House telegraph. By the next day, there would be an onslaught of messages: "SHOCKED MAY I COME DOWN FOR FUNERAL," wired correspondent and illustrator S. J. Woolf from New York. "IN MY PROFOUND MOURNING FOR THE PRESIDENT DEATH I WOULD LIKE TO ATTEND FUNERAL TOMORROW COULD YOU GIVE ME DIRECTION," telegraphed flutist Rene Le Roy, who had once performed at the White House.[19]

Some of those who wrote had enjoyed genuine ties of friendship to the president, such as Mrs. George Barnett, whose husband had been Marine commandant back when FDR was acting secretary of the Navy. If no space could be found for her, the gracious Mrs. Barnett promised, "I will be there in loving thoughts."[20] Many others, though, attempted to trade on little more than chance meetings and decades-old acquaintanceships to get onto the guest list. With an efficient but merciless stroke of a pencil—probably Helm's—these piles of requests soon bore a small inscription: "No." Ralph W. Varney had been a classmate of Roosevelt's at Harvard; Gerard Beeckman once looked after FDR's stamp collection; George H. Maines was an "old friend" of the family from Poughkeepsie. No, no, and no.[21]

Most everyone would be told no, and there was an overriding reason for it: The East Room, where the service would take place, could hold only two hundred people. While Supreme Court justices and foreign heads of state would find chairs, most everyone else would not.[22] Edith Helm soon devised a boilerplate apology—succinctly frank, not unkind, and wholly truthful—then wired it back to the hopeful masses: "ON ACCOUNT LIMITATIONS OF SPACE INVITATIONS CONFINED TO OFFICIALS AND FAMILY. MRS. ROOSEVELT GREATLY REGRETS THAT IT HAS BEEN NECESSARY TO MAKE THESE RESTRICTIONS AND THAT SO MANY FRIENDS OF THE PRESIDENT MUST BE DISAPPOINTED."[23]

With the committee having decided on how to turn people away, it then confronted the painstaking task of whom to invite. Diplomats, justices, cabinet members, a delegation from Congress, state governors, and FDR's personal staff—181 of them would see their names on the invitation list.[24] (It was made clear that the invitations did not include spouses.) Roughly an equal number of additional guests would be escorted by ushers to other rooms in the White House—the State Dining Room, the Movie Room, and various parlors—which the maintenance crew would wire for loudspeakers.

Helm's meeting notes make no mention of how long the group spent conducting its business. Most likely it had taken them many hours and the adjournment did not come until late into the night. When the meeting finally ended, Daniels rose and made his way down to the Executive Wing. Taking one of the White House ushers into the Oval Office with him, Daniels began wrapping up the trinkets on FDR's desk.

The following day, Friday the thirteenth, as the funeral train slowly threaded its way through Georgia and the Carolinas toward Washington, Edith Helm and the officers of the Social Bureau encamped in the West Wing, dispatching messengers with envelopes containing funeral invitations and the admittance cards that guards would require to allow entry to the White House. Some invitations were mailed by special delivery.[25] Everything had to be done in a matter of hours. When Justice Robert H. Jackson returned home that afternoon, his wife, Irene, told him she'd received a call from Helm, reminding them both to be at Union Station to meet the train the next morning. Helm "thought the request had been mailed to us," the justice recalled, "but might not have reached us."[26] Clearly, the white-gloved efficiency of the White House Social Bureau had been brutally taxed by the need to hurry.

In the West Wing, amid the din of shuffling papers, slamming doors, and ringing phones, an outsider had to tread carefully to keep out of the way. One of those outsiders happened to be Harry Truman, who had arrived early that Friday morning and was doing his best to conduct his first full day as president.

Entering the Oval Office, Truman paused to take in the intimidating majesty of FDR's mess. His eyes swept past the ship models, the maritime prints, the cozy chairs upholstered in a scallop-patterned plush. Shiny floor ashtrays stood like sentries on the green-blue carpeting.[27] The place looked as if the big man himself might roll in at any moment, adjust his pince-nez, and light up a Camel at the end of his long, wooden cigarette holder. Even Roosevelt's desk, despite Jonathan Daniels's visit of the night before, was still "laden with mementos," Truman would recall. "Everywhere were signs of the man who had labored there so long."[28] It had, in fact, been twelve years, one month, and nine days that FDR had labored as president. During that time, the Oval Office and the man elected to serve four terms within it had become as inextricable as the gray-green paint that had long ago dried on its walls.

Truman would eventually redecorate the office to his liking, but this morning he had no desire to change anything.[29] He might even have avoided sitting in the Boss's chair, had there been any other suitable place in the room. There wasn't. "I was forced to use the desk," Truman confessed in his memoirs years later, but first he asked an aide to wrap up what remained of FDR's desktop menagerie and put all the objects safely away.[30] This gesture would hardly be the limit of Harry Truman's deference that morning. An anxious hive of FDR's staffers swarmed just outside the Oval Office door, and "I even attempted, as much as possible, to keep from interfering," Truman would recall later. Even with a country to govern and a world war to conduct, Truman sympathized with Roosevelt's assistants. They were, he wrote, "overwhelmed... with the plans for the coming funeral."[31]

That Friday, the weightiest duty rested on the shoulders of Colonel Richard Park, FDR's military aide, who spent most of the day drawing up plans for the ceremony itself—an elaborate armed forces procession from Union Station, followed by a brief service in the East Room. As the late-afternoon shadows lengthened across the White House lawn, Colonel Park called a general meeting of the funeral committee. They met in the "Fish Room"—a nickname inspired by Roosevelt's having used the conference chamber across the corridor from the Oval Office to display his aquarium and fishing trophies.[32]

Thirty-two people filled the tall, windowless space[33]—brass from the State Department, the military, and the Secret Service formed an unlikely mix with the primped and precise people from the social and protocol offices.[34] Agents Mike Reilly and James Rowley had flown up from Warm Springs ahead of the funeral train aboard an Army Air Transport Command plane, touching down in D.C. at 7:30 P.M. and then taking a car straight to the West Wing.[35] Most likely, the men were latecomers to a meeting that had begun without them. Reilly took a seat at the conference table and Rowley slipped into a chair along the wall.

Some of those assembled thought in terms of crowd control, others about flourish and historical precedent. But all were aware that the largest event in Washington's history would have to be discussed, revised, and finalized before anyone could leave the room. Park rose and began to read his draft of the proposed ceremony aloud, paragraph by paragraph.[36]

Sitting in the room as Colonel Park spoke was White House transportation man Edwin Fauver (transport chief Dewey Long was at that moment on the funeral train en route from Warm Springs). Most of the other officials concerned themselves with the procession of the cortege and East Room services; Fauver, however, faced a specific task. The funeral train was due in from Warm Springs Saturday morning at 10:00. By Saturday evening, the train had to be ready for its second leg: the run to Hyde Park.

It would be no simple affair. First there was the question of how many people could be taken to the Hudson Valley estate. Each would have to be given a Pullman berth, as this was an overnight run of over three hundred miles. The drafting of the passenger manifest was a tedious, piecemeal effort that stretched from Friday evening until well into the next day.[37] Everything would begin with a core list of sixty-six names chosen by Eleanor Roosevelt, working with Grace Tully on the funeral train bound for D.C.[38] From there, the roster would immediately begin to fatten with the names of must-haves for both the Roosevelts and the Trumans. There were old friends and still older relatives to be included, colonels, majors, and long-suffering assistants. Trusted political allies like Chicago's mayor Ed Kelly and New York's governor Herbert Lehman could not be left out; Edith Helm, Colonel Park, Edwin Fauver, and the many others who'd have a hand in drafting the manifest made sure they were not. At some point, early in the list's development, an alert staffer recalled that the Trumans had a daughter, and so a "Miss Truman" appeared in pencil near the top of the roster.[39]

On successive sheets of paper, the Pullmans filled—with justices (all nine of them), with journalists (including the "Three Musketeers" of Oliver, Nixon, and Smith), and with advisors like Edwin Pauley and George Allen, whose lack of official titles at least left them with a "Mister" typed before their names. For White House assistants who happened to have dark skin, that show of respect was denied. By Saturday afternoon, the revised funeral train list would grow to eighty-two names.[40] The final manifest that Dewey Long wired to agents in the field, three and a half hours before the train would leave—contained 102.[41]

The guests selected to attend both the funeral and the burial would receive notes from Edith Helm furnishing all the necessary details. The invitation dispatched that Friday to the Shoreham Hotel for Secretary of State Edward Stettinius, for example, requested that he and his wife meet the funeral train for its arrival at Union Station the next morning and then return to the terminal that night: "Mrs. Roosevelt wishes me to notify you that the train will leave from the same track at 10:00 P.M. Saturday," Helm wrote. "You are invited to go to Hyde Park."[42]

Everyone wanted to go to Hyde Park, and this left Fauver and the transportation men with a problem of diplomatic proportions, quite literally. Space limitations inside the White House were a tactful, and indisputable, reason to exclude many mourners—even a good many important ones. But a train is different. Extra sleepers could (and would) be added, but with so many members of Congress—even those who loathed FDR when he was alive—now clamoring for seats, it became clear that only one thing could be done about it. When it steamed out of Washington the following evening, the Franklin Delano Roosevelt funeral train would be *two* trains.

Thus would become the hierarchy of the rails: The original funeral train of eleven cars on its way up from Warm Springs would be lengthened to eighteen as soon as it reached the Union Station yards in D.C. Retaining the Pullmans *Ferdinand Magellan* (for Eleanor's use) and the *Conneaut* (to carry FDR's remains under guard), the augmented train would be large enough to accommodate the Supreme Court, the press corps, as well as FDR's cabinet, staff, family, and friends.

The second funeral train—dubbed, appropriately enough, the *Congressional*—would consist of eleven cars, to be filled with delegations appointed by the House and Senate. Remaining berths would go to various diplomats and overflow members of the media.[43] As a show of respect, both trains would be treated as equals. Both would have sleeping compartments for everyone. Both would be stocked with food and liquor. Yet it was quietly understood that the train carrying FDR's coffin was, of course, *the* funeral train.

The plan was logical and straightforward. It satisfied the technical demands of railroading and tiptoed successfully across the minefield of protocol. Its true genius, however, lay in its solution of a rather sticky problem: where to put the Trumans.

The *Ferdinand Magellan* was, in all circumstances, the president's private Pullman. It was the only railroad coach in America equipped to serve as both a rolling executive mansion and an armored car. For the trip up from Warm Springs, with a deceased FDR reposing aboard the *Conneaut*, there was of course no difficulty with Eleanor's occupying the *Magellan*. But once the train reached Washington, the situation would change. With Truman duly sworn in as the thirty-third president, the *Magellan* was his to use. But putting the car at his disposal would have meant asking a grieving widow to move her things into an ordinary Pullman sleeper. It was a socially uncouth request and, fortunately, one that would not have to be made.

Which is why, that Friday night, somewhere in the 226,696 miles of America's railroad grid, the *Roald Amundsen* was making its way to Washington for a rendezvous with destiny—which is to say, with President Harry Truman.

It had been a while since the stately old Pullman—a five-bedroom car complete with lounge, dining room, pantry, and staff quarters—had done any official duty. The *Amundsen* had rolled off Pullman's manufacturing line on December 19, 1928, right alongside the *Ferdinand Magellan*.[44] They were the last two cars in the "Explorer Series," the informal name for lots 6037 and 6246—six opulent business cars all named for famous pathfinders, including Robert Peary and Marco Polo.[45] Available for charter by anyone with sufficient means, the *Amundsen* soon began appearing at the tail of the presidential train.[46]

Roosevelt had become smitten with the *Amundsen*'s comforts during his 1936 reelection campaign and, four years later, the White House leased the car to serve full time on the POTUS consist. But then came Pearl Harbor, and Steve Early's insistence that FDR should have a specially built, armored railroad car. The White House picked the *Magellan* for the overhaul, a move that sent the *Amundsen* back into Pullman's regular charter fleet in 1942.[47]

But now the *Roald Amundsen* would be returning, if briefly, to presidential service—specifically to Truman's, but symbolically to Roosevelt's, too.

⊶⟾ ⟾⊷

Another issue that Fauver—together with the Secret Service—faced was the routing of the train itself. When the war had begun, FDR's rail trips up to the Hudson Valley estate had been changed to a backwoods route to keep the train out of the public eye. POTUS would leave Washington on the Baltimore & Ohio's main line and take it as far as Philadelphia, where it would switch to the Reading line's tracks as far as Bound Brook, New Jersey. From there, the train would creep through the grimy waterfront of Jersey City on freight tracks before knocking onto the New York Central's West Shore line and taking that all the way up to Highland, New York. Limousines whisked the party across the river to Hyde Park.[48]

This arrangement had worked well—but the route was scrapped for the funeral train, probably because motoring all the passengers across the bridge from Highland would have required hundreds of cars and closing too many roads. And so it was decided: From Washington, the train would take the Pennsylvania Railroad's main line into New York City and then the New York Central's east shore trunk—the famed "Water Level Route"—up to Hyde Park. Thanks to a private track that the Roosevelt family had put in years before, the funeral train could offload FDR's coffin right at the foot of the Roosevelt estate. The *Congressional* would continue further north and stop at the village depot.

The ground plan for the second leg of the funeral train would not be finalized until the following evening, Saturday the fourteenth, just hours before the actual trains slipped out of Union Station. The surviving pages of undated notes—scribbles, question marks, and cross-outs scrawled in an unknown hand below Secret Service letterhead—only hint at the myriad problems that needed solving: "5 truckloads only of flowers are desired here and it is requested they be put on *Congressional* to ease unloading," reads one line. A few pages later: "Dewey's list had 28 names coming up on train as guests and family. 18 press etc." And above that, the cryptic notation: "Can Nat Car 100 Trck 5 Pkp Supt NYC Car for him need agent." This note referred to the Canadian prime minister, Mackenzie King, who would be arriving at the Poughkeepsie train station on Track 5 aboard his private Pullman, *Car 100*, and required a New York Central Railroad agent to drive him to Hyde Park.[49] The logistical problems were endless, but one issue towered above all the others: that of protecting the train itself.

Looking back on the event from a time in which terrorism on domestic shores is no longer theoretical, the very idea of what took place on the fourteenth and fifteenth days of April 1945, borders on the ludicrous: The new president and his cabinet, the most senior and influential members of Congress, the nine robes of high judicial bench, and the highest-ranking officers of the armed forces—in sum, the entire leadership of the free world—elected to board a single train and take a trip together. It was an excursion that took them through some of the most densely populated urban centers of the United States, along a route that had been announced in advance—and it all happened during the largest global conflict in recorded history. It is difficult to imagine any occasion of state today—joyous or tragic—that could galvanize so many men and women of variant callings and opposing views and bring them together for such a visible, spectacular, and altogether dangerous undertaking. Even in 1945, the thing felt momentous. "In the history of the American government," noted Thomas Reynolds of the *Chicago Sun*, "there probably never before were so many top-ranking officials of the government in one single place."[50]

Whether in deference to the dead president or for fear of planting ideas in the minds of subversives, few remarked publicly about how the funeral train—profound and historic a mourning ritual as it was—represented an unprecedented imperilment to national security at a time the country could least afford to play games with fate. Hindsight, however, would loosen lips. Writing twenty-seven years after she rode aboard the *Roald Amundsen* as the comely young daughter of the new president, Margaret Truman reflected: "In retrospect, it seems a terribly dangerous thing to have done in time of war. If sabotage or an accident had wrecked that train, the nation would have been crippled."[51]

Indeed, it would have—and such an accident actually had come close to happening once before. On November 14, 1943, the battleship *Iowa* was steaming through the Caribbean, taking the president to Cairo for a conference with Winston Churchill and Chiang Kai-shek. Several of America's most important military commanders were also aboard, including General George Marshall and Admiral Earnest King. Fifty miles east of Bermuda, the destroyer *William D. Porter*—which had been conducting a drill—mistakenly fired a torpedo at the *Iowa*. The warhead narrowly missed the *Iowa*'s hull and exploded in its wake. The close call prompted this entry in Roosevelt's log: "Had that torpedo hit the *Iowa* in the right spot with her passenger list of distinguished statesmen, military, naval, and aerial strategists and planners, it could have had untold effect on the outcome of the war and the destiny of the country."[52]

The train ride was a security undertaking of a size and scope never before attempted on American soil: a martial lockdown of 328 miles of railroad track, some 30 of which snaked through New York City, whose population exceeded 7.2 million. It would involve everyone from plain-clothes detectives to armed infantrymen. It would also amount to one of the darker ironies in the shadow world of government: The Secret Service, whose sole purpose was to maintain the well-being of a live president, now faced the biggest challenge of its existence over a dead one.

Beginning with the fortification of the *Ferdinand Magellan* in 1942, POTUS was arguably already the most secure train on earth. (The only possible exception was Hitler's special train, the *Fuhrersonderzug*—which went by the code name *Amerika*, of all things. The Fuhrer's personal Pullman, car No. 10206, was, like FDR's carriage, armored, though the *Ferdinand Magellan* outweighed it by some 20 tons.[53]) The mandated security protocols for Roosevelt's train trips had been end-less, ranging from the tasting of every victual stocked in the dining-car pantries, to the selection of a particular grade of coal to be used in the locomotive firebox.[54]

On its regular runs to Hyde Park, the train usually left the platform beneath the Bureau of Engraving and Printing in D.C. just shy of mid-night. But to allow track workers the time to check every foot of rail in advance of the president's train, the railroad's main line might be shut down as many as six hours in advance. As the security men swept through, they'd often tow away automobiles left parked anywhere adja-cent to the right-of-way, just in case a saboteur had elected to hide himself or anything inside.[55] Historically, the Secret Service's most effective measure for protecting POTUS had been stealth; most of the wartime journeys had been "blackout trips" for which no announcement would be made, no newspaper story written.[56] This time, of course, no such stealth was possible. Everyone in America knew the funeral train would be traveling from Washington to Hyde Park. The Associated Press did not help security matters by laying out the entire schedule of the funeral train—including exact arrival and departure times—for syndication in national newspapers.[57]

If the funeral train forfeited the advantage of secrecy, it would turn the odds back to its favor with both its itinerary and the hours it traveled.

Between Washington and Hyde Park, the train would be making only three stops: Philadelphia, Pennsylvania Station in New York, and the New York Central Railroad's Mott Haven yards in the Bronx, a sprawling interlocking near Yankee Stadium where the Central maintained its Pullman fleet. Because the hazards of running the train through a metropolis went without saying, it would be happening at a time when most citizens were in bed. The train was scheduled to slip into Penn Station at 4:40 A.M. and pause for twenty minutes; the Mott Haven stop was slated for 6:25 to 6:45.[58] The layovers had been added only because the crews needed to switch out the locomotives. By the time most New Yorkers would be up and about, the Secret Service hoped, the train would be long gone.

Still, the funeral train's first leg—in progress even as the second was being planned—demonstrated that Americans were more than willing to stand all night just to get a glimpse of the *Conneaut*. It was clear the Washington-to–Hyde Park section of the route had to be secured.

As a preliminary step, the division superintendents of both railroads received orders to move all freight and passenger trains clear and have their road workers double-check every switch and turnout under their jurisdiction.[59] Plans called for the Roosevelt section and the *Congressional* to maintain a margin of 1.5 miles between them all the way up the line. If anything went wrong, the trains would be a safe distance apart. The sections would take turns at the lead, and the railroads would post emergency standby locomotives along the route, just in case any of the engines failed.[60]

For the Secret Service to have any hope of guarding over three hundred miles of train track, it would have to rely heavily on the help of the railroads (which marshaled track gangs and their own police force), the FBI (which helped to coordinate city police), and the armed forces. The Secret Service was already depending on just about any man with a uniform to help protect the train on its first leg. In Greenville, for example, the guards posted along the tracks had come from Fort Jackson, the Greenville Police Department, the sheriff's office, and the State Highway Patrol. Even the local American Legion sent some vets over.[61]

Even if it had wanted to—and the author has found no evidence that it did—the government could probably never have guarded the funeral train's entire route through the southern states. Not only was the distance—722 miles from Warm Springs to Washington, D.C.—prohibitively long and isolated, the indelicate truth was that, with the notable exception of Eleanor Roosevelt, the funeral train that left Warm Springs carried few living souls of sufficiently high military or civic rank to warrant such extreme protection. But that picture would change for the run north of Washington. Not only would most of the federal government be aboard, the funeral train would be knocking along the heavily populated industrial corridor connecting New York City and the capital. Guarding the funeral train's second leg, therefore, was critical—and the Secret Service was determined to guard every single mile of it.[62] Thousands of soldiers would stand, evenly spaced, along the Pennsylvania Railroad's four-track main line all the way up to New York. From there, the Army would post thousands more to stand along the New York Central's track up the Hudson.[63] In the cities, the FBI and local cops would take over. Philadelphia's mayor Bernard Samuel ordered his entire police force into uniform.[64]

In New York, the security would be unrivaled. The NYPD marshaled eight hundred officers for duty, including what the press called the "the sabotage and alien squads." They stood on the streets, in Penn Station, and even bobbed in patrol boats.[65] (The funeral train would be taking tunnels under the Hudson and East rivers.) Mott Haven Junction in the Bronx would be turned into a literal police state. On Sunday morning, residents of the apartment houses near the railroad yards might have thought for a moment that they lived in recently liberated Paris: American soldiers were patrolling the 153rd street viaduct over the layup tracks, machine guns drawn.[66]

As for the top agents, they would be fanning out. Secret Service chief Michael Reilly—one of the few who'd been trusted to physically carry FDR when he was alive—would take eleven of his best men and fly out of Washington ahead of the funeral train on Saturday afternoon. Nearly six hours before the train even left Union Station, the Secret Service agents would be landing at Stuart Field near West Point. Army cars would take them across the Hudson River to Hyde Park, where Reilly's men would spend the night of the fourteenth with Agent McGrath of District No. 2, figuring out how to lock down the town of Hyde Park. George Drescher and his men, meanwhile, were put in charge of protecting Truman.[67]

Today, sixty-five years after the death of Franklin Roosevelt, parts of the Secret Service file pertaining to the protection of his funeral train still remain classified.[68]

FOUR

THE MAIN LINE

At 2:15 P.M. Friday, as the Atlanta skyline disappeared in the distance through the *Ferdinand Magellan*'s observation windows, Eleanor Roosevelt and Grace Tully sat beside each other in the lounge's deep plush chairs. The First Lady had summoned her down to the *Magellan* not long after the funeral train steamed north out of Warm Springs.[1] Now, as the gray concrete of Atlanta gradually ceded to the undulating greens of Chattahoochee, the women could resume their work.

There was plenty of it to do. So many arrangements had to be made: a service in the White House, a burial in Hyde Park, and a funeral train—bigger and more elaborate than this one—to travel between the two. Up in Washington, Colonel Park's meeting in the Fish Room would not convene for another few hours, so it was unlikely the women knew of the plans, soon to be in the offing, to add an entire second train for the run to Hyde Park. In practice, though, it did not matter. The guest list for the journey's next leg had to be started. Though Edith Helm and the Social Bureau staff would contribute a great deal to that enormous task, so long as the two minds they needed most—the president's wife and his personal secretary—happened to be aboard Pullman cars clacking through the middle of Dixie, some of the planning would have to be done here, on the rails.

Before beginning the passenger list, however, Eleanor decided to take care of a more immediate order of business. She wished to find some way of responding to the thousands of condolence messages pouring in by telegram and post. The First Lady had seen them as they'd begun arriving at Warm Springs and, though she could not see the ones accumulating in Washington, they were now forming a small mountain in the White House.[2]

Grace Tully and Eleanor decided that a response should to be sent to everyone who had written—but something standardized would have to be composed. The two settled on a simple sentence: "Mrs. Roosevelt and family thank you for your condolences and kind thought." It was to be printed on white card stock with a black border.[3]

At the head of the train, the lumbering tonnage of B&O communications car No. 1401 swayed beneath the smoke trail of the locomotives. Grateful to be of use, the Signal Corps men warmed up the circuitry for Grace Tully's telegram, bound for Mr. Tolley of the White House Social Bureau. In a message of extravagant length—138 words, not an abbreviation among them—Tully relayed the precise wording of the card, then asked Tolley to place an initial print order for 2,500 of them. "It is impossible at this moment to know how many we will need," she wrote. "But the Government Printing Office could get started."[4] When the telegram arrived in Washington, it was printed on official White House letterhead and stamped: "Rec'd. 4/13/45 4:00 PM."

The condolence issue dispatched, the women in the *Ferdinand Magellan* shifted their attentions to more difficult matters. The First Lady hesitated, then spoke: "Did Franklin ever give you any instructions about his burial?"[5] For a moment—the only time Tully or anyone else would recall seeing for the entire train trip—Eleanor Roosevelt's voice broke and her eyes welled. She recovered instantly.[6]

All that Tully could remember was a conversation that she and FDR had had about a year before, when he had told her that he liked the idea of being buried at sea. The former U.S. Navy undersecretary had been in one of his nostalgic, seadog moods. Tully, who did not often get her Irish up with the Boss, not only told him she thought idea awful but that everyone in America would agree with her. He dropped it.[7]

As the *Magellan* advanced northward, Grace Tully recalled something else: The president had in fact dictated his funeral instructions to a previous secretary some years before—but the typed sheets had been lost. Tully had searched all the files months ago, she recalled to Eleanor, but had come up empty. The president had said he would dictate his wishes a second time, but he never had.[8] The women had to start from scratch.

Unbeknownst to either, at that very moment four sheets of paper lay folded in an envelope and locked inside a White House safe—FDR's personal one, located in his bedroom on the second floor. The papers contained typewritten, detailed instructions on how the president wished to be buried.[9]

Eleanor already knew, at least, how her husband did *not* wish to be buried. "We had talked often," the First Lady would remember years later, "when there had been a funeral at the Capitol in which a man had lain in state and the crowds had gone by the open coffin, of how much we disliked the practice; and we had made up our minds that we would never allow it."[10] The casket would remain closed.

As the train pressed on, Eleanor asked Tully to do her best to remember to whom FDR had promised the myriad paintings hanging in the Oval Office as "personal gifts."[11] The president had mentally earmarked many to distribute to his assistants—presumably, once his fourth term ended—as expressions of gratitude for their service. As the *Magellan* bobbed along the southern rails, Tully committed her memories to paper. She recalled that Roosevelt had meant to give his portrait of John Paul Jones (a junk-shop find that, following a careful cleaning, revealed itself to be a fine painting) to typist Dorothy Brady. Tully also took this opportunity to reveal that the Boss had selected a painting to give to her, too, and jotted down her own name beside that of a small seascape that hung just to the right of the Oval Office fireplace. To FDR's Secretary, the gift was tantamount to priceless, for she remembered always looking at the canvas as she sat on the big leather sofa with Roosevelt, taking shorthand.[12] At length, Tully and the First Lady worked their way to the biggest undertaking of the journey: the list of those whom Eleanor wished to take on the funeral train's second leg to Hyde Park.

As the miles of sweltering countryside rolled slowly by outside the air-conditioned *Magellan*, the women penciled a list of the people to be honored with a Pullman berth. (This was, actually, the second time Eleanor had made a list like this. At the cottage in Warm Springs the previous night, William Hassett had sat with her to determine who would be aboard for *this* leg of the train ride. Fala's name appeared near the top of the roster.[13]) The sixty-six names that would be wired to the White House formed the core of the "Roosevelt people" aboard the train bound for Hyde Park.[14] There would, of course, be Truman's people, too. But apart from making sure that "the President and Mrs. Truman" were included on the list (fortunately, the Social Bureau at the White House would remember to add Margaret), the guests of the thirty-third president were not their concern.

Leading off the manifest were the names of FDR's intimates— Hassett, press secretaries Steve Early and Jonathan Daniels, Margaret Suckley, and FDR's sons James and Elliott. Farther down came the members of the Roosevelt cabinet. The four-page list also included the former director of war mobilization, James F. Byrnes, a man whose arrogance and ambition placed him outside the realm of those whom Eleanor trusted, and presidential aide Lauchlin Currie.

Though the train had an entire day to ply the 722 track miles between Warm Springs and Washington, there was no way it could stop at the smaller towns along the route; a running speed of 25 mph simply would not permit it. Nonetheless, Steve Early had asked the engineers to ease off the throttle at the depots so that people's respects would not be repaid by a face full of track dust.[15]

One such slowdown took place at Clemson, South Carolina, 123 miles up the line from Atlanta. Clemson University was a military school, and the commander in chief's death had affected the cadets deeply. With their banners aloft, the young men had marched in long, sinuous columns down to the railroad tracks. Now, high up in locomotives Nos. 1409 and 1394, Claude Blackmon and L. B. Griffith, the graybeards who'd been entrusted to take the funeral train onto the main line in Atlanta, were preparing to turn everything over to the next crew in Greenville, 30 miles ahead. But the engineers slowed their machines down to 10 mph as the Spanish-tile roof of the Clemson depot came into view. A field of uniforms stretched out beneath the eaves. Holding out flags trimmed in fringe, the cadet color guard— four peach-faced lads young enough to resemble Boy Scouts—stood at attention as the Pullmans slipped past. At length, the *Conneaut* drew up. Hands rose to foreheads in salute.[16] And then the train was no more.

For hours, the smoky engines had lugged the funeral train over miles of Georgia clay, past groves of Leyland cypresses and live oaks, and through cotton fields girdled with weathered timber fencing. "The

President would have enjoyed the ride," wrote Merriman Smith. "He loved to sit beside the broad window of his private car and comment on the condition of the soil and forests."[17]

Smith, who had torn so many dispatches from his typewriter that he'd reached "the saturation point when it came to writing anything more about the grieving South,"[18] still found himself awed by the emotional displays. In field after field that the train had passed, farmers in rags had tugged their mules to a halt and then walked slowly toward the tracks, clutching their dust-caked hats in their hands. At the highway crossings, motorists had slid out from behind their steering wheels to stand like sentries beside their trucks, coupes, and four-door sedans.[19] On the approach to Gainesville, fifty miles out of Atlanta, Smith had stared out the windows in disbelief as the train passed a group of women picking cotton under the merciless sun. At the sight of the train, they dropped to their knees in the tilled dirt, their palms stretched up to the heavens.[20]

Engineer Blackmon reached for his brake valve. The funeral train's wheels hissed as their flanges rubbed the railheads for the gradual westward sweep into the Greenville Station. Now, after a full day's run, Washington was 153 miles closer than it had been at Atlanta. In the gathering dusk, trees and woodframe houses of the South Carolina city threw long shadows across the embankment. Ahead, what looked like a row of fence posts flanked the main-line track on both sides—but these were not fence posts. They were uniformed servicemen standing at attention as the hot, dripping engines hissed down the canopied platform. Behind them stood thousands of civilians. Many of them balanced atop the rails of layup tracks nearby to get a better view. For the U.S. Army photographer aboard the Air Force plane soaring high above the scene, it created the illusion of train tracks made of people.

Twenty-five thousand had come, and their number stretched half a mile on either side of the main line. The funeral train rolled to a stop a few minutes shy of 7:00 P.M., and Steve Early stepped onto the platform to shake hands with C. Fred McCullough. Greenville's mayor had two floral arrangements with him. The first, an elaborate spray of lilies and red roses, was from the citizenry—most of whom were standing right behind him. Mrs. Kate Finley, whose son had died in the war, had produced the other, a wreath of red and white carnations. Two policemen carried the tributes aboard the *Conneaut*, setting them down near the floral eruption taken aboard in Atlanta, which covered the entire forward wall of the Pullman's lounge.[21]

At the roundhouse, foreman "Dot" Schultz was putting the final spit polish on the new pair of locomotives, Nos. 1401 and 1385, that would be cutting in to relieve Blackmon's and Griffith's machines.[22] No. 1401 embodied the pride of the Southern's locomotive fleet. She was 92 feet long and 281 tons, and the tops of her six 73-inch driving wheels stood well over the heads of many men. But it was the livery of No. 1401 and her main-line sisters—borrowed from the engines of Britain's railways—that dazzled. The length of her enormous boiler wore a coat of apple-green paint trimmed in gold, while a glimmering aluminum adorned her nose drum, rims, and running boards. The Southern Railway's system totaled 8,000 miles of train track; nowhere in that iron maze could be found locomotives better dressed than these.[23] Their reversers thrown and throttles cracked open, Engineers Richard "Easy" Cooksey and O. B. Surratt backed their opulent machines down the track.[24]

The funeral train had left Warm Springs wearing no outward sign of its duty. On Schultz's watch, that was about to change. Taking an American flag down from the rafters of the shop, "Dot" and his men tacked it across No. 1401's nose, then stood for a photograph with the locomotive before letting it on its way.[25] With the new engines coupled onto the train, "Box" Childers, the fireman back in the second engine, stared up the tracks. An unbroken multitude of people packed both sides of the main line as far as he could see. Later, Childers said: "I believe you could have walked on their heads all the way to Salisbury."[26] At 7:05, with most of the daylight gone from Greenville, No. 1401 led the funeral train out of town.

At 7:17 P.M., a telegram from the train arrived at the White House, attention of transportation man Fauver: "FOLLOWING IS APPROVED LIST OF MEMBERS OF OUR PARTY WASHINGTON TO HYDE PARK AND RETURN."[27] At some point late in the day, the communications car cabled another message from Eleanor Roosevelt, this one far more personal. It caught up with James Roosevelt somewhere during his hopscotch across the Pacific toward New York and told him the funeral would be Saturday afternoon. "Our plane was bucking head winds," the young Roosevelt remembered. "I knew in my heart I was going to be too late."[28]

⊶⟌⟍ ⟍⟌⊶

North of Greenville, No. 1401's head light knifed through the warm, inky darkness, the American flag stuck flat to the smoke box hatch by the wind. One by one, the funeral train's cars coalesced with the southern night as attendants pulled down the heavy canvas shades.[29] Only the lights back in the *Conneaut* remained visible, the shades in the lounge lifted up into their pockets, so that those who stood trackside as the train rumbled past could see Roosevelt's catafalque.[30] The old Pullman lounge car looked like a ghostly lantern as it swayed gently on its way; there would be no mistaking it.

At some point, Steve Early decided to allow the three wire reporters a brief visit to the *Conneaut*[31]; there was only so much even the best reporter could write about weeping crowds. The newsmen filed slowly down the length of the train, passing through the dining car and into the *Ferdinand Magellan*, where they found Eleanor Roosevelt in the lounge. She was knitting.

While Robert Nixon had developed a deep respect for FDR, it was one that, as an employee of William Randolph Hearst's unapologetically right-leaning International News Service, he would largely keep from coloring his prose.[32] But the president's death had changed things, even at the Hearst papers. Earlier this day, Nixon had written with genuine reverence a description of Roosevelt's final moments. "He was stricken at his desk," read Nixon's dispatch (presumably referring to the portable work table that had been drawn up to FDR's chair in the cottage), "still striving for his great goal—to banish the threat of war and warfare from the world for generations to come."[33] The copy desk let it be.

One by one, the reporters expressed their condolences to the First Lady. It was their first chance to address her following FDR's death. Eleanor took the time to speak to each of the men personally. "You have been very kind," she said to Oliver.[34] Then the reporters took their leave, passing through the *Magellan*'s rear door and out onto the open platform where the hot, humid wind whipped through their shirts. The *Conneaut*'s door shut heavily behind the newsmen, sealing them in a kind of sanctum. After passing down the narrow corridor past the stateroom doors, the chaperoned group reached the chamber where the Boss's coffin lay beneath the stony gaze of the guards. Frosted-glass wall sconces bathed the room in light. Enormous floral wreaths and sprays rubbed their backs up against the Pullman's metal walls; it looked as if the armed forces had posted sentries in the Garden of Eden.

About an hour out of Greenville, the funeral train slowed for a ten-minute service stop at Hayne, South Carolina, where the nimbus of light spilling from the *Conneaut*'s rear windows washed the faces of young soldiers who stood guard along 500 yards of track. Performing a duty that was second nature by now, Steve Early stepped down to the platform to receive another enormous wreath of flowers. This one was from the people of Spartanburg, 1.7 miles up the line, where 11,000 people had gathered to watch the train pass.[35]

In the *Magellan*, Eleanor found herself suddenly exhausted,[36] as if her own burning filament of strength and fortitude had suffered its plug pulled. Making her way up through the car, she stepped into the oak-paneled meeting room where she took a seat at the table. There, the waiter served her dinner.

A mere three years had passed since the *Magellan* had emerged from its makeover and fortification at the Pullman car barns in Chicago. And yet, in that space of time, Franklin Roosevelt had traveled over 50,000 miles in the car, many of them without his wife.[37] The treads of his wheelchair had rolled over the same dark-green carpet on which Eleanor now stepped; he'd sat countless times at this very table, the room filled with his laugher, smoke, and the scent of liquor, every eye gazing at the quick-witted president in the Brooks Brothers oxford who could host a party as well as he could run a country. But on this evening, as the 142 tons of presidential Pullman ventured into the night, the only sounds came from the wheels rumbling below as the wife of the late Franklin D. Roosevelt picked up her silverware and dined alone.

Though Stateroom "B" had been hers, Eleanor had asked porter Fred Fair to make up the president's bed instead. The First Lady closed the door of "C" behind her, changed, and slid between the sheets. Try as she did to sleep, however, Eleanor found that she could not. "I lay in my berth all night with the window shade up, looking out at the countryside he had loved and watching the faces of the people at the stations, and even at the cross-roads, who came to pay their last tribute all through the night," she would write later on. "I never realized the true scope of the devotion to him until he died."[38]

It was not lost on Eleanor Roosevelt that her husband's remains were making their way home nearly eighty years to the day that Abraham Lincoln's own interment train had done the very same thing. FDR, ever aware of the importance of precedent, tradition, and how history would record his legacy, would have been pleased at the coincidence. The First Lady remembered a poem just then. It was Millard Lampell's "The Lonesome Train," written to commemorate the death of Lincoln.[39] Its haunting lines about the loneliness of a train on its way to bury a president found a new definition within Stateroom "C" of the *Magellan*.

In the compartment he shared with the Associated Press's Harold Oliver, Merriman Smith was hunched over his typewriter again, hammering out another story for the UP. As he felt the train's pace slacken, he looked out of the window. He didn't know the name of the town—only that the train was somewhere in North Carolina, and there was no scheduled stop here. Below the Pullman's floor, the brake shoes gave a quick squeeze to the wheels, and the funeral train slowed to walking pace. It was nearly 11:00 P.M. Smith left his compartment, padded down the sleeper's corridor, and, yanking open the heavy vestibule door, poked his head outside.

The entire city of Charlotte—or damned near to it—had turned out. Every street reaching away from the railroad track was, for three blocks, a solid mass of people. They stood in the darkness staring at the train as Smith stared back at them.

No one knows who started it, or whether it was planned or spontaneous, but as the train drew up to Charlotte's tiny station, a clutch of Boy Scouts began to sing "Onward Christian Soldiers." A handful of adults around them joined in, then the ones behind them, and then the ones in earshot of those. In the next few moments, the bleary-eyed reporter heard thousands of voices rise in unison, such as no churchgoer had ever heard. It was, Smith later wrote, "the most impressive moment of the trip." Though the newsman felt it was "heartening to hear the little town tell itself that everything would be all right,"[40] he understood what lay just beneath those triumphal voices. "Those people were scared to death," Smith reflected. "They weren't singing for a departed soul. They were singing for themselves, to hold themselves up, as though they were asking, 'What are we going to do now?' "[41]

Leaving Charlotte behind, the train hastened back into the night. Aboard the *Conneaut*, the guards stood erect and silent, shifting their feet only to counterbalance themselves against a sudden pitch as the train leaned into a banking curve. As the car heeled, *Newsweek* wrote, the servicemen "glanced uneasily at the flag-draped casket."[42] At Patterson's direction, the carpenters had fitted the bier with a half-inch retaining lip,[43] but the coarse wool Marine blanket covering the pine made a slippery pedestal for a polished copper box that weighed nearly a third of a ton. As the *Conneaut* swung back to level trackage, the men exhaled.

Their anxiety proved groundless; the bier performed flawlessly. Four inches shy of two feet off the Pullman's floor, it brought the casket lid to three feet and nine inches—sternum height on the young men. The thousands of spectators who "saw" Roosevelt's coffin in reality viewed only the flag covering it—but they could see it perfectly. The bier had been a simple, intuitive, and yet wholly inspired piece of foresight.[44]

Even eleven cars back, the men in the *Conneaut* could hear the lead locomotive's whistle each time the train passed over a crossing. The distant, haunting wail "cut mournfully through the Southern countryside," *Newsweek* reported, "deepening the sense of loneliness and pain as the funeral train moved northward with the dead President."[45]

⊶⇌ ⇌⊷

Sometime during that Friday night, as the train bearing FDR's body rumbled through the darkened fields and thickets of the South, Elizabeth Shoumatoff's Cadillac was sputtering along the tangle of roadways on its way back to New York, drinking its wartime cocktail of watered-down gasoline.[46] Shoumatoff had let her assistant, Nicholas Robbins, do the driving. The painter sat in the passenger seat in silence. She had welcomed the refuge of Lucy Rutherfurd's stately brick Federal in

Aiken the previous night, but Shoumatoff and Robbins had left early in the morning. Shoumatoff's home in the affluent New York City suburb of Locust Valley loomed at the end of a 670-mile drive; the Russian artist—heartbroken, carrying FDR's unfinished portrait with her—found herself aching to get there.[47]

For this entire day, Shoumatoff's convertible and the Roosevelt funeral train had meandered northward, each on its separate route. Robbins, behind the car's big steering wheel, had tried to comfort Shoumatoff, but the Russian artist felt herself slipping with every mile. She was wretched for having to leave Lucy in a state of grief and imprisoned within her own grief, too. Shoumatoff had not known the president as Lucy had, but Roosevelt had won the painter completely over with his charms. Shoumatoff cherished the memory of a sunny afternoon in July 1943, when FDR had invited the painter to Hyde Park—for no other reason than to thank her for having painted his portrait a few weeks before. They'd enjoyed a lunch of Polish ham and chicken cream soup, and when Roosevelt took the wheel of his dark-blue 1936 Ford—equipped with hand controls just like his convertible down in Warm Springs—he had careened around the hairpin curves of the estate roads so fast that Shoumatoff had giggled like a schoolgirl.[48] The memory could not have been in starker contrast to this drive, now. Unable to bear the news reports of the president's death, Shoumatoff had refused to turn her car's radio on. Instead, she stared silently out the window. After a day's worth of driving, the sun had disappeared to the west, abandoning her to the gloom.

As the white convertible's headlamps cast their arc down the dark road, Robbins noticed the lights at a railroad crossing ahead begin to blink. He slowed the car to a stop. Seconds later, two enormous green locomotives flashed by, and then a string of cars—first baggage, then Pullmans. All of the train's windows were dark. As the last car rolled past, Shoumatoff noticed its lights ablaze. The windows framed a meadow of flowers, and in the center was a flag-draped casket.[49]

That night, long after most of the train's passengers had retired, housekeeper Lizzie McDuffie lay in her berth on one of the Pullmans, probably the *Imperator,* the old open-section sleeper coupled behind baggage car No. 549.[50] Down in Warm Springs, McDuffie had shared a room with Daisy Bonner, the local cook who'd discovered the white dove in Roosevelt's cottage. The two lived above the garage. McDuffie could sleep amid the smell of gasoline and exhaust; she could sleep beneath a baking tar roof; but aboard the funeral train, she could not sleep. McDuffie had twice walked through the train, all the way back to the *Ferdinand Magellan*, to ask Mrs. Roosevelt if she needed anything. Both times she was thanked but sent away. ("She is the most considerate person that was ever born, Mrs. Roosevelt is,"[51] McDuffie thought, after ambling back through the swaying Pullmans and easing herself into the cotton sheets of her berth.)

With the heavy green curtains closed, McDuffie flicked off the reading lamp and lifted her window shade to peer into the passing night. "Lying in my berth, and knowing the President's body was lying in the back," she said, "I couldn't get away from thinking of conditions of things when Mr. Roosevelt became President. I lay there and thought about the bread lines."[52]

Back in the *Conneaut*, where the guards stood at attention over the president's body, Hassett had lain in his bed since a few minutes after 10:00. Over the years, Roosevelt had come to call Hassett his own personal "Bartlett, Roget, and Buckle" for his unfailing ability to pen the president's most eloquent letters.[53] Bill Hassett struggled with his grief on this final trip, but as a bookish New Englander, isolation and solitude remained his natural states. When FDR had been away at Yalta, leaving only Jonathan Daniels and Hassett on duty in the White House, Daniels had observed to his journal: "In such interludes as this one Hassett sometimes retired to his books and the bottle."[54] Presently Hassett picked up his diary and scribed the evening's final lines: "F.D.R. made his last journey from Warm Springs this morning—the strangeness and unreality of all that has happened in so brief a time."[55]

The funeral train plunged through the darkness, changing engines and crews again at Salisbury, North Carolina, where 8,000 people (including 145 honor guards from Fort Bragg) stood in silence—and presented still another floral wreath. Sometime after midnight, the train rumbled slowly through Greensboro. The countryside between the big cities was land that one journalist later termed "Noplace in the Carolinas."[56] With a schedule to keep, the funeral train simply could not stop in such locales, where tenant farmers slept in shacks, their sagging burros tied up nearby.

The exception was a place—never identified—where the railroad tracks slipped into a narrow cut of earth with farm fields abutting the crevasse on either side. Behind the throttles of Nos. 1400 and 1367, the engineers choked off the steam to the reciprocating chambers. The driving rods made a few slow revolutions before the locomotives chuffed to a halt beneath a tall wooden tank: a water tank. The engines needed a drink.[57]

As the fireman wrestled the filling spout over the hatch of the first tender, an elderly black sharecropper—awakened by the hiss and clang of iron monsters below—wandered over to investigate. He peered down into the open cut and saw the train paused in the ghost light, its windows all dark except for those of the last car, where he saw the flag and knew what it meant.

Shocked and humbled, the man began to sing "Hand Me Down My Walkin' Cane."[58] His sonorous baritone boomed across the moonlit fields, drawing other farmhands out of their shanties. One by one, they added their voices to the chorus. One of the engineers looked up, certain he could hear singing from somewhere above and away. But the train had no time to dally. Yardmen were prepping the final pair of locomotives up the line in Monroe at milepost 165.1; the train was due in D.C. by 10:00 that morning; and the Boss, even in death, could not be kept waiting.

At 2:00 A.M., the funeral train bore down on Danville, Virginia, where the locomotives would rest long enough to take on coal and water while a service crew filled the ice bunkers. With the passing of an obscure milepost back near Lexington, North Carolina, the train had finally halved the distance to Washington. The capital city loomed closer now: 236 miles—but still eight hours—away.

Though the engineers held the train's running speed to 25 mph, the wheels tripped across the rail joints fast enough to send a lulling *clickety-clack, clickety-clack* up through the carpeted floor. Since the dawn of railroading, that soothing, marvelous sound had helped countless passengers to fall asleep. On this night, it may also have been the sound that gently reminded Merriman Smith, pecking at his typewriter in the cushioned solitude of a Pullman car, that he had not slept for two entire days. Enough, he thought; it was time for bed.

As two of only three reporters permitted aboard, Smith and Oliver paid for the privilege of covering the century's most important funeral by nearly being worked to death themselves. At each stop, without fail, a bureau rep had been waiting on the platform, demanding fresh copy. Most all of the stories carried the same dateline: "Aboard the Roosevelt Funeral Train." The exact geographical location was unimportant; the train *was* the place.

The thin-mustachioed Smith and his reedy colleague were fortunate in one respect: They'd been quartered in a drawing room—spacious digs on a train. The compartment had two berths along the windows, folding tables for working, a separate couch, and a lavatory and closet. Soon Smith fished into his duffel, kicked off his trousers, and slipped his tired legs into a pair of dirty pajamas. As he set foot on the ladder to climb into the upper bunk, he stared at Oliver, who was "beating his typewriter industriously."[59]

"Harry, for God's sake, let's get some sleep for the first time in forty-eight hours," he said.[60] Oliver tore the sheet from his typewriter carriage, slumped down, and began pulling off his socks. "You know what?" he said in his high, soft voice, looking up at Smith. "For the first time I realize that the old man is dead."[61] The AP man deposited himself into the lower berth as Smith, above, found the light switch and flicked it off. The compartment went dark.

For his part, Merriman Smith had already realized the old man was gone; shaking the memories would be another matter. While the official record would immortalize Roosevelt's final words as "I have a terrific pain in the back of my head," Merriman Smith preferred his own version. The last time Smith saw the president alive had been April 10. Stuck in a news blackout with no copy to write, Smith had gone to the Warm Springs general store and rented a horse for the afternoon. It proved a temperamental beast, and as Smith struggled with the reins on one of the foundation's winding roads, FDR roared up behind the wheel of his '38 Ford, the Secret Service car in an anxious tailgate. Taking one look at Smith, the president bowed dramatically and summoned a baritone louder than the car's engine. "Heigh-O, Silver!" FDR yelled, and drove on. "As far as I was concerned," Smith would write years later, "those were his last words."[62]

Smith had only been in his bunk for a few minutes when the train lurched to a halt at Danville. Just then a buzzer jolted the men up from their blankets. Oliver rose and opened the door. Smith heard the car's porter explain that there was a man on the platform asking for a reporter named Harold Oliver. The man was from the Associated Press's Richmond bureau; he was there to pick up a story. Smith chuckled to himself, grateful that the United Press had decided to give him an hour of peace.

Just then the buzzer sounded a second time. It was a man from the UP. He was there to pick up a story.[63]

The rising sun of Saturday, the fourteenth day of April, made its appearance as the train neared Charlottesville, Virginia. Morning light had just begun to mist the skies with tentative hues of blue. In the train station, electric lamps bolted to the timber canopies threw orbs of ocher light into the cavities beneath West Main Street, which crossed the main line on a viaduct. Along the surrounding overpasses, 1,500 people peered down at the glinting ribbon of rails. Their train station was 112 miles from Washington.

On the cordoned-off platforms, armed sentries stood at twelve-foot intervals, the butts of their rifles resting on the brick. Mayor Roscoe Adams had not joined them. He had no wreath of flowers to present, either, because the funeral train would not be stopping. Instead, Adams stood up on the street with his electorate and waited.[64] He had no more idea of when the train would show up than anyone else did. By now, word had spread that Roosevelt's coffin was in the last Pullman, and many in the crowd had shivered in place since 2:00 that morning to make sure they would get to lay eyes upon it.

At 6:20 A.M., their chance came. Swept in behind a cloud of sparks and coal smoke, the train, most all of its windows dark, hissed beneath 10th Street, then 9th, and then finally West Main. In the tenebrous light, the *Conneaut* rolled into view, swaying at the train's tail. People caught a glimpse inside: flowers, guardsmen, flag. Men sighed and women wept. Then, as suddenly as it had come, the train was gone again, heading for its final stomachful of coal up at Weyburn.

At 8:15, the sun was high and the air warming quickly near the Virginia town of Bealeton. Up inside engines Nos. 1366 and 1406, engineers C. R. Yowell and H. D. Hansborough, who'd taken over the train back at Monroe, cut the steam and eased the long string of Pullmans onto a siding. Once the *Conneaut* was clear of the switch, the hoggers waited. R. K. McClain's schedule had been followed to the minute, and now train No. 48—a Washington-bound express—blew past on the main line.[65] The import of the moment was not lost on the veteran engineers: For the first time anyone could remember, an ordinary passenger train had been routed in front of the president.

Back in the dining car, the pause afforded the waiters the luxury of delivering trays of food without the balancing act required when the train was under throttle. Though they were very close to Washington now, a number of passengers were lingering over breakfast—those, at any rate, who had decided they could eat.

Merriman Smith's slumber had proven ephemeral; he'd been at his typewriter most of the night, standing after sunrise only to shave, change, and stuff his disheveled clothes into his bags.[66] William Hassett had risen early and gone forward to the communications car. From the White House, Edith Helm had wired the train in the middle of the night asking what hymns the First Lady wished to be included in the service. As soon as Hassett was certain that she was up, he'd gone to ask her. Presently, standing amid B&O No. 1401's massive transmitting equipment, Hassett relayed Eleanor Roosevelt's two choices back to Washington: "Faith of Our Fathers" and "Eternal Father, Strong to Save." Before the Signal Corps men finished the reply telegram, Hassett added an additional request from the First Lady. "The only thing we have to fear is fear itself"—these were the words she wished to be inscribed on Roosevelt's tombstone.[67]

In Washington that morning, the air was already muggy and still as Engineer Yowell took his lumbering charge across the Potomac River a few minutes past 9:30. Near Virginia Avenue, he slowed the funeral train to a crawl. Over the fireman's shoulder, Yowell could see layup tracks fanning off to the left. One of them led to the siding beneath the Bureau of Engraving and Printing. POTUS was home. When the signal cleared, the funeral train knocked over onto Union Station's approach track, slicing an arc through Washington's grid of brick and white stone on its gradual sweep to the north. Every train nearby, even ordinary switch engines, had been held behind double-red signals until the funeral train disappeared under New Jersey Avenue.[68] The Pullmans crept up the narrow tunnel beneath First Street just behind the Capitol, then emerged in the daylight of Union's massive interlocking.

It was 9:55. The funeral train rolled slowly northward, past the limits of the umbrella sheds, beneath the signal bridge by H Street, then beyond the railway express building. Up inside signal tower "K," a switchman took hold of the handles below the big board. Outside, in the maze of converging tracks, a brief release of pressurized air preceded a heavy clink of shifting rail. Slowly, the train began to creak backward toward the arch-roofed concourse of Union Station.

Behind the security line drawn and held by young Marine guards, crowds had filled the station plaza and gotten as close to the arrival track as the uniformed men would let them—which was not close. The crowd of 12,000 that stood at the terminal half an hour before the funeral train arrived had swelled to 25,000. At the Columbus Memorial out front, people sat on the heads and backs of the marble lions for a better look. Nearby, a group of nuns stood and murmured the rosary. In the East Concourse, two redheaded boys read aloud from Book XV of *The Odyssey*: "Welcome the coming, Speed the parting guest."[69]

It was not only the largest crowd ever to assemble in Washington, it was the quietest.

FIVE

TWELVE HOURS

T*welve hours elapsed* between the funeral train's arrival at Washington's Union Station on the morning of Saturday, April 14, and its departure for Hyde Park late that same evening.

In the end, only 378 people had been selected to attend the White House service, whittled down from thousands.[1] Those who received an invitation also found a simple, typewritten note from Edith Helm tucked inside their envelopes. It was a request to meet the funeral train at Union Station at 10 A.M.[2] The Secret Service probably would have preferred to shut the station down, but that would have been impossible. With the war at its peak and the capital surging with government workers and military men, 100,000 people coursed through the train gates every day.[3] But the Roosevelt funeral could, at least, commandeer part of the terminal, which is why Helm's directions were specific. "Will you," the invitation requested, "go to the 'Team Entrance' of the station which is at the north end of the station (extreme right) and proceed down to the tracks."[4]

A white granite Beaux Arts shrine to the railroad, Union was the largest train station on the face of the earth.[5] The Baths of Diocletian had inspired its barrel-vaulted Main Hall, which gave onto an immense concourse covered by an arched, coffered ceiling. The gates for the concourse's thirty-three tracks—twenty that terminated on the main level and thirteen on the lower level that merged into a tunnel winding south below Capitol Hill—were numbered from west to east.

Although Track 33 (on the concourse's "extreme right," where Helm had directed the attendees) was the last numbered gate, it was not the last track in the boarding area outside. There was one more: the well-worn freight spur of the Railway Express Agency that branched off Track 33 near the dead end of H Street. Newspapers (and, later, books) put the funeral train's arrival at Track 1, which sounded suitably regal, though it was incorrect.[6] The Associated Press was among the few news sources to get the facts straight, reporting that "the funeral train was parked on a Union Station siding near a bustling freight depot."[7] The truth was that the body of the most important leader in the free world would, on this day, arrive on a track normally used to load and unload boxcars.[8]

The Express Agency's spur enjoyed the security advantage of relative seclusion (a stand of trees even flanked it on one side) and an expanse of unobstructed ground area that stood between it and the neat comb of passenger tracks in the train shed. No other approach could afford enough room for the five-foot-tall plank-wood platform erected to receive the coffin from the *Conneaut*'s window or for the horse-drawn caisson, which could never have maneuvered around the umbrella-shed support columns that lined all the platforms.[9]

Just before 10:00 that Saturday morning, the funeral train had emerged from the mouth of the tunnel that cut through the terminal's foundation, rolled far north past the signal bridges—nearly out of sight—and then stopped. Three hundred of Washington's power elite, massed at the foot of the receiving track, watched in silence.[10] (So did tens of thousands more, but regular citizens were kept in the open plaza behind the police lines.[11]) Far away, a switch clinked, there was a cough of smoke from the locomotive stacks, and then the train began its slow creep backward toward the terminal.

When the *Conneaut*'s rear wheels reached the turnout for the freight spur, the car swung sharply into the contour, then the others followed like an enormous steel caterpillar turning a corner. The freight spur was worn and uneven, but it held. The crowd could see a flagman perched on the back of the train. His eyes narrowed for the moment when the *Conneaut*'s port-side rear lounge window would line up with the wooden scaffold. Six feet...four...one....Suddenly the flagman thrust his lantern straight out.[12] Up ahead in the lead locomotive, Engineer C. R. Yowell saw the signal and dumped the pressure from his brake pipe. There was a deafening rush of air from the valves, and then the funeral train was still. Those who glanced at their watches saw the minute hand at just a sliver past 10:00.

The assembled dignitaries had begun arriving about half an hour before, amid a commotion of shuffling feet and slamming car doors. Around the station, "a great crowd had gathered," Justice Robert H. Jackson remembered, "a silent and solemn crowd, with many moist eyes."[13] The Secret Service scrutinized each invited guest before allowing him or her through the cordon. Beyond it was the sort of assemblage that only state weddings and funerals can produce: cabinet members, Congressmen, military brass, diplomatic attachés, and every robe from the Supreme Court bench.[14]

Included in the crowd were men from Joseph Gawler's Sons, undertakers, who had gone to the nearby stationmaster's office to check if the funeral train was on time.[15] During several long-distance calls from Atlanta, Fred Patterson had recounted to thirty-six-year-old William A. Gawler that the embalming of the president very nearly didn't happen; Roosevelt's arteries had been so calcified that Patterson's men could hardly inject the preservative fluids.[16] Gawler also knew that Patterson had—above the protests of the Secret Service men—hidden some embalming equipment beneath the Marine blankets covering the bier in the *Conneaut*, in case the body required additional attention along the way. Although Eleanor had decreed that the lid of the coffin would not be opened for public viewing, Patterson had presumably wanted to ensure that the remains would be presentable for members of the family in Washington, should any desire to look. The Atlanta mortician had been concerned enough to request that one of his men be allowed to accompany the coffin on the funeral train. Admiral McIntire had refused to even consider it.[17]

In the West Wing of the White House, the funeral committee had already dispatched much of its work before the train's arrival in Washington, even though the planning for the funeral train's second leg to Hyde Park was far from complete. That morning, the White House staffers and family boarded the official cars at 9:30 and arrived at Union Station a few minutes later. Harry Hooker, FDR's old friend, stepped through the police line along with Eleanor's secretaries, Malvina Thompson and Edith Helm. Pale and hollow-eyed, Anna Roosevelt walked toward the arrival track with her husband, the former newspaperman and now colonel, John Boettiger. Their little boy, Johnny, was recovering from his throat infection at Bethesda Naval Hospital, just outside the city.

If the funeral sported a glamour couple, it was Brigadier General Elliott Roosevelt and his wife, actress Faye Emerson. Though Interior Secretary Harold Ickes would later record that Elliott looked gaunt and fatigued, the bomber pilot was still handsome in his dress uniform, with two rows of service bars on his left breast and his hair oiled and combed back.[18] He was looking well for a man who had flown across an ocean, arrived at the White House at 3:15 A.M., and barely had time for a nap before accompanying his wife to the station.[19] Faye Emerson, who had recently starred in the Warner Bros. picture *Hotel Berlin* opposite Peter Lorre, had draped her delicate face with netting and wore a simple black dress, as did the other young and pretty Roosevelt wives, who clustered as the press photographers took aim and popped off their magnesium flashbulbs.

Everyone in the crowd was worth a picture that morning. Uniforms were everywhere. The shutterbugs snapped a photo of Army Chief of Staff General George C. Marshall talking with Secretary of War Henry Stimson, aged seventy-eight and visibly ailing, while Admiral Ernest King looked on.[20] Standing with them was still another admiral, William D. Leahy, a seventy-year-old piece of maritime steel who, though "being of a conservative mind"[21] and disagreeing with most of Roosevelt's domestic policies, nonetheless had been his trusted advisor, and personal friend, for thirty-six years.

Eleanor Roosevelt composed herself in the lounge of the *Ferdinand Magellan* and waited. Anna led the family to the train, climbing first up into the *Conneaut*. Its tiny lounge was so choked by seven enormous wreaths that flowers pressed their heads to the window glass like anxious children. Inside, the group paused before the flag-draped casket. Through the windows, some of the women could be seen weeping.[22]

Only after all the Roosevelts had gone aboard did President Truman follow, taking two handpicked companions—James F. Byrnes and Commerce Secretary Henry Wallace—into the Pullman with him.[23] The men had arrived at Union Station just four minutes before the funeral train had appeared and, as they'd stepped from the limousine beneath the station's cavernous vaults, the press photographers had scrambled into position to get the three into a shot. The journalists were surprised to see Byrnes, his unmistakable, craggy visage crowned by a wide-brimmed fedora. Hadn't FDR's old war mobilization director quit just a few weeks ago? What was he doing back in Washington? As the Speed Graphic cameras swung into position and the shutters clicked, Truman had to have felt inwardly pleased. He had planned this photo op carefully and wanted the shot in the next day's papers.[24] Aboard the *Conneaut*, the group gazed down at the flag-draped coffin silently for a few moments. Then the burly figure of Arthur Prettyman, FDR's trusted valet, appeared in the corridor. He turned and escorted the family forward into the *Magellan*.[25] Truman and his two companions lingered, allowing a respectful distance before following the young Roosevelts ahead.

When the new president saw Eleanor waiting to receive him in the *Ferdinand Magellan*'s lounge, he apologized immediately for his wife and daughter's absence ("Mrs. Truman and Margaret were making arrangements to leave with me that evening for Hyde Park," Truman would later reveal in his memoirs).[26] Eleanor was gracious as always. Her handshake for Wallace was noticeably affectionate[27]; Wallace—a good liberal—had always been her favorite.[28]

As for James F. Byrnes, well, Mrs. Roosevelt did not like Jimmy so much. Byrnes was, in Elliott Roosevelt's blunt appraisal, "a wheeler-dealer whom Father had never trusted."[29] With his enormous yet easily bruised ego, Byrnes had required exhaustive maintenance as Roosevelt's director of war mobilization, brilliant as he'd been. When Byrnes had resigned from the government in a huff after losing the VP's slot to Truman, Roosevelt's only words had been: "It's too bad some people are so prima-donnaish."[30] Over the years, Byrnes's histrionics had "taxed Roosevelt's strength more than most people realized," Grace Tully recounted.[31] And now that the Boss was gone, here was Jimmy, polite as a schoolboy, shaking the First Lady's hand.

Truman had to have felt the unctuousness of Byrnes's presence. But he had had a good reason for bringing both Byrnes and Wallace with him. Though Wallace had been FDR's vice-presidential running mate in 1940, the Iowan's far-left views had failed to win him sufficient backing for the 1944 ticket. By contrast, Byrnes—a rare political bird who had served in all three branches of the government—was supremely qualified for the post. But organized labor could not be made to accept him.[32] When Truman appeared shoulder to shoulder with his two rivals in the Sunday edition rotogravures, he looked equal parts peacemaker and power broker.[33] The fact was that the new president needed all the help he could get, even if it meant that a little maneuvering had to take place at a funeral.

The cabinet and Supreme Court filed aboard the *Magellan* next, where the assembled Roosevelts—Eleanor serving as matriarch and spokeswoman—waited to receive them. "I was very much touched by Mrs. Roosevelt's bearing under these most trying circumstances," Agriculture Secretary Claude R. Wickard confided later in his diary. "There are only a few people who could have had the deep grief and cares that she had without breaking under the strain."[34]

Meanwhile, the *Conneaut*'s rear observation window came out. Nine noncommissioned officers hoisted the casket and passed it slowly through the opening. Each man's share of its weight was over eighty-four pounds. The men positioned their burden atop a ceremonial black artillery caisson, its fringed swags and tassels wagging as one officer rested his boot on the wheel hub, leaned over the casket lid, and pulled the leather straps tight. Seven white horses stood passively in their harnesses. As the Army Air Force band struck up the National Anthem, the men in the crowd gently slid their hats off and pressed the felt to their hearts.[35]

Because the caisson and the official limousines would be bringing up the rear of an excruciatingly long procession, it was necessary to start the march right away. At eight minutes after 10, the shrill pitch of a bosun's whistle split the air—a nod to Navy tradition—and the front of the column set off.[36] Colonel Park, entrusted with planning most of this day's ceremonies, had chosen a direct route from Union Station to the Executive Mansion, but he had also picked the grandest avenues to get there—Delaware, Constitution, then Pennsylvania. Even with modest-size contingents marching, so many branches of the government and military had been included that the cortege stretched a mile long—half the length of the route itself. Twelve separate formations, plus forty-eight scout cars and a cluster of howitzers, would pass by spectators lining the route before the coffin even appeared.

A squadron of Washington motorcycle police, arranged in an inverted V, rolled down into Union Station's crescent-shape plaza to take the lead. As the caisson waited, the contingents swung into the march, one by one: the U.S. Marine Band and the Navy Music School Band, battalions of Naval Academy midshipmen, the Army Air Force and Army Service Force, Marines and Bluejackets. There was a company of African American troops, and contingents of WAVES (Women Accepted for Volunteer Emergency Service), WACs (Women's Army Corps), and SPARs (*Semper Paratus*—Always Ready)[37]—acronyms many enlisted men could not translate but knew nonetheless because these particular enlistees were female.

At long last, the gun carriage bearing FDR's casket, its spoked wheels turning under equine power, joined the procession. Behind it, tucked into the upholstered quietude of black limousines, came the Roosevelt family, Truman's contingent, and the retinue of Roosevelt staffers and friends. Soon the cars' motors were drowned by the snarl of twenty-four heavy bombers—Liberators and Flying Fortresses—laying exhaust trails low overhead. The procession moved at a crawl; bystanders who wished to watch it pass completely waited thirty-five minutes.[38]

The Secret Service estimated that half a million people had turned out along the procession route, where in the swampy air they stood ten deep at the curbstones behind a human partition of troops standing three paces apart. Tree limbs sagged under the weight of boys who had climbed up for a better view. Some people brought empty boxes to stand on. Some fainted. The mercury had crept to 76 degrees and beads of sweat ran down the soldiers' cheeks as they stood beneath their steel helmets. Many of the uniforms, worse for the wear of deployment overseas, were stained and wrinkled. The young enlisted men smelled of sweat; they smelled of war; they smelled like men even though most were just boys. Executives in pricey suits stood silently beside mothers carrying babies. Old women watched the passing contingents with tears in their eyes. Tradesmen in aprons shared the sidewalk with civil servants.[39] The city brimmed with all kinds of people—too many of them.

"If the war lasts much longer," *Life* magazine had said two years earlier, "Washington is going to bust right out of its pants."[40] Some

300,000 people had flocked to D.C. in search of wartime civilian jobs since 1942—young office girls alone at the rate of 10,000 a month. Jobs they found, but little else. There were no apartments to be had for any price, and the erosive combination of overcrowding and rationing meant waiting in lines—long, wrap-around-the-block lines—for everything: a bottle of Old Charter at Milstone's Acme cut-rate liquor, a table at the Colonial Cafeteria, a movie at the Earle downtown. No doubt so many people went to watch FDR's funeral because there were so many people already there to begin with. The grief, however, was no matter of coincidence.

As the cortege crossed 9th Street and approached the Justice Department, an elderly black woman broke across the police line and ran out onto Pennsylvania Avenue. "Lord God," she wailed, "take care of us now."[41] At a time when public tears were generally reserved for melodramas at the movie houses, people stood on the sidewalks of Washington and wept openly. Newspapers even ran photo clusters devoted solely to anonymous, tearstained faces. Most were women; the grieving of men was different, though no less public. Labor Secretary Frances Perkins would remember for years the young soldier who'd returned her knowing look with a sigh as he stood by the White House's high iron fence, staring through the bars in a protracted daze. "I felt as if I knew him," the soldier told her. "I felt as if he knew me—and I felt as if he liked me."[42]

With the tall black caisson trundling behind, the horses clopped to a halt on the White House's circular driveway. Hoisted high on the shoulders of the servicemen, FDR's coffin disappeared into the North Portico doorway with the Roosevelts following behind. In the entrance hall, the ushers from Gawler's Sons pulled open a collapsible casket truck, which received its polished copper charge at 11:14. The truck's rubber wheels rumbled over the bronze relief of the presidential shield sunk into the lobby floor, turned left, and rolled down the long corridor past the Green Room and into the East Room. Inside, on the Oriental rug beneath the glow of three immense tent-and-bowl chandeliers, Gawler's men had set up a catafalque, two and a half feet high, draping it in brown velvet.[43] Gently, the bearers set the coffin down on top of it.

Florist vans had been driving up all day, even though Eleanor Roosevelt had requested (and the radio stations had broadcast) that people not send flowers.[44] No doubt she considered it wasteful, extravagant. Besides, that kind of money could be spent on war bonds. But nobody had listened—not even the U.S. Senate, which had motored over a wreath of carnations and lilies.[45] The United Steel Workers sent a spray of carnations, lilies, and irises. Even the *florists* sent flowers; up to the gates had come a costly spray of orchids from the Allied Florists of Chicago. One delivery truck arrived with a simple spray of pansies that had been ordered by a woman in Normandy, France, where Allied troops had landed ten months and ten days before. "Greetings to one who never turned his back," read the card, "but marched breast forward; Never doubted clouds would break; Never dreamed though rights were worsted, wrong would triumph."[46] Stacked against the four walls of the East Room, the wreaths and sprays formed a hillock of cut blossoms that teetered ten feet high.[47]

Outside, the motorcade's other passengers began to trickle into the mansion. Arthur Prettyman, stooping in exhaustion and sadness, disappeared through the servants' entrance.[48] Hassett had come from the train, too. "My telegram never reached Mrs. Helm, as I learned when I phoned her upon reaching the White House," he recalled. Over the line, Hassett repeated the First Lady's choices of the hymns. Then he dug up a copy of Roosevelt's first inaugural address and sent Helm a copy. The Right Reverend Angus Dun, Episcopal bishop of Washington, would need the Boss's exact lines in order to weave them into his oration.[49]

As the other automobiles waited out front, Harry Truman's car pulled away from the queue and stopped before the West Wing entrance, where he slipped inside.[50] Truman had no wish to disturb the family's privacy. Plus, the new president was anxious. The East Room services would begin at 4:00 P.M., and the funeral train would be leaving at 10:00 that evening. That allowed him two windows of time—small but significant windows—in which he had much to do. His hat in his hand, Truman stepped briskly down the corridor.[51]

$$\rightleftharpoons \quad \leftrightharpoons$$

As Truman sat at the Oval Office desk that afternoon, his mind was still attempting to wrap itself around an immense secret that he had known about for less than forty-eight hours—one that would change his presidency, the outcome of the war, and the fate of the world itself.

Already, the trail it had left was mysterious and confusing. On Thursday evening, not an hour after he took the oath of office, Truman had been approached by Secretary of War Henry Stimson, an aristocratic man with a salt-and-pepper mustache and a worry-worn face. Stimson had asked to speak with the new president about "a most urgent matter." Truman nodded. Then, lowering his already tense voice, Stimson proceeded to tell Truman about "an immense project that was under way—a project looking to the development of a new explosive of almost unbelievable destructive power."[52] Stimson's words were the perfect preamble to a startling revelation—but the secretary said no more. Seemingly eager only to fulfill his duty by briefing the commander in chief (the detailed talk could wait), Stimson respectfully took his leave.

Later that first night of his presidency, as Harry Truman's limousine came to a halt in the courtyard of his apartment building at 4701 Connecticut Avenue, the new commander in chief was overwhelmed. The vague knowledge of this "project," whatever it was, was merely the most substantive of a quickly accumulating pile of evidence that frightened him. It was proof—as if Truman needed any—that FDR had systematically excluded him from the most important secrets of state. "The weight of the government had fallen on my shoulders," Truman wrote later. "I knew the President had a great many meetings with Churchill and Stalin. I was not familiar with any of these things and it was really something to think about."[53]

There was plenty more to think about. Truman had, in fact, worried about this moment coming for some time. As he and his old World War I sergeant Eddie McKim had left a White House party the previous September, McKim—who'd been startled by Roosevelt's cadaverous appearance—motioned to the mansion and said, "Hey, bud, turn around and take a look. You're going to be living in that house before long." Truman had paused, then answered: "Eddie, I'm afraid I am. And it scares the hell out of me."[54]

Truman's primary use to FDR had been his popularity in the Senate. He had been a compromise choice for VP, and Roosevelt had planned to avail himself of Truman's allegiances on the Hill once it was time to officially end the war. "That was the biggest consideration," FDR advisor Harry Hopkins admitted later. "The President wanted some-body that would help him when he went up there and asked them to ratify the peace."[55]

Until then, FDR was content to let his deputy do what vice presidents have always done: don tuxedos and attend cocktail parties. Margaret Truman recalled that her father "cheerfully accepted more invitations than any other vice president in recent memory."[56] Roosevelt had done essentially nothing to prepare the Missouri senator for executive lead-ership, even though he understood the inevitable consequences of his own failing health. The previous summer, in fact, as Truman and Roosevelt shared lunch at a folding table set up beneath a White House magnolia tree, the president had admonished his running mate to avoid air travel in favor of the safety of the railroad. "Harry," he had said. "I'm not a well man. We cannot be sure of my future."[57] Truman shuddered inwardly as he watched the president's trembling hand pick up a little pitcher of cream and proceed to splash more onto the saucer than in his tea.[58]

Nonetheless, that brief breakfast meeting—a photo-op for *Life* mag-azine, mainly—had been one of only eight times that the president and Truman had so much as seen each other in the year prior to Roosevelt's death.[59] Most of the other occasions had been cabinet meetings, and "Roosevelt never discussed anything important at his Cabinet meet-ings," Truman later admitted.[60] Now, the afternoon of Roosevelt's funeral, as Harry Truman sat in the Oval Office, he pondered what he knew but mainly he pondered what he did not.

American forces were fording the Rhine and would soon be in the outskirts of Berlin; Josef Stalin was reneging on many of the agree-ments—particularly over Poland—over which he, Roosevelt, and Churchill had shaken hands at Yalta; the inaugural session of a new dip-lomatic venture to be called the United Nations would soon be under way in San Francisco; and a secret city of physicists quartered on a windswept mesa somewhere in New Mexico were three weeks away from hoisting something they called "the gadget" to the top of a steel tower in the desert and seeing what would happen when they imploded a ball of plutonium inside of it. Harry S. Truman scarcely possessed a detail about any of these developments.[61]

"Here was a man who came into the White House almost as though he had been picked at random from off the street, with *absolutely* no usable background and no usable information," Robert Nixon of the International News Service would later observe.[62] Even Winston Churchill expressed surprise over FDR's failure to groom his vice president in any way: "It seemed to me extraordinary, especially during the last few months, that Roosevelt had not made his deputy and potential successor acquainted with the whole story."[63]

There were, however, a handful of men who *were* acquainted with the whole story, and Truman had been doing everything in his power to speak with them. The previous day, Friday the thirteenth, as the funeral train made its way to Washington, Truman had packed his appointment calendar. At 10:15 A.M. he had met with the Joint Chiefs of Staff and asked Secretary of State Stettinius to give him a detailed report of where U.S. relations stood with every major international power.[64] When the meeting had broken up, the president approached William Leahy, the grizzled admiral on whose experience FDR had depended for making most every decision about the war, and asked him to stay on as his advisor. Leahy accepted, then withdrew to his office to build the stack of top-secret documents Truman would need to digest.[65] At noon, Truman went over foreign dispatches with Admiral William Brown and Colonel Richard Park.

Later that Friday afternoon, word had come to Truman that James F. Byrnes was in Washington, staying at the Shoreham Hotel. (Before climbing onto the Navy plane at Spartanburg, Byrnes had wired the White House that he was coming. He saw fit to address the president of the United States with "Dear Harry."[66]) Byrnes's notorious arrogance notwithstanding, Truman was happy to hear that Roosevelt's old war henchman was in town.[67] For a new chief with no time to learn the lessons of state, Byrnes was probably the best tutor he could hope for. Truman told him to come right over.

Byrnes was there in minutes. As the sly political dog stepped onto the plush green carpet of the Oval Office, Byrnes no doubt thought—and hardly for the first time—that by rights he should be there as its occupant, not a visitor.[68] Byrnes had, after all, been Roosevelt's initial choice for VP for the 1944 campaign. But the men of the Democratic party's smoke-filled rooms had deftly maneuvered Truman onto the ticket, and eventually Roosevelt stopped fighting them.[69] The fact was that the Congress of Industrial Organizations (better known as the CIO—among the most powerful unions in America) wanted nothing to do with Byrnes.[70] Back in 1943, when he was FDR's Economic Stabilization director, Byrnes had frozen the wages of factory workers, and CIO leader Sidney Hillman apparently never forgot it.[71] Given the union money and votes controlled by the CIO's new political action committee, Roosevelt risked throwing the whole election if he failed to embrace Truman.[72]

If jealousies still smoldered within Byrnes on that fateful Friday, however, he managed to cloak them. Both men had ample reasons to be civil to each other: Byrnes had seen his chance to chum up to a new president, and that new president saw his chance to learn what the old one had never told him. About domestic policy, about Yalta, about the Soviets, Byrnes knew everything there was to know. He had, after all, been FDR's confidant—the "assistant president"—and his mind was still a trap. As soon as Byrnes took a seat before Truman that afternoon, the two began to discuss "everything under the sun."[73]

Pleased with Byrnes's near-flawless recall of facts (as a young man of twenty-one, Byrnes had been a court stenographer and still knew shorthand), Truman told the South Carolinian that he planned to appoint him secretary of state as soon as Edward Stettinius could be tactfully extracted from the job.[74] Truman's ex officio reasoning had to do with ensuring that a qualified man would, should Truman die or become incapacitated, succeed him to the high office. (At this time, the Constitution designated the Secretary of State as next in the line of presidential succession.) But it was Byrnes's having been jilted by Roosevelt for the running mate's post back in 1944 that drove the decision just as much. "Byrnes, undoubtedly, was deeply disappointed and hurt," Truman wrote. "I thought that my calling on him at this time might help balance things up."[75]

For Truman, that afternoon's business with Byrnes had been concluded—but his guest was not finished speaking. Beneath Byrnes's perennially furrowed brow, his dark, pensive eyes fixed themselves on the new president who sat in the enormous brocade swivel chair that Roosevelt had filled for so many years. Byrnes took a breath and spoke.

"Mr. President," Byrnes said, "we are perfecting an explosive great enough to destroy the whole world." He paused a moment, and continued: "It might well put us in a position to dictate our own terms at the end of the war."[76]

There it was. Stimson's disclosure had been, technically, "the first bit of information that had come to me about the atomic bomb," Truman recalled in his memoirs, but the secretary of war "gave me no details. It was not until the next day that I was told enough to give me some understanding of the almost incredible developments that were under way and the awful power that might soon be placed in our hands."[77] That understanding had come from Jimmy Byrnes.

If Byrnes was right about the bomb's ability to shorten the war, the implications would be enormous. The way things looked in mid-April 1945, World War II was far from over. The Joint Chiefs of Staff had recently estimated that Germany would hold out another six months. As far as Japan went, the brass predicted that that country could not be driven to its knees in fewer than eighteen months; without the atomic weapon, America would be fighting World War II until October 1946.[78]

Before Friday's meeting had broken up, Truman made another decision about Jimmy Byrnes: He'd need to spend more time in his company—much more time. So the new president made a request. "He asked," Byrnes remembered, "that I accompany him the following morning when he went to meet the funeral train on which Mr. Roosevelt's body would arrive, and then ride with him on the journey to Hyde Park."[79]

The journey to Hyde Park was already shaping up to be far more than the obligatory attendance of one president at the funeral of another. On this Saturday, April 14, in the twelve-hour window between 10 A.M. and 10 P.M., Truman was doing his best to work in as many meetings as possible with key Roosevelt men. But the opportunities were fleeting. Truman had already spent three precious hours in the company of Byrnes and Wallace, met the funeral train at Union Station, and been driven back to the White House in a procession so painfully slow that he could have returned quicker on foot. At 4:00 P.M., his day would be interrupted once more by the East Room services—and by 9:30 he'd be in a limousine bound for Union Station yet again.

The blocks of time between those obligations were already full; FDR's ailing confidant Harry Hopkins was due for lunch. Admiral Leahy would be returning at 2:15—with Byrnes in tow—with dispatches from Churchill and to discuss the Stalin situation.[80] These meetings would be critical, but the truth was that Harry Truman simply did not have enough time to keep conferring with people. And, without question, he certainly lacked the time to prepare for another important event to which he had committed himself: President Truman had decided to deliver an emergency State of the Union Address on Monday, two days hence.

Like the fateful discussion with Byrnes, this development too had begun the previous day. On Friday, around 12:30 P.M., shortly before Byrnes had come to the White House, Truman had decided to run up to Capitol Hill for a bite of lunch with his former colleagues. For the new president, this wasn't just a social call; something was bothering him.

Truman understood the implications of millions of Americans looking to their new president for leadership and seeing only a former Missouri senator who'd been VP for barely three months looking back at them. (Indeed, Truman's political profile had been so modest that when FDR had chosen him as his running mate, a common refrain soon became: "Who the hell is Harry Truman?"[81]) Clearly—and quickly— Truman would have to speak to the nation and make it evident that he was a leader. The war effort could not afford uncertain feelings about a new commander, or rumors of a change in strategy. "As the new Chief Executive," Truman recalled, "I wished to assure our people, our armed forces, and our allies that we would continue our efforts unabated."[82] In the marble passageways of the Capitol, behind a closed door to one of the larger offices, thirteen senators and four House members assembled for Truman's visit. When he raised his plan to deliver a big speech, a good number of them opposed the idea. It was, they argued, much too soon. Roosevelt had just died. The citizenry was not ready. Truman listened politely, then informed them: "I am coming. Prepare for it."[83]

The speech Truman promised would be the most important congressional address since Pearl Harbor. On the home front and overseas, the unified, motivated pursuit of victory depended on its success. And yet the very boldness of Truman's plan was what painted him into a corner; there was a speech of inestimable importance to deliver, and nearly no time to write it. As Truman contemplated how much of his time would be squandered by the mandate of getting to and from Roosevelt's burial—some eighteen hours, most of which would find him secluded in the Pullman car *Roald Amundsen*—a strategy emerged, and there could be no alternative to it.

Truman would have to use the funeral train as his classroom, both to work on his speech and to receive certain men—Roosevelt men, and some of his own, too—whose counsel he needed to cut the pattern of his leadership. The journey aboard the funeral train was obligatory, but it was also an ideal staging area. Seldom before and never since would railroad travel so favor the fate of the country with its inadvertent gifts of solidarity and isolation.

Democratic party chief Robert Hannegan and treasurer Edwin Pauley were among the men in the Senate office when Truman had paid his lunchtime visit. The two men accepted Truman's offer to drop them off at the Mayflower Hotel on his way back to the White House. During the ride, Truman asked them to join him on the funeral train.[84] The speech would have to be written aboard, and Truman wanted them both to contribute. The president, as Pauley recalled in his memoirs, "had to take immediate steps to bind the nation together, to keep its unity of purpose, and to allow no crevasses of misunderstanding that our enemies could exploit. For this reason the funeral trip to Hyde Park had perforce to take on the nature of a working party."[85]

At 4:00 P.M., Saturday, April 14, 1945, telephone and telegraph lines throughout the United States fell silent and radio broadcasts ceased. Engineers stopped their trains. Riveters in bomber plants laid down their guns to stand in silence beside unfinished fuselages. New York City subway trains ground to a halt. Firehouse bells tolled in Boston. Newspaper presses stopped in Chicago. At sea, ships heaving in the waves opened the throats of their pneumatic horns. In these and myriad other ways, the people of the United States honored the passing of Franklin Delano Roosevelt.

At that moment, beside FDR's coffin, Bishop Dun began the service in the East Room. The bishop stood straight as a monument; it was impossible to tell that beneath the folds of his purple cassock was an artificial leg, a replacement to the one he had lost, as a boy, to polio.[86] Dun looked out over the room. Every one of its bentwood chairs was occupied. Diffused through the crystal ropes of the chandeliers, electric light glistened on foreheads and cheeks, wet with perspiration and tears. On the walls, only the heavy gilt mirrors and swags of crimson drapery interrupted the undulating palisade of roses, orchids, and ferns.[87] The Trumans and Roosevelts, in the front row on either side of the center aisle, sat in oval-backed French armchairs.

The humidity verged on intolerable. Margaret Truman, dizzy from the thick floral perfume, feared both claustrophobia and faint. She stayed conscious by staring intently at a bead of sweat that clung to Bishop Dun's nose.[88] The cleric prayed: "O God, from Whom every good gift cometh, we thank Thee for the qualities of heart and mind which this Thy servant brought to the service of our nation and our world."[89]

"It seemed to me," Eleanor Roosevelt later wrote, "that everyone in the world was in the East Room for the funeral services except three of my own sons. Elliott was the only one who, by luck, could get back."[90] But for their absence, however, no one who had meant anything to FDR had failed to arrive—except for Lucy, of course, though her absence was a foregone conclusion. There was FDR's closest advisor, the gravely ill Harry Hopkins, who had left his sickbed at the Mayo Clinic to come to Washington; British foreign secretary Anthony Eden, whose journey from London allowed Churchill to stay home and eulogize Roosevelt before Parliament[91]; and Norway's crown princess Märtha, whom FDR had personally housed at his Hyde Park estate after she'd fled the Nazis in August 1940.[92] Only one seat in the room was empty: Positioned at the front was the simple wooden wheelchair of Franklin D. Roosevelt.[93]

Honoring the request that Hassett had attempted to cable from the funeral train, the bishop punctuated the ceremony with FDR's own words: "In his first inaugural, the President bore testimony to his own deep faith," Dun intoned. "He said: 'So first of all let me assert my own belief that the only thing we have to fear is fear itself.'" Roosevelt's most famous words echoed throughout the chamber where Princess Märtha wept silently and Prince Faisal Saud of Saudi Arabia, dressed in his long white "robes of the Arabs," said the newspaper, sat stoically through the strange Episcopal rite.[94] "As that was his first word to us," the bishop continued, "I'm sure he would wish it to be his last. So, we may go forward into the future as those who go forward without fear of the future, without fear of our Allies or our friends, and without fear of our own insufficiency."[95]

And then it was done. Its hymns, words, and symbols carefully chosen, the service was a twenty-three-minute wonder of brevity. Even the cantankerous Ickes was pleased with its decorum and understatement.[96] The only blemish, perhaps, was a fleeting detail imparted by the following day's *Baltimore Sun*. As the choir began to sing the hymn "Faith of Our Fathers," James F. Byrnes had joined in "lustily."[97]

—————

Immediately after the service, Truman walked into the Cabinet Room in the West Wing. Portly advisor George Allen, having flown in from Las Vegas, and his assistant, Ed Reynolds, looked up from the long table, its polished surface strewn with paper. Reynolds had picked Allen up early that morning at the apartment he kept at the stately Wardman Park Hotel about two miles from the White House. In the West Wing, Matthew Connelly, Truman's appointments secretary, immediately set them up in the room with everything they needed.[98] "Where have you been?" Connelly had joshed Allen when he had telephoned after landing. "We're addressing Congress Monday.... You probably won't be much help, but you'd better get down here anyway."[99]

In fact, Connelly knew just how badly Truman needed George Allen. Like all savvy officials, Truman understood that a good speech, while ultimately the politician's own, was the work of several trusted men—usually ones far more articulate than he. Truman was known and liked for his frank, midwestern plainspeak (upon learning he'd been chosen as FDR's vice president, Truman's response had been: "Oh shit"[100]). But a State of the Union address—Monday's address in particular—demanded more, and the new president knew it. George Edward Allen, Esq., was what was known as a fixer (today, "lobbyist" is the glossier term); major corporations like Republic Steel had installed Allen on their boards, entrusting him to maintain smooth relations with the men who ran the country, men whom Allen called his friends.[101] Allen's well-greased political past had imbued him with a tongue of pure silver.

Truman had already scribbled down a few phrases for the speech early that morning in his apartment,[102] and Byrnes had breezed in an hour before the funeral began with a few key points,[103] but Allen and Reynolds would be doing most of the writing. Truman told them he wanted the speech to emphasize two themes. "First, that he intended to go down the line on President Roosevelt's policies," Allen recalled. "Second, that Roosevelt's unconditional-surrender terms to Germany and Japan would stand."[104]

About this second point, Allen and Reynolds decided to engage Truman. Ever since Roosevelt and Churchill had met in Casablanca in January of 1943, Joseph Goebbels had been using their unconditional-surrender demand as fuel for propagandist bonfires. If the Axis resolve weakened and allowed the Allies to win, Hitler's propaganda minister bellowed, the unconditional-surrender demand was proof that the German people would be enslaved, exterminated, or both.[105]

Now the speechwriters queried Truman about the possibility of cooling the rhetoric, which might theoretically lessen the near-suicidal German resolve, shorten the war, and save American lives. Truman refused; the Roosevelt-Churchill line would not soften.[106] With that, the president turned and left the room.

When the funeral services came to an end, Eleanor Roosevelt rose and departed the East Room with a heavy, determined step. Emerging into the first-floor corridor, she turned and, making a quick right into the entrance hall, climbed the half-turn stairway to the second floor, where the family quarters were.

What happened next has been recounted, re-created (and, in some cases, considerably embellished) by historians for decades. What is beyond question is that Eleanor, behind the closed door to Anna's bedroom, confronted her only daughter about Lucy Rutherfurd's presence in Warm Springs—and about whether Rutherfurd had visited the president on other occasions. Cornered, Anna saw no point in prevaricating. While denying she'd known that Lucy was in Warm Springs during the previous week, Anna admitted that she had helped to engineer the wealthy widow's visits to the White House while Eleanor had been away. Anna "dissembled like child," Elliott later wrote, but finally confessed that she had even played hostess.[107]

What reason could Anna possibly give for facilitating her mother's betrayal in such a way? According to one account, Anna told Eleanor that she'd orchestrated Lucy's visits because "Father asked me,"[108] hastening to add that FDR was lonely—painfully lonely—and that she, busy with a husband and a child, could not "fill Father's gap of loneliness."[109] Presumably, then, Anna had sent invitations to the one woman in the world who could.

To say that Eleanor Roosevelt was devastated by this bit of intelligence is to state the obvious. But although Elliott Roosevelt wrote that his sister's complicity in Lucy Rutherfurd's repeated visits "added immeasurably to Mother's anguish," he termed the news a "realization," not a revelation.[110] Indeed, that Eleanor Roosevelt knew, on her own, even to ask Anna if Lucy Rutherfurd had been to the White House in the past suggests that she had either known or suspected the visits already, most likely as a result of the ruminative hours the First Lady had spent in the lonely confines of the *Ferdinand Magellan* during the funeral train's journey to Washington. Regardless, according to Elliott, it would take Eleanor Roosevelt years to fully forgive her only daughter.[111]

Leaving Anna's bedroom, Eleanor Roosevelt returned downstairs, where she sought out usher J. B. West with two requests: She wished the casket to be opened, and she wished to be left alone with it. The East Room guards withdrew, leaving the First Lady beside her husband's body. It lay in the folds of velvet, clothed in a gray suit, white shirt, and the same blue-and-white tie that FDR had worn to his 1941 inauguration.[112]

Eleanor Roosevelt's recollection of her concluding moments with the casket is spare and emotionless. She recorded only that she "put a few flowers in it before it was closed finally."[113] The First Lady was perhaps not as alone as she thought, however, for West would later recount the event in detail. He also disclosed that something far more significant than a cluster of flowers was buried with FDR: "Mrs. Roosevelt stood at the casket, gazing down into her husband's face," the usher wrote. "Then she took a gold ring from her finger and tenderly placed it on the President's hand."[114] Eleanor and Franklin's troubled marriage of four decades was truly over.

That Saturday afternoon, in the smoke-laced haze of Union Station's yards, men in overalls had set to work disconnecting hoses and shunting cars; they were dismembering the funeral train. Not only would the consist have to stretch to accommodate over a hundred passengers, the second leg of the route would carry the train over the iron of the Pennsylvania and New York Central railroads; it was time for the Southern Railway to bow out.

As the pair of green and silver locomotives relinquished their charge, helper engines towed away the Southern's dining car, three of the Pullmans, and the baggage car, their brake hoses swinging limply as wheel trucks rumbled over the switches. Since there would be no presidential motorcade used up in Hyde Park, there was no need to transport the limousines, so B&O automobile car No. 748 would be staying behind, too. Only five cars from the original funeral train would continue on the run out of D.C.: communications car B&O No. 1401, sleepers *Glen Doll* and *Wordsworth*, and the *Ferdinand Magellan* and *Conneaut*—the latter two retained, respectively, to accommodate Eleanor Roosevelt and the coffin of FDR. By now, the *Roald Amundsen* had arrived to join couplers with the *Ferdinand Magellan*. Counting all the rolling stock behind the engine, the funeral train would have eighteen cars—seven more than that of its predecessor on its leg from Warm Springs.[115]

Two hours after the East Room services had ended, White House transportation man Dewey Long sent a four-page telegram to Secret Service Agent Robert H. Lowery, care of the Western Union office at the New York Central Railroad station in Poughkeepsie, about six miles south of Hyde Park. Park was wiring the finalized list of the funeral train's passengers—102 names, together with the all-important car assignments.[116] The final passenger list (which included both sleeper and berth numbers for each guest) was, in turn, typed onto three legal-size sheets and combined with the official itinerary of the train, complete with a list of stations and corresponding arrival and departure times. Easily the most sensitive and important record created in the planning of the funeral train, this incredible document—subsequently titled, "Trip of the President, Washington to Hyde Park, N.Y., and Return. April 14–15, 1945"—was typed over sandwiched sheets of carbon paper, the resulting copies distributed to Secret Service agents.[117] The roster also showed the White House transportation men's grace under pressure; with mere hours to plan the most complicated railroad journey of their careers, they still managed to arrange the accommodations with respect and discernment.

Omitting the dining cars, the funeral train's carriages were numbered from rear to front, and the train's hierarchy generally followed the same order beginning with FDR himself, whose remains would again rest aboard the *Conneaut*, now car No. 1. Eleanor Roosevelt would be staying aboard the *Ferdinand Magellan* (car No. 2), accompanied by her daughters-in-law, Anna, and Elliott. The *Roald Amundsen* (No. 3) would be the private domain of the Truman family and a few handpicked guests. Pennsylvania Railroad diner No. 4497 demarcated the tail section, which, in keeping with railroading tradition, because it was farthest from the noise and smoke of the engine, had always been the penthouse of the train.

Stretching ahead of Diner No. 4497 was an uninterrupted string of six Pullmans—car Nos. 4 through 9—forming the train's midriff. FDR's staff, close friends, and a few family members would find berths aboard car Nos. 4 and 5—the *Howe* and *Glen Brook*. Car No. 6, the *Wordsworth*, was assigned to Roosevelt's cabinet. The *Glen Canyon*, No. 7, would become the judicial branch on wheels, quartering all nine justices of the Supreme Court.

Although the sleeping cars had been pushed, pulled, and knocked over millions of miles of railroad track in the preceding twenty years, they were still handsome quarters that Pullman kept in good repair. The cars were heavy, quiet, and comfortable. Opening off the carpeted corridors of each were a series of compartments and drawing-room suites, usually six of the former and three of the latter. The drawing rooms were spacious enough to receive guests.[118] For a suitable tip, a willing porter would fetch some glasses and ice from the dining car and, with a passenger's stash of whiskey and cigarettes to offer around, a small, melancholy party could be easily under way.[119]

Forward of the midsection was a second dining car—Pennsylvania Railroad No. 4478—and then four more sleepers, Nos. 10 though 13. Though the company here was still distinguished, the political blue blood was thinning. Car No. 11, the *Treonta*, had been given to the newspaper and radio correspondents. The passenger list showed a mere four occupants in car No. 13, the Pullman nearest the locomotive, even though there was far more space available. The reason soon becomes evident: Aboard were berths for White House valet Arthur Prettyman, chief butler Alonzo Fields, messenger John Boardley, and Eleanor Roosevelt's Hyde Park cook Alice Palmer; the *Glen Willow* was the segregated car. Ahead of car No. 13 rode the signal communications car; the *Crusader Rose*, an open-section dormitory car for the crew; and No. 1310, a battered old New York Central passenger coach. This last piece of rolling stock was listed as a "buffer car," an old railroading contrivance developed to separate passengers from dangerous cargo—in this case, presumably, the most powerful men and women in the United States government from one very large steam locomotive.

Though the official guest list stood at 102 names, the *New York Herald Tribune* would put the passenger load at 140. Obviously, a number of the funeral train's passengers finagled a berth at the last minute or via channels that left no paper trail. Car No. 12, for example, shows only one passenger on the official list. It is highly unlikely, however, that the *Glengyle*'s remaining six compartments and two drawing rooms went to Hyde Park empty.

Interspersed throughout the long passenger list were also members of the "Missouri Gang"—the moniker that Roosevelt's staffers had coined for Truman's uncouth political friends. True, some of the men lacked the patrician polish of FDR's crowd—but Truman had picked them, and they were coming along. Ed Pauley and speechwriter George Allen would share Compartment "I" up in car No. 9, the *Glen Doll*. DNC chairman and ace strategist Robert Hannegan occupied Drawing Room "B" in the *Glen Gordon*, one car farther ahead past the diner.

Two other names appeared on the roster that failed to raise many eyebrows at the time. Later, the newspaper stories whose headlines screamed their names would prompt many to wonder how either man had been permitted aboard the funeral train—and so close to Truman—in the first place. In car No. 4, Compartment "D" quartered one John F. Maragon, whose pull with Truman's military aide Colonel Harry Vaughan was enough to part a Pullman curtain for him. And, up in the *Glen Lodge*—No. 8—West Wing aide Lauchlin Currie and his wife would make the long trip to and from Hyde Park in Compartment "G."

If there were whispers about the lowbred Maragon being aboard, they amounted to little. Currie attracted even less attention. Certainly no one suspected he was working for the KGB.

Funeral director Gawler's men entered the East Room at 8:00 P.M. After bolting down the inner lid of the coffin, one of the morticians applied a bonding compound to seal the outer one shut.[120] At 9:00, the undertakers wheeled FDR's casket out to the circular drive, where a 1941 Cadillac Superior hearse waited beneath the portico.[121] The long procession with the gun carriage and team of white horses would not be repeated for the return trip to Union Station. It was dark outside. The train was waiting. Even the crying seemed to be over, for now. Tailed by a twelve-car entourage of police and soldiers, the hulking black car motored down the sixteen blocks that stretched between the executive mansion and the train terminal. This time the trip took less than a quarter of an hour.[122]

It was now nearly 10:00 P.M. The Team Entrance at Union Station was a clot of police and Secret Service, long sedans, and Pullman porters. As the passengers arrived, security men checked their names against the passenger manifest that had come over from the White House. A sense of restlessness now weighted the sorrow that had hung over the platform only twelve hours earlier. Tonight the guests had come not to meet the funeral train but to board it. The sounds of distant train bells and announcements echoing through the concourse only added to the sense of unease. Even though the sun had set, a sticky heat still hung in the air; the heavy breeze carried the threat of rain.

Its windows aglow in the darkness, the funeral train loomed on the Railway Express freight track that had received it that morning.[123] Passengers milled about by vestibule doorways, squinting their way down the phalanx of railroad cars that stretched nearly a quarter of a mile. Colonel Park had seen to it that attendants—each with a copy of the passenger list—were on hand to help everyone to find his assigned sleeper and compartment number.[124]

Grace Tully arrived with assistant secretary Lela Stiles. They had deliberately come well in advance of the hearse to spare Tully from having to see FDR's coffin being hoisted again, but they were losing time. "So many thousands of people jammed the station and the plaza that we were delayed for many minutes before we could push our way through the vast throng," Stiles later wrote.[125] When a Secret Service man spotted Tully, he quickly waved the ladies through, but it was too late. "A shaft of light shot from somewhere behind us," recalled Stiles. The casket had arrived.

Gawler's big hearse growled to a halt abreast of the *Conneaut*. The Army Air Force band began to play softly as the car's rear door swung open on its hinges, its curtains dangling over the ground as the men slid the casket down the rollers. From the observation window of the *Conneaut*—its glass again removed—young faces peered out. Then pairs of young, strong hands followed, carefully feeling for a sturdy purchase on which to hold and pass the heavy casket through.

Grace Tully began to cry. Stiles looked around helplessly. Just then, she remembered, "John Boettiger, the President's son-in-law, stepped swiftly from the shadows at this moment and escorted us down the side of the train until we could get aboard and find our car."[126]

With the hearse's arrival, the boarding of the train began in earnest. The Roosevelt family was safely installed aboard the *Ferdinand Magellan*. In a crush of Secret Service men led by George Drescher, President Truman and his family found themselves whisked into the *Roald Amundsen*.

Only after it was apparent how many people would be aboard for the funeral train's second leg did the run from Warm Springs two days before seem so small and intimate. Sleep deprived, overworked, and mired in grief, some of the veterans of the funeral train's southern journey may have privately wished they could have begged off the northern one—but they came, and the train began to fill. William Hassett, Grace Tully, and Dorothy Brady would all find reserved compartments in car No. 5, the *Glen Brook* (Tully and Brady were to share their quarters); a drawing room for Steve Early waited in the *Howe*, one Pullman behind. "Hacky," the switchboard operator, was also coming. Her compartment was up ahead in the *Glen Lodge*.

The Musketeers had returned, too: the AP's Harold Oliver, the INS's Robert Nixon, and the UP's indestructible Merriman Smith. The three men would find their compartments up in car No. 11, the Pullman *Treonta*, which would hold them and thirteen other reporters from the newspapers and radio networks. FDR himself probably would have laughed at so big a media turnout. Privately to Admiral Leahy, Roosevelt had often referred to reporters as "ghouls who are just waiting for me to fall out of the automobile, or get shot, or something."[127]

Across the wide loading area, the funeral train's second section—the *Congressional*—was accepting its own passengers—delegations from the House and Senate, diplomats, and still more journalists.[128] Its occupants were important but not among the elite. What's more, although the egos of its passengers might have been bruised to know it, the *Congressional* had also been put on the rails to carry flowers. Most of the East Room's wreaths had been stripped of their cards and taken to local hospitals, but no fewer than five trucks' worth of flowers would travel to Hyde Park aboard the baggage cars of the "other" funeral train.[129]

Although safely aboard the funeral train, Grace Tully and Lela Stiles could not find their berths. Tully was assigned to car No. 5, and Stiles would be three cars ahead, but the women had no idea which of the eighteen cars John Boettiger had helped them into. Which way was forward? Because the funeral train had been entirely reassembled after arriving from Warm Springs, Tully's sense of POTUS's usual layout was useless.

Passing through a heavy door, the two women found themselves in a soft-lit sitting room paneled in wood. It took Tully a moment to grasp what had happened. She and Stiles had somehow stumbled into the *Roald Amundsen*—and were suddenly in the company of President Truman, his wife and daughter, and Jimmy Byrnes. Tully froze. "At first I didn't realize I was bursting in on the President of the United States," she remembered. "Though I had seen Mr. Roosevelt's coffin, my mind had not yet accepted the fact that he was dead."[130]

Shaking herself into awareness, Tully stammered an apology—but she did not step off the president's Pullman. Instead, harnessing the mettle that came with twelve years of assisting the most powerful man on earth, FDR's secretary marched straight up the *Amundsen*'s corridor and out through its vestibule door.

Inside the vast terminal, the hands of the clock crept toward 10:00 P.M.

SIX

THE TRAIN OF SECRETS

The minute hand swept past 10:00 P.M.; five minutes remained
until the scheduled departure time. Aboard the funeral train,
the familiar sounds of muffled voices and suitcases bumping off
the metal bulkheads signaled that people were settling in. Fortunately
for them, Washington's glucy air could penetrate no further than the
vestibules; Pullman had hauled the old heavyweight sleepers back into
its shops in the mid-1930s and installed 7,000 pounds worth of air-
conditioning equipment in each.[1] It was a comfort to Mrs. Price Collier,
ancient social lioness of Tuxedo Park and Roosevelt's maternal aunt,
who was arranging herself in spacious Drawing Room "B" of car No. 5,
the Pullman *Glen Brook*. She had come to Union Station, as she put it,
"to ride home with Franklin."[2]

One car behind, in the *Howe*, Daisy Suckley, FDR's cousin who had
been at the cottage when he died, had found her way to Compartment
"H." Although Fala had been left to her care even since the train had
departed Warm Springs two days before, it was understood that the First
Dog would enjoy his customary privileges of the *Ferdinand Magellan*.
The Scottie knew the Pullman at least as well as its attendants did.

Having spent the previous day and night aboard, Eleanor Roosevelt
had gotten to know the beautiful old car quite well, too, and no doubt
appreciated that President Truman would be quartered aboard the
Roald Amundsen for this trip. Whether she realized it or not, Eleanor
also owed a debt of gratitude to Dewey Long and his men, for the
Magellan had been coupled next to last on the train, one car ahead of
the *Conneaut* and just behind the *Amundsen*. That location meant that

all the glad-handers, power brokers, and favor-seekers who would be coming down through the train to see Truman would not be trooping through the Roosevelts' coach.

In the *Magellan*'s softly lit compartments, Elliott Roosevelt, along with his mother, sister, and sisters-in-law, were settling in. Bolted to the wall to the left of the lounge's rear doorway was a brass ship's clock. The hour confirmed the worst. "My brother Jimmy should have been here by now," Elliott thought.[3] Jimmy—at that moment flying some-where over the Great Plains—had done all he could to traverse an ocean and a continent to reach Washington in time, but he had missed a con-nection. The funeral train would leave without him.

It would also leave without Harry Hopkins. FDR's most trusted advisor was to have occupied Drawing Room "B" in the *Howe*, but the compartment was instead given to author, *New Yorker* contrib-utor, and Roosevelt speechwriter Robert E. Sherwood and his wife.[4] "Hopkins felt too exhausted to make this last, sad trip," Sherwood later wrote.[5] Doctors had removed two-thirds of Hopkins's can-cerous stomach in 1937; the resulting hemochromatosis would very soon kill him.[6]

Shortly after boarding, Interior Secretary Harold Ickes was angry to discover that the few available berths aboard Roosevelt's train had been opened for the likes of Truman advisors Robert Hannegan and Edwin Pauley—Democrats, yes, but, in his view, no friends to the Roosevelt people. Later, Ickes grumbled in his diary that there were no doubt gate-crashers who had also managed to finagle berths.[7] He was prob-ably right. But the Roosevelt reign was over, and no better proof existed than what could be seen through the windows of the *Roald Amundsen* just minutes before the funeral train pulled away. Sitting in the cozy, wood-paneled nook of the Pullman, Harry Truman was already deep in conversation with James Byrnes.[8]

As Merriman Smith lugged his satchel aboard, a porter told him that he could find the other newspaper men in the dining car.[9] The funeral train had two dining cars, but the closest for the reporters was one Pullman back from the *Treonta*, where most of them were sharing berths.[10] Pushing open Diner No. 4478's heavy vestibule door, Smith stepped into the warm pocket of cooking smells, liquor, and cigarette smoke. He found his colleagues at the tables. Smith sat down next to William C. Murphy, Jr., the White House correspondent for the *Philadelphia Inquirer.*

Seven cars up, on the head end of the train, the yard lights glinted off the polished skin of a GG-1 locomotive, its 36-ton body resting motionless on twenty wheels. Nothing like the Pennsylvania Railroad's G engines roamed the rails anywhere else in the world. Their wholly electric guts and sleek, steeplecab body—a high center motorman's compartment flanked by symmetrical, sloping hoods—made them the earthbound answer to Flash Gordon's spaceship. Industrial designer Raymond Loewy, who had given the G its avian lines, had called the locomotive "a monster of power,"[11] and at 10:05 on the night of April 14, the monster awakened. As the engineer notched his controller forward, the engine's pantograph (the spring-tensioned arm that pushed up against the live catenary wire above) sucked its first gulp of power. In a millionth of a second, 11,000 volts surged down into six hungry pairs of 25-cycle, single-phase traction motors geared to the driving axles. With barely a lurch, the bulk tonnage of eighteen railroad cars began to inch forward.

The initial tractive force of a GG-1 engine equaled 72,800 pounds, an enormous strain on the linkages. Somewhere down the length of the funeral train, a coupler between two of the cars agonized under the torque. The steel held for a second. Then it flew apart.

The pilot locomotive had already taken off in the lead with the *Congressional* following it. Now both would have to wait until the yardmen could replace the fractured knuckle. Normally, a GG-1 could make quick work out of an eighteen-car limited—but the funeral train was no ordinary limited. Many of its cars (the armor-laden *Magellan* especially) were seriously overweight.

Its spine broken, the funeral train lay still atop the rails. At 10:30 P.M., a drenching rain lashed across the terminal tracks. Questioning faces peered from the rain-streaked windows of the Pullmans. The downpour did nothing to disperse the thousands of people still watching from behind the police lines.[12]

Looking back from the GG-1's open window, the engineer got the all-clear at 10:42 P.M. and reengaged the motors. The funeral train crept ahead, the forward Pullmans entering the interlocking as the *Conneaut* slowly slid away from the casket's wooden loading platform. All seemed well. About 300 feet up the line, a caterwaul of tearing metal echoed back through the umbrella sheds. The coupler had broken a second time.[13]

And then it happened a third time.[14]

In the forward dining car, news of this last coupler fracture was too much for reporter William Murphy. "The Republicans have always known it would be hard to get Roosevelt out of Washington," he cracked. At this, one of his colleagues suggested that he might spare himself his obvious aggravation by getting off the train while there was still time. Murphy waved him off. "You guys will be coming back as soon as the old man is buried," he said. "But not me. I'm going to sit by his grave for three days and see if he really rises."[15]

Merriman Smith, by contrast, was not the sort of man who'd appropriate FDR's mortal remains for the sake of a joke. Even so, his respect for Roosevelt did not keep him—once the train was finally under way at 11:01 P.M.—from indulging a few complaints of his own. Some of Smith's colleagues maintained that they had been deceived. The White House, they said, had been lying to them about Roosevelt's health all this time. For example, following FDR's late-February return from the Crimea, where he had met with Churchill and Stalin in the Black Sea resort of Yalta, the official line was that the president was in "tiptop" shape.[16] Anyone could plainly see that he was not.

There was another thing that the White House had never shared with the reporters. As Harry Truman arrived at his Capitol office one afternoon earlier that spring, he noticed a handsome, well-dressed man sitting outside his door. The vice president assumed he had a visitor, until Colonel Vaughan informed him that the man had—apparently without Truman's having noticed—been holding vigil outside for the past two days. The mysterious visitor seemed to have no interest in coming inside to see Truman, either. "Well what the hell is this?" Truman asked.[17]

It was the Secret Service, and the young man was George Drescher— the agent who now was riding with Truman aboard the *Roald Amundsen*, eight cars back from the dining car where Smith and his colleagues were talking. In January 1945, the Secret Service brass had quietly informed the ranks that Roosevelt "was in serious ill health," and put Truman's guards on standby. Then, on March 1, another directive came down: "President Roosevelt might go at any time."[18] At that point, Truman's security detail clicked over to 24/7 duty. Clearly, the highest echelons of the executive branch understood that FDR's days were numbered. The press had been told nothing.[19]

Rivulets of rain splayed horizontally across the diner's windows as the train picked up speed. Had the couplers not broken, the train would have been well past Baltimore by now. Instead, running late, the engineer would palm his controller handle one or two notches higher than he'd planned; the train had an hour to make up before New York—some 220 miles ahead in the darkness.

In many ways, the funeral train's second incarnation—which would travel well under half the distance of the first—was a wholly different train. There were now two sections instead of one, twenty-nine cars instead of eleven, and a long list of distinguished guests. The atmosphere aboard would be different, too. Those who had accompanied the funeral train on its southern run had moved about the corridors like phantoms, stunned into stupor and silence. But FDR had now been dead for over two days. For many, the shock had slackened its grip; feelings of confusion and uncertainty ensued, so that everyone felt the need to talk. Among the passengers, thoughts that had previously centered only on the passing of the Boss could now begin to turn inward. The mourners could ponder their own futures now—and be frightened by them.

Another important difference was the presence of Truman and his entourage. Ostensibly they mourned, but most had boarded the train in order to conduct business. For them, the primary activity on the funeral train was maneuvering, not grieving. Its compartments and corridors were places to confer. Not the least of these men was Truman himself who, while feeling the loss of FDR acutely, had come aboard to work on his address to Congress and discuss matters of state known but to a handful of men anywhere on earth.

The train was fuller, longer—and yet still too small. It pushed strangers together. It did what trains so often do, perhaps with the help of a highball and the lulling sound of track thrumming beneath: It provoked thought, and it opened lips. In terms of its dark-green Pullmans, the funeral train looked much the same. But within it, something had changed. The train of sadness was now the train of secrets.

Aboard Diner No. 4478, the reporters continued to talk and drink. Soon another contentious topic crept into the conversation—that of the dead man himself. "One reporter made the point that it was a mistake not to have performed an autopsy on the President's body," Smith recalled, "and with a full, public disclosure of the results. That would have been a sure antidote for the rumors that swept the country in the days following his death."[20]

The rumors had begun almost immediately—that FDR had been murdered, that a look-alike had been posing as the president for years, and even that Roosevelt had died by his own hand. One yarn, prevalent in New York City's Harlem neighborhood, held that FDR had not died at all but was still alive and being kept somewhere, having gone insane.[21] Most prominent among the conspiracy theorists was a man who had never even set foot on American soil. Within a day of FDR's death, Josef Stalin made it known from Moscow that he believed FDR had been poisoned.[22] Of all the back-fence talk, however, none was more spectacular than the belief that the body aboard the Roosevelt funeral train was actually not that of Franklin D. Roosevelt.

Conspiracy theories and rumors have long attended the deaths of the famous, but in FDR's case, they were inadvertently permitted to flourish by the conspicuous lack of a postmortem. This, combined with the fact that the president had died in a secluded cabin in the company of few witnesses—and then been placed in a coffin that remained closed to members of the general public—succeeded in prying open the gate of doubt.

That gate would stay open a long time. So insistent was the talk about a cover-up that, even years after Roosevelt's burial, agitators still felt strongly enough about their theories to publish them. In 1947, a subversive pamphlet would emerge titled "The Roosevelt Death: A Super Mystery." This pulp-paper missive lent credence to most of the alternate-death ideas—even ones that contradicted some of the others. (That the author of the pamphlet identified himself only as "Mr. X" said as much about the publication's integrity as any of the prose within it.) "The casket was left closed because somebody had something to hide," intoned Mr. X. "What it was we may never know exactly but some of us have some well-founded suspicions."[23] Though the foundations were dubious, the suspicions were indeed plentiful. These included the inside-job theory ("the Secret Service men . . . put a pistol to his head and pulled the trigger"[24]) and the suicide one ("He had helped to set the whole world on fire. There was nothing left to ignite"[25]).

At least Mr. X's readers were led to believe that the body that had made its way to Hyde Park on the night of April 14 was in fact that of the president. Another theorist—who would also bring his canards to print—posited that a surrogate corpse had been placed inside the casket down in Warm Springs. "A gross deception has been practiced on the nation," warned Emanuel M. Josephson in his 1948 book, *The Strange Death of Franklin D. Roosevelt.* "It [is] highly probable, almost a certainty," pronounced the author, "that the person who died [in Warm Springs] *was not President Roosevelt.*"[26]

Josephson, a purported medical doctor whose other works include *Breathe Deeply and Avoid Colds,*[27] contended that FDR's coffin had been permanently sealed down in Warm Springs (which it had not) and then taken—an unidentified impostor's body resting within—to the White House. After the East Room services, the coffin was allegedly removed to a funeral parlor in East Fishkill, New York. Josephson claimed that the mortician had granted him an interview and informed Josephson that he had been "given strict orders not to dare to open the coffin, and was told that the armed guard was under orders to shoot anyone who would attempt to open it."[28] The following day, with the poseur safely interred below the garden in Hyde Park, the ruse was complete. (Or nearly so, since Josephson never managed to explain what he believed happened to the real Roosevelt.)

If true, Josephson's theory essentially meant that the highest echelons of the United States Government had been assembled aboard an eighteen-car train for the sole purpose of traveling 328 miles with an unknown corpse.

Kindly put, in terms of both substance and style, the words in these publications constitute pure dross. But the contentions they made were taken seriously by thousands of Americans. What's more, the con-spiracy authors were correct about a few things. The circumstances of FDR's death—the mountaintop hideaway, the mysterious Russian woman as witness—did seem plucked from a murder novel. The casket was closed for most of the three days that separated Warm Springs from Hyde Park. And an autopsy had never been performed.

But there were good reasons for all of these things. In his 1946 book, *White House Physician,* Admiral McIntire wrote that an autopsy would have served "no useful purpose," as the three doctors present—two of whom were coronary specialists—"were in agreement [about] the cause of death."[29] Even if the medical men had gotten a forensics team involved, a formidable obstacle would have blocked them: the First Lady. "Mother would not dream of allowing pathologists to perform their acts of mutilation,"[30] Elliott later said.

And though comparatively few people had seen FDR's body, they were sufficient in number to eliminate any possibility of producing something so ludicrous as a substitute corpse. In Warm Springs alone, those who viewed the remains included Eleanor Roosevelt; undertaker Fred Patterson and his four assistants; FDR's cousins Daisy Suckley and Polly Delano; and numerous presidential staffers including Prettyman, Hassett and Tully; and housekeeper Lizzie McDuffie, who subsequently related: "They had the casket lying open in the living room near the President's bedroom door. There was a glass over him. Oh, he was handsome. You wouldn't have thought he had a day's illness."[31]

The National Seamless Copper Deposit casket in which the body of FDR lay was what was called a twin-seal model. A top-of-the-line casket, it boasted two lids: an outer "couch" lid that ran the length of the top and two inner panels that could be closed in Dutch-door fashion—the foot panel over the legs and the head panel over everything above the deceased's waist.[32] Although the casket was closed before being put aboard the funeral train bound for Washington, it was sealed permanently only after Bishop Dun's service, which means that still more people—including undertaker William A. Gawler—had observed FDR's remains in the East Room. On Saturday, Fred Patterson recalled, "Mr. Gawler 'phoned me stating that the tissues were firm, complexion was fine and those who saw him remarked: 'He looks like his old self again and much younger.' "[33]

It also must have escaped the conspiracy theorists' attention that a description of FDR's corpse had even appeared in the *Chicago Daily News* under the byline of Walter Trohan, whose story included this passage: "Against the bank of flowers the lid of the coffin was raised. Mr. Roosevelt looked younger in death than on his last appearance here. The lines of care and strain had lifted. The body was clothed in a gray-blue business suit, a white soft collared shirt, and graying blush four-in-hand tie."[34]

How exactly Trohan was privileged to that firsthand view—assuming it *was* firsthand—is difficult to say; the instances in which the undertakers opened the casket lid were few, fleeting, and only in the presence of the Roosevelt inner circle. Why was the body never revealed, even briefly, to the public? As Eleanor had told Grace Tully during the first leg of the funeral train's journey, she and FDR both considered lying in state a distasteful practice.[35] However, even if Mrs. Roosevelt had not felt that way, the postmortem realities could simply not have been avoided: The severity of the cerebral hemorrhage had disfigured the president's handsome face—contorting it until it bore scant resemblance to the living FDR[36]—and left his skin a disturbing shade of purple.[37]

Why, then, were those who were able to view FDR's remains so complimentary about his appearance? Quite possibly for the same reason that journalists had for years ignored the president's paralysis and looked the other way when Lucy Rutherfurd was around: They were being gracious to a man they liked. There can be no doubt that the morticians' efforts to preserve and cosmetically improve the body down in Warm Springs had been heroic. In the early hours of Friday the thirteenth, Fred Patterson's embalmers had labored for well over five hours[38] and had also sought the aesthetic counsel of valet Arthur Prettyman in the proper parting and combing of Roosevelt's hair.[39] Patterson also recollected that Eleanor Roosevelt, after being allowed into the cottage's bedroom to see her husband's prepared remains, had thanked him for all he'd done.[40] Privately, however, Eleanor had experienced "shock" upon seeing her dead husband, according to Elliott.[41] And in his diary entry for April 13, press secretary Jonathan Daniels noted: "Later I learned from Anna or John Boettiger that Mrs. R. thought a bad job had been done by the undertaker."[42]

Given the severity of the hemorrhage that claimed the president, a very reasonable argument can be made that there was not much that any funeral director could have done to cosmetically mask the obvious. But one point is beyond dispute: There was simply no way, at least within the limits of good taste, that there could have been a public viewing of FDR's remains—which also meant, by default, that there was no way that the allegations of conspiracy theorists could have been conclusively silenced.

As the hour crept toward midnight, the funeral train passed through Odenton, Maryland, and then aimed its head light for Baltimore. In the

Conneaut's lounge, the wall sconces—each dangling a pair of blown-glass flutes—were all turned on, bathing the car's interior in a warm glow. The attendants had lifted the shades up into their wall pockets, opening the windows to full view from the outside. Just as they had in Georgia and the Carolinas, people had gathered trackside to wait in silence for the train to pass. The only difference now was the temperature; the mourners in the North had built bonfires.[43]

Young Margaret Truman noticed the fires—flares, many of them—from her compartment window aboard the *Roald Amundsen*, and they unsettled her. The eerie glow "illuminat[ed] thousands of grief-stricken faces," she wrote. "Sleep was practically impossible. When I did sleep I had nightmares about trying to open a window and escape from a small suffocating room."[44]

One car behind her, aboard the *Ferdinand Magellan*, Anna Roosevelt was bedding down with her own demons. As she prepared to retire, Anna discovered that she'd been given Stateroom "C"—FDR's old bedroom. "I've never known who assigned it to me," she recalled later. She could not sleep in the bed. "All night I sat on the foot of that berth and watched the people who had come to see the train pass by. There were little children, fathers, grandparents. They were there at 11 at night, at 2 in the morning, and 4—at all hours during that long night."[45]

Anna was not the only occupant of the *Magellan* who could do nothing but stare at the clusters of people slipping past outside the windows. "No one could sleep," Eleanor Roosevelt recalled. "So we watched out the windows of the train the crowds of people who stood in respect and sorrow all along the way."[46]

If the mourners on the train read uncertainty and dread in the faces of those who stood shivering along the tracks, it might have been because they felt it themselves. No one was immune from the sense of foreboding, not even the president's widow.

Elliott watched his mother closely. He was only thirty-four, but as a bomber pilot, he had matured beyond his years. Elliott knew that beneath the brave face and seemingly effortless poise the press had praised again and again was a woman deeply wounded. "At the moment," he said, "Mother was incapable of assessing the surgings of affection, disappointment, indignity and anger."[47]

Her future loomed ahead of her, and it held few comforts. She feared having nothing useful to do; she worried about feeling old.[48] Eleanor

Roosevelt had been the most dynamic, independent, and influential First Lady in history. Her travels had taken her across three continents, through world's fairs and munitions plants, lecture halls and Army hospitals, and even to the bottom of an Ohio coal mine. And now it was all over. "She would be sixty-one in October," Elliott recalled, "and she could see no future for herself except as a widow in retirement."[49] So complete had Eleanor Roosevelt's elegant self-possession been at the East Room services on Saturday afternoon, few could have guessed at the gnawing feelings of loneliness and fear that assailed her that night, as she lay within the rolling fortress of the *Ferdinand Magellan*.

For everyone aboard, the funeral train's destination was the grave site on the Roosevelt estate in Hyde Park, but for Eleanor it was something more. It was Springwood—the Georgian-colonial mansion in which her husband had spent his boyhood and from which her mother-in-law, the imperious Sara Delano, had exercised her self-righteous sway over Franklin and Eleanor's lives even unto her death in 1941. Sara's power rested not only in the fact that the purse strings of the family fortune were coiled tightly around her cold, knobby fingers; Franklin, an only child, had been mother's boy until the end: He either did not notice—or failed to acknowledge—Sara's ill-concealed disappointment over her son's choice of a wife.

From the moment in 1903 that Franklin had told his mother that he'd fallen in love with Eleanor, his fifth cousin once removed, Sara had schemed to get him to fall back out of it. She packed her twenty-one-year-old son off to a bluestocking job in London, then spirited him away on a cruise to the Caribbean.[50] Neither plan worked. Eleanor's pedigree was not the problem (she was a Roosevelt, after all, and her uncle Teddy was President of the United States), but Sara was alarmed by Eleanor's unladylike, socially progressive streak.[51] Plus, Eleanor was a bit on the homely side, with a rounded chin and regrettably protuberant teeth. Her only son, Sara felt, could do better.

The passing years had failed to soften Sara's judgmental views. At times, Granny (as the Roosevelt children knew her) had been simply cruel. "Franklin" could easily have wed "so many pretty girls," Sara would lament at a table full of dinner guests—Eleanor seated among them. Even when Eleanor would flee the dining room in tears, FDR kept chewing in silence.[52] The Roosevelt children, as Anna would recount, were too young at the time to see Sara's maliciousness for what it was.

But later on, as they grew old enough, Anna said, "we all realized that Granny was just 'an old bitch.' "[53]

As the funeral train crept its way through the night toward the estate, Eleanor Roosevelt reached a decision: Though the big house was now hers to live in if she pleased, she would not. "The presence of our commanding grandmother was almost tangible within its walls,"[54] Elliott remembered. But his mother had more immediate reasons, too.

Money was a problem. According to the terms of FDR's will, Eleanor's share of what remained of the Delano family fortune would be $8,000 a year[55]—a respectable sum, but hopelessly inadequate to maintain a thirty-five-room mansion complete with gardens, stables, and a full-time staff. But the inheritance, plus a modest side income earned through speaking engagements and her nationally syndicated newspaper column, "My Day," would be enough to pay the rent at 29 Washington Square West, Eleanor's Greenwich Village apartment. It would also allow her to keep Val-Kill, the fieldstone cottage that FDR had built for her on the Hyde Park property back in 1924—a compassionate gift that Eleanor would treasure not only for its simple, rustic charm but for its being located two miles away from her mother-in-law in the main house.[56]

The rest of Springwood—manse, gardens, stables and all—Eleanor would eventually hand over to the Parks Department.[57] A magnanimous gift to the public, it still did not free her from the considerable estate taxes she owed. To pay those, Eleanor would have to turn to FDR's stamp collection, a staggering caboodle of a million and a quarter pieces that the president, wielding his scissors and a magnifying glass, had lovingly built and cataloged over most of his life.[58] It would all go under the auctioneer's gavel, allowing the First Lady to settle accounts with the Internal Revenue Service.[59]

That night, as she lay awake in the gently pendulating bed of Stateroom "B," Eleanor wrestled with anxieties beyond those of her own future, and the future of the family of which she was now the head; she worried how Harry Truman would manage the reins of power so suddenly dropped from her husband's hands and thrust into his. Prior to Eleanor's retiring, some of the Roosevelt faithful had endeavored to keep her apprised of the doings aboard the *Roald Amundsen*, one car ahead, where the new president was holding court. "A parade of Father's followers kept passing between our coach and Truman's,"

Elliott recalled, "bringing back tidbits of information."[60] For Roosevelt's widow, the news carried few comforts. It was clear that DNC president Bob Hannegan and treasurer Ed Pauley in particular had Truman's ear. Pauley was a petroleum tycoon, and Eleanor believed that his private deals did not suit him to a life of public service—much less a seat of influence beside the new president.[61] Worse still was the rumor that Jimmy Byrnes would soon become Truman's choice for secretary of state. When she heard the news, Eleanor muttered to herself, "This is the worst mistake in the world."[62]

If Eleanor Roosevelt's words were unusually raw, she had a better reason for them than even Elliott knew. According to Trude Lash, the wife of Eleanor Roosevelt's young activist friend Joseph P. Lash, not long before the train departed Union Station, Byrnes had informed the First Lady that she would have to ride in the same railroad car with the new president. When Eleanor refused, Byrnes lost his temper because he, apparently, wanted the second Pullman for himself and the leaders of Congress. It's not clear where and when this episode took place, but Lash reported that several members of the cabinet had been "completely stunned" by Byrnes's callousness and self-importance. Of the incident, Eleanor Roosevelt said later that Byrnes had proven himself "a very small human being, indeed."[63]

What gossip the Roosevelts learned from loyal couriers drifting back into the *Ferdinand Magellan* from the car ahead was only a fraction of all that was actually going on up there. Indeed, the funeral train had barely rumbled past the Ivy City roundhouse north of Washington before Truman had assembled Colonel Vaughan, Edwin Pauley, Bob Hannegan, and Admiral Leahy in the *Roald Amundsen*'s lounge, where he and Byrnes had already begun meeting before the train had even departed.[64] Whatever work that might otherwise have been done in the Oval Office Truman had transplanted to the clubby domain of his borrowed Pullman car—and it was clear he intended the work to go on, regardless of the hour. "The rest of the night," Pauley would recall afterward, "continued a fairly continuous conference."[65]

Second only to Truman himself, the man at the center of that conference was Byrnes. But even as Jimmy was shaking hands inside the *Roald*

Amundsen, he was managing to blacken eyes—figuratively, at least—on the rest of the train. The Roosevelt faithful regarded Byrnes's having taken up quarters in Truman's car as a betrayal—even a threat,[66] for Byrnes had swung into the right-hand position with Truman so quickly that his maneuverings reeked of ambition. True, Byrnes had resigned the government prior to FDR's death, and he was, on this train, a private citizen. But he was still a "Roosevelt man" in the view of many, including Harold Ickes.[67] As the interior secretary would later confide to his diary, Franklin Roosevelt had virtually made Jimmy's political career. It was FDR who'd appointed Byrnes to the Supreme Court in 1941. It was FDR who then, by making Byrnes his director of war mobilization in 1943, essentially anointed him as his second in command. Now, aboard the funeral train, for Byrnes to distance himself so visibly from the Roosevelt camp was in bad taste, Ickes felt, and that was all there was to it.[68]

Of course, Byrnes—"a politician to the finger tips," as the *Atlantic Monthly* would call him[69]—was only doing, if a bit too obviously, the kind of maneuvering that any shrewd statesman could be expected to do. If the Roosevelt men felt resentment, it may well have stemmed from the fact that they themselves had few maneuvers left. Indeed, as they rode the funeral train that night, most of FDR's appointees were awaiting their turn at the political guillotine; before Truman's first hundred days were up, two-thirds of the Roosevelt cabinet would be sacked.[70]

Soon the all-too-visible disparity between the chosen and the vanquished forced a rift that cracked figuratively right up through the corridors of the Pullmans. Edwin Pauley sized it up bluntly: "The elements of the train quickly separated themselves into the Roosevelt people who remained in a state of shock, and kept very close to their own quarters throughout the whole night of the trip, and the Truman people who could not afford any such isolation."[71]

Shock was certainly one way to describe the state of affairs aboard the *Wordsworth,* the Pullman reserved for Roosevelt's cabinet. Voyage of the damned might be a better one. Facing political careers that were suddenly at an end, many of the men drank heavily—enough to make up for the few who did not.[72]

"The Cabinet were all together in car 6," Wallace recollected. Treasury Secretary Morgenthau, he wrote, "was completely tired out and had almost nothing to say. Ickes was bent over and had plenty to say, most of it uncomplimentary to the new President."[73]

About Postmaster General Frank Walker "was an air of doom and defeat,"[74] Wallace said, even though Wallace himself, sedate and distant, chose to sit alone. Morgenthau remarked to one of his colleagues that Secretary of State Stettinius looked "nervous as a witch."[75] He had every reason to be. Jimmy Byrnes was enjoying Truman's attentions aboard the *Amundsen* and the dashingly gray-haired Stettinius knew well enough what that portended for him.

"It seemed almost impossible for us to believe that this was the last journey which was to be taken by the President,"[76] Agriculture Secretary Claude Wickard would write in his diary. Wallace, as was his gift, summed up the situation aboard car No. 6 with the finest words: "The cord which had bound the Cabinet together had snapped."[77]

As the *Wordsworth* rocked its way northward, FDR's men continued to puzzle, debate, and drink their way through the long evening. One car back, in the *Glen Brook*, Grace Tully sat quietly in Drawing Room "A." At one point, she looked up to see Jane Ickes, the young, red-haired wife of the famously cantankerous Harold Ickes, standing in the compartment's doorway. In the poisonous atmosphere one car forward, Ickes had fought openly with his spouse after she had objected to the rich tapestry of invective he had woven about Truman. "You don't understand the time we're living in," Ickes had barked.[78] Perhaps she didn't; Jane Ickes was the thirty-two-year-old wife of a seventy-one-year-old statesman. But she did understand that she cared little for carrying on an argument in public, so she abandoned her husband to his liquor and stalked down one car to sit with Grace Tully. The two would end up talking until 1:30 A.M., when Jane Ickes apparently decided it was safe to venture back into the *Wordsworth*.[79]

The newspapers had announced that the funeral train would arrive in Philadelphia at 1:19 A.M. and lay over for thirty-six minutes.[80] As the hour approached, 30th Street Station gradually filled with "men and women representing every conceivable strata of the city's life," the *Philadelphia Inquirer* reported.[81] They stood beneath the eight enormous pendant chandeliers that dangled like art deco icicles over the

Tennessee marble floor. Not that anyone could *see* the floor: There were 5,000 people inside the building.

A few minutes shy of 1:00 A.M., a loudspeaker crackled to life with the announcement that the funeral train was running far behind schedule. No one made for the doors to leave. There would have been no place for them to go; outside on Market Street were 50,000 more people, waiting to get inside. Minutes after the first announcement came another. This one informed the crowd that they would not be permitted to the platform area below the station (the police were fearful that all the pushing and shoving would result in people falling down onto the tracks). The only way to actually see the train, Philadelphians were told, was to go to the river bridges. Only then did a shuffle toward the exits begin.[82]

An hour later, a GG-1's headlamp flashed out of the darkness and the *Congressional* rolled into the station. Minutes behind it, the funeral train bore down on its final approach, blue sparks popping atop the engine's pantograph as it skidded beneath the catenary wire. Ahead, sprouting from the main line's eastern embankment, the windows of switching tower "Arsenal" glowed in the darkness beneath a gabled roof. Inside the GG-1, the engineer notched his controller down and shed a few pounds of air from the brake pipe as the train rounded a tight curve and slid in between the fingers of the station's subterranean platforms. Its crossing bell echoing off the concrete walls, the locomotive slowed the long string of cars to a stop. Mayor Samuel stood on the platform with a white-gloved contingent of 300 police. Samuel was ready with the same token that seven big-city mayors in the South had presented before him: an enormous wreath of flowers.[83] It took its place aboard the *Conneaut*.

The funeral train rested only nine minutes—enough time for passengers to take a few quick breaths of night air before hurrying back inside. No sooner were the vestibule doors closed and latched than the Pullmans were slipping down the platform. As the station's limestone facade faded into the distance, the train nosed its way northward through a maze of retaining walls before elbowing to the east by the city zoo, then rumbling over the shimmering blackness of the Schuylkill River.

Now, a few minutes after 2:00 A.M., the depth of night had finally set in. Throughout the train's ten sleepers and three private cars, the Pullman porters had come through at various hours to make down the berths for those who decided they would attempt sleep; white cotton sheets, two pillows, and a chrome decanter of ice water were theirs as the compartment doors clicked closed. But many passengers—out of choice, or perhaps lack of it—stayed awake the entire night.[84]

Having risen at the crack of dawn on Saturday, Harry Truman had now been awake for twenty hours.[85] The new president—fond of naps—did not like to work when he was groggy (the very night he had become president, Truman had gone home, eaten a ham sandwich, and turned in around 10:00 P.M.[86]). The lights of the *Roald Amundsen* remained burning as the train cut its way up through the sooty industrial core of North Philly. "I don't think even Dad got more than a few hours' sleep that night," Margaret Truman remembered. "For one thing he was still working. He spent much of the night outlining his speech to Congress and discussing it with Jimmy Byrnes and others."[87]

They had been at it for hours already. Everyone Truman had convened in the *Amundsen* wanted to air his ideas about the future direction of the country, but for the moment there was really only one issue that mattered: Monday's address before the legislature. In his journal, Truman would later say little about this night spent at work on the most defining policy declaration since Roosevelt's "Day of Infamy" speech. "We had outlined it going up"[88] was about the extent of it. But the president's token description belied a situation that was, in fact, a small crisis.

In terms of its importance, the speech was nothing less than monumental. "It is an address," said the *Washington Post*, "which the entire world is awaiting eagerly for indications of the course [the president] will chart for winning the war and guaranteeing peace."[89] The speech also had to be finished by Monday morning and was nowhere near that point now as the funeral train began to chew up the ninety-odd miles that remained before it would dive beneath the Hudson River and slip into New York City.

All through Saturday afternoon and into the evening, George Allen had worked on the script in the West Wing. As 9:00 P.M. neared, Allen recalled, he and Ed Reynolds "transferred operations to the Roosevelt funeral train."[90] Though largely isolated in the Pullman *Treonta*, the press corps was well aware that work on the speech was going on and that Allen (the man who had helped write Truman's first speech as vice president[91]) had his hands in it. One of Truman's "assistants" (never identified in the AP dispatch) would later ascribe to Allen only a minor, tributary role: doing "spade work" and "whipp[ing] together the first draft from suggestions made by various individuals."[92]

In truth, the speech was largely the work of Allen and Reynolds alone. Though plenty of ideas had come from the advisors Truman assembled around the big oak table in the *Amundsen's* dining room,[93] those men—judging from the diaries they left behind—could hardly be called wordsmiths. Twenty-four years would have to pass before George Allen finally took credit for what he could do with a typewriter: "We went up to Roosevelt's funeral in an upper berth," he told an interviewer, referring to himself and Reynolds. "We worked on [the speech] all the way up there, nobody else worked on that."[94]

As the night wore on, Allen eventually sent Reynolds nine cars up to polish the draft in the solitude of Drawing Room "A" of the *Glen Gordon* while he stayed behind, listening for nuggets to drop into the speech as Pauley, Hannegan, Leahy, and Byrnes talked.[95] George Allen was good at cherry picking like this—very good at it. Though men like Byrnes could probably have trounced him when it came to the minutiae of law or policy, Allen had a knack for knowing what truly mattered to people. When FDR had appointed him commissioner for the District of Columbia back in 1933, Allen had set off across America to study living conditions brought on by the Great Depression. For good measure, he dressed like a hobo.[96] "Washington has never seen anything quite like George Allen," a profile in *Time* magazine would later observe.[97] He would roll his eyes, boom with laughter, and keep serious men in stitches with his stories. But the true talent of George Allen lay in his knowing the value of telling stories to begin with. As the men aboard the *Amundsen* weighed and measured what Truman's speech should contain, Allen seemed to know that the narrative's key ingredient would have to be the man from Missouri himself.

The 80 tons of the *Roald Amundsen* swayed gently beneath the men's feet as the funeral train clattered across the industrial face of New Jersey—Trenton, New Brunswick, Elizabeth. The train was due in to New York at 4:35 A.M., but not everyone at the dining-room table would hold up for that long. At some point (probably around 3:00 A.M.) what Pauley termed the "steady round the clock conference"[98] finally proved too much for the president. Truman rose, bade his advisors a good night, and slipped into his compartment.

FDR's correspondence secretary Bill Hassett had gone to bed hours ago. But first he had walked back four cars from the *Glen Brook* to the *Ferdinand Magellan* to check on Mrs. Roosevelt, as he had so many times. She thanked him, once more, for everything he had done for her, but needed nothing more.[99] Hassett turned and made his way back—through the smoke-filled *Roald Amundsen* where Byrnes was holding court, up through the dining car, the Pullman *Howe*, and finally into car No. 5.

Hassett opened the door to Compartment "G" and found FDR's old friend Leighton McCarthy looking at him. Apparently they would be roommates. That was fine with Hassett; the two men had known each other a long time, and both shared a deep-rooted affection for the Boss. McCarthy—former Canadian ambassador to the United States, whose own son John had been stricken with polio—was perhaps the only man who had even seen a paralyzed Franklin D. Roosevelt very nearly walk. It was sometime in 1927, when Roosevelt had spent months religiously submersing his wasted legs in the 88-degree thermal pool at Warm Springs. One day, McCarthy returned to his cottage to find Roosevelt alongside a wall with his arms stretched out, concentration and wonder etched into his face. "Look, Leighton," FDR whispered fiercely. *"I'm standing alone."*[100]

Now, eighteen years later, inside a Pullman compartment hurrying through the troubled night, the two men looked at each other sadly. The memories were too painful to discuss; the only thing to do was go to sleep. McCarthy offered repeatedly to take the upper berth—a toilsome climb up a ladder—while Hassett repeatedly insisted he take the lower. Eventually, the sixty-five-year-old Hassett ordered his seventy-six-year-old bunkmate into the bottom berth.[101]

Sunday, April 15, 4:00 A.M. In the small hours of the morning when railroad terminals are usually just drafty echo chambers of marble,

New York's Pennsylvania Station was filling with people. They came alone, in pairs, and in small groups. Hundreds of New Yorkers stood beneath the concourse's umbrella vaults of iron and glass, soaring to unseen, grimy heights above the floor.[102] Because the newspapers had said nothing to the contrary, the mourners presumed they would be permitted to descend to the platforms to see the funeral train pass. Instead, at the tops of the ornate, brass-railed staircases, the people saw only the glinting badges of policemen, who informed them that they had come as far as they would be allowed to go.[103]

A headlamp flashed from the darkness of the North River portal as the funeral train slipped into the predawn chill of the deep, open cut between Tenth and Ninth avenues. Here the Pullmans were visible for just a few moments before they disappeared into the forest of columns supporting the foundations of the General Post Office. At Ninth Avenue, the main line fanned into twenty-one tracks to feed Pennsylvania Station's eleven platforms. Watching the progress of the funeral train and the *Congressional* on his model board, the dispatcher lined both straight into Penn's center lanes—the tracks on either side of Platform No. 6.[104]

Pulling the pair of trains along like toys, the powerful GG-1 engines had easily made up the hour delay out of D.C., then shaved off another twenty minutes for good measure.[105] The funeral train came in on Track 11 at 4:15 A.M. The *Congressional* slid through the switches seventeen minutes later, coming to a rest on Track 12.[106] Upstairs on the concourse, the train gates turned to scenes of despair as cops turned away battalions of the tearful. Having coaxed themselves from bed at an ungodly hour, these New Yorkers had come to pay their respects— but now there was simply nowhere else to pay them. The funeral train would not be visible again anywhere in Manhattan. Some people were not even sure for whom they were crying. Just as stories gain embellishments with each new telling, word of the president's death had mutated as it spread through the city, spinning off absurd and unrelated rumors—among them that fighter Jack Dempsey had also died, and Frank Sinatra, too.[107]

But down in the recondite world of the tracks, things were calm. Parked across from each other, the long trains reposed in the half-lit, subterranean realm where police patrolled the platforms. Up at the head end, the GG-1 engines cut off to make way for a pair of New York,

New Haven & Hartford Railroad electrics. By 5:03 A.M., both sections trundled into the East River tunnel, sixty feet below the sidewalks of 32nd Street.[108] Notwithstanding the stalwarts who had made the early-morning pilgrimage to the station, most of Manhattan's residents were still asleep as the train pulled out. The hundreds of thousands of people in Midtown hotels and apartment houses never were aware that Franklin D. Roosevelt was leaving them.

Picking up speed to make the 1.22 percent grade climb from under the East River, the funeral train rocketed out of the tunnel at Vernon Avenue in Long Island City, a neighborhood of factories and warehouses on the industrial shoulder of Queens. Starting on a long, sweeping climb to the west, the funeral train knocked onto the flyover track that skirted the Pennsylvania's sprawling Sunnyside Yards.

Clustered at the tops of high poles, the yard's spotlights enveloped the massive interlocking in a soft, milky light as the funeral train sped clear of it, high on an embankment of traprock and earth. Despite the seeming stillness of the place now, an hour before daylight, wartime Sunnyside was alive with activity. The Pennsylvania Railroad had marshaled virtually anything that rolled to accommodate the 109 million people who'd pass through Pennsylvania Station in 1945.[109] The yards swelled with the stopgap measures the railroad had taken with the outbreak of war: clusters of new locomotives, freight cars converted to passenger coaches, and even luxury limiteds rechristened as roving hospitals.[110] Coiled up together in the predawn chill, the rolling stock stood ready—coaches, troop sleepers, and, in the North Yard beyond the Pullman commissary building, a sea of boxcars. As the war made its incessant demands—for men, for guns, for trucks and tanks and food— nothing in Sunnyside would sit still for very long.

The New Haven locomotive flexed its electric muscle and the funeral train thrummed farther up the ribbon of rails. At the Gosman Avenue cutoff, the train shunted over to the approach tracks for the Hell Gate Bridge. Its enormous bow truss loomed ahead to the northwest, a latticework summit soaring over the angry river currents below.

⊶⇌ ⇌⊷

Few aboard realized it, but as the funeral train—and the *Congressional* trailing it by a few minutes—skirted the limits of the Sunnyside Yards, it was in the process of going twenty-eight miles out of its way. The detour was unavoidable. In Midtown Manhattan, Penn Station and Grand Central Terminal were a mere nine blocks apart, but for a train to pass from the tracks of the Pennsylvania onto those of the Central, its archrival, the only option was to run over Hell Gate, taking the New Haven's trackage up into Westchester County as far as New Rochelle Junction. There, a connecting line branched to the southwest as far as Woodlawn, where the funeral train would cross onto the New York Central's Harlem Division.[111] The final step would be getting the train onto the Central's Hudson River main line leading up to Hyde Park. That junction point lay farther to the south, in the Bronx neighborhood of Mott Haven.

Mott Haven is what had the Secret Service genuinely scared. Sunk into the belly of the Bronx, the yards' fifty-one layup tracks stretched for eight city blocks, surrounded by an unbroken grid of apartment buildings, warehouses, and stores. On the previous service stops, the funeral train and the *Congressional* had been hidden underground and enjoyed the additional protection afforded by the night. Here, both forms of camouflage would disappear. The schedule allowed the trains enough time to change engines—twenty minutes, and not a moment more.[112]

The first light of Sunday broke over the horizon of apartment house roofs at 6:18 A.M. The trains arrived in Mott Haven seven minutes later, creeping around the wye—the crescent-shape track that linked the Harlem to the Hudson divisions. As the wheel flanges scraped and hissed around the curve, a phalanx of military police, Secret Service men, and New York City detectives took up positions near the train, keeping curious civilians (and quite a few had come) at a distance. As the New Haven electrics slipped off the consist, two enormous steam engines—J1-d Hudson-class locomotives, each fifty-four feet long and 177 tons[113]—stood at the ready. On the first leg out of Warm Springs, the Southern's steam locomotives, magnificent machines as they were, had to be paired up to manage the train's weight. The Hudsons required no such doubleheading; a single J1-d could easily manage the eighteen-car train on its own. No. 5283, with C. J. Potter at the throttle,[114] backed down onto the funeral train until the heavy clink of locking couplers echoed off the brick backs of the apartment houses. On the 153rd Street bridge, soldiers paced the asphalt with machine guns slung around their shoulders.[115]

Though Potter, with the funeral train's engine under his hand, was arguably America's most important engineer at this moment, he would be waiting for the other train to pull out first. The *Congressional* would use its thirty-minute lead to run to Hyde Park and begin unloading passengers to automobiles that would drive them to the burial site. Meanwhile, the funeral train would be rolling onto the private siding at the riverfront foot of the Roosevelt estate at 8:40.[116] The plan had been worked out well in advance, as had the appearance, at Mott Haven, of a third locomotive—a deadhead to chuff off a mile ahead of both trains as a first line of defense against whatever dangers, natural or manmade, might lie in wait.[117]

According to the timetable, the train was to remain in Mott Haven only until 6:45 A.M. Despite the clusters of early-risers rubbernecking along Sheridan Avenue and Terrace Place, much of the Bronx was still asleep at this hour, though the passengers of the funeral train—especially those stirred from slumber by the train's coming to a halt—had been gradually waking up.[118] In the *Roald Amundsen*, Harry Truman was already dressed to receive Harold Ickes for a briefing.[119] FDR's interior secretary had presumably exhausted his vitriol of the night before and was in sufficient humor to speak to the man he'd denounced. The dining-car cooks had put on plenty of coffee—an immense reward for those not too hung over to rise early, dress, and make their way down to breakfast. Sitting at one of the tables was Henry Wallace, his hand cupped around a fresh brew that he periodically brought to his lips as he stared out the window.

Suddenly, Wallace's face froze in terror as he saw a wall of gray water about to slam into the train. The secretary of commerce ducked. Then he realized that the crisis was nothing more than a team of car-washers; the water had been merely the soapy contents of a bucket.[120] The New York Central was not about to have a dirty train pulling two presidents. Wallace understood. He smiled through the wet glass.[121] Everyone aboard was, perhaps, a little jumpy.

At 6:40 A.M., the passengers in Dining Car No. 4497 felt a lurch beneath their feet. The locomotive's 4,075 horses had begun pulling.

The sun was powerful and brilliant on its slow climb from the east. It shone on the dewy grass growing at trackside. It also lit up thousands of faces. They were all new and yet sadly familiar, for thousands just like them had stood along the route all the way up from Georgia. "Even more impressive than the clusters of people standing in the early Sunday dawn," observed the *Washington Post*, "were the solitary onlookers who knew the train was coming and had donned coats to watch it from their own yards."[122]

The very same thought occurred to Claude Wickard aboard the Pullman *Wordsworth*, who had awakened in Compartment "H" and gazed out the window from his berth. "People were standing along the railroad tracks in every village and town along the way, and even in the rural areas," the agriculture secretary would recall. "This was all the more remarkable because it was so early and on Sunday morning."[123]

Aboard car No. 5, Hassett had risen early as well. As soon as he was dressed, he decided to check on Mrs. Roosevelt. Walking aft through the train, he passed through the rear door of Dining Car No. 4497 and was about to enter the *Roald Amundsen* when the Secret Service men stopped him. They soon waved Hassett onward, but the detainment—however brief—had meant something. The distance between the Roosevelt and Truman people was widening.[124] Hassett made his way down the *Amundsen*'s narrow corridor. In the observation lounge, he saw Truman sitting with Byrnes, who was reading his notes from the Yalta summit aloud to the new president. Hassett apologized for disturbing them as he passed on through.[125]

As Hassett stepped into the chilled air of the *Ferdinand Magellan*, he found that Eleanor Roosevelt had already risen and dressed. She was sitting by one of the windows, seemingly hypnotized by the blur of passing rail and ties on the adjacent track. Of the funeral train's entire route, this stretch—the seventy miles that the New York Central's four-track main line hugs the rocky eastern shore of the lower Hudson Valley—was the most beautiful by far. Across the mile-wide, blue-gray river, sheer cliff faces of diabase rose from a deep, verdant bed of oaks and maples, their branches dappled with the bright green of spring buds. The sun crafted complex shadows from the undulating rock face, which it cast upon the river surface. There was a reason why the lush, sweeping landscapes of painters Frederick Church and Thomas Cole would later define a genre known as the Hudson River School.

And yet Eleanor Roosevelt seemed to notice little of it, preferring instead to submit to the mesmerizing blur of the tracks. Then, suddenly, she broke free of the trance, smiled at Hassett, and bid him good morning.[126]

As the sun refracted off the Hudson River's shimmering surface that Sunday morning, the man in possession of still another of the funeral train's secrets rose, dressed, and put on his rimless spectacles. Lauchlin Currie, the forty-three-year-old economics advisor to FDR, had been assigned to Compartment "G" of the *Glen Lodge*, the Pullman at the center of the long string of cars, along with his wife, Dorothy Bacon. A brilliant economist with a Ph.D. from Harvard, Currie possessed a disposition that spoke well of his ivy-league breeding. Composed and even-tempered, even in the face of angry dissenters, Currie had quickly won the respect and admiration of FDR shortly after the two met in 1937.[127] At the time, Currie was a tenderfoot at the Federal Reserve. Roosevelt quickly realized that his New Deal policies would benefit from a man with Currie's easy manner and considerable intellect. By 1939, Lauchlin Currie was working in the West Wing.[128]

Currie's unremarkable demeanor might have been part of the reason why his name can be located nowhere in the many recollections of those who rode the funeral train. The contemporary observer has no choice but to presume that Currie's behavior aboard the train was customary and forgettable. He was, after all, merely waiting out his last days as a Roosevelt aide before his inevitable replacement.[129]

In all probability, however, Currie had much more weighing on his thoughts than the necessity of finding a new job. As one of numerous presidential assistants, Currie had been a member of what one historian has termed "an anonymous and shifting group."[130] Some staffers who had gotten to know and like Currie called him by his nickname, "Lauch." But Currie had another sobriquet that no one in the West Wing knew. This was "Page"[131]—the code name selected by the KGB, for which Lauchlin Currie had been spying since roughly 1939.[132]

At first, Currie's assistance to the Soviets had been both cautious and limited. Currie was described by an associate as a "fellow traveler"—meaning, a Communist sympathizer—who "never went the whole way."[133] Currie's leaks usually took the form of conversations with Gregory Silvermaster, a man Currie knew as a friend but who also happened to operate a network of informers that was among the richest pools of information for the KGB in wartime Washington.[134] Currie's defenders (and Currie himself) would later protest that Silvermaster and other contacts were merely social acquaintances; that he had not known that they were Soviet operatives and, hence, that his actions had not constituted spying.[135] This explanation fails, at the very least, to address the significant question of why Currie was sharing confidential government information—with anyone—in the first place.

While the specific nature of the intelligence he disclosed in the early days remains largely unknown, Currie did, on one occasion, warn the Soviets that the Americans were making formidable progress toward breaking their secret code.[136] The first actual document on record as having come from Currie was dated April 1941. It was a report on his recent economic mission to China for FDR.[137] Soon other papers would follow, outlining America's policies regarding the Far East—a matter of tremendous interest to Moscow.[138]

More recently, however, Currie's aid to the Soviets had shifted into a higher gear. During the summer of 1943, Currie had handed a secret document over to George Silverman, an operative in the Silvermaster ring. The precise contents remain a mystery, but it is known that the report concerned a political subject and it had originated in the State Department.[139] Then, ten months later, in June 1944, Currie dropped off a document of critical importance—the contents of which would eventually make it all the way into Stalin's hands in Moscow.[140]

It was a report informing the Soviets that FDR—despite his public fist-pounding to the contrary—would in fact be willing to acquiesce to Stalin's demand that the U.S.S.R. be able to keep the half of Poland granted it in 1939 under the pact the Soviet leader had made with Hitler. From Currie's intelligence, Stalin further learned that FDR would pressure the Polish government (then a body in exile in London) to grant concessions to the Soviets. The information was nothing short of an ace slipped into the cuff of the Communist strongman, who could then be assured that, once the war was over, he could keep his hands around Poland's neck with no significant interference from Washington.[141]

As Currie rode the funeral train to Hyde Park on this April morning, the big drop was nearly a year in the past. But he had continued to pass on information.[142] Early in 1945, he had also met several times with a man named Anatoly Gromov, a KGB officer who masqueraded as a Soviet diplomat and worked out of the Soviet Union's embassy in Washington.[143] Somehow, incredibly, all the subterfuge was still intact. What Currie could never guess was just how close he was to the end. His peace of mind, such as it was, would last for only three more months.

On a humid day in August 1945, a curly-haired woman named Elizabeth Bentley—pretty, fluent in Italian, and educated at Vassar and Columbia—walked into the Hartford, Connecticut, office of the Federal Bureau of Investigation and turned herself in as a spy. Then she began naming names. Currie's was among them.[144]

Until 1943, Bentley had been the secretary and lover of a man named Jacob Golos, an official with the Society for Technical Aid to Soviet Russia—a front for Soviet espionage activities.[145] Bentley claimed that Currie was a key member of a spy ring operated by Silvermaster, a ranking government official who had held successive posts in multiple New Deal agencies since 1935; as of 1944, he worked at the Treasury Department. Gregory Silvermaster's house was allegedly used by spies in his network—including Currie and assistant treasury secretary Harry Dexter White—as a drop point for documents purloined from various agencies. Silvermaster, Bentley claimed, used a camera and darkroom in his basement to photograph all the documents.[146] Bentley—known to the KGB under the code name "Good Girl"[147]—would take the train down from New York every two weeks to pick up rolls of film from the Silvermaster ring and from several others then operating inside the city.[148]

Bentley's accusations were sensational, but they constituted the avowal of only one person—one whose word could be doubted simply because she had been a practitioner of deception herself. Nonetheless, FBI chief J. Edgar Hoover would later personally vouch for Bentley's integrity.[149] Yet absent documentary evidence or corroborative testimony, little could be done with her testimony on its own.[150] When the FBI hauled in those whom Bentley had named, most were evasive and said nothing useful.[151]

Not that that mattered much. By 1947, the Red Scare was on—ignited partly by Bentley's claims—and the House Un-American Activities

Committee (HUAC) set out to ensnare (or at least terrify) everyone on her list. By that time, Lauchlin Currie's document-dropping days were over. KGB documents later showed that Currie had one final contact with the Soviets in November 1945, a one-on-one conversation with a Soviet operative in which Currie "after some hesitation...agreed to cooperate" further.[152] By that time, however, Currie no longer worked in the White House. He'd resigned in April 1945, shortly after FDR's funeral, and Elizabeth Bentley's turning informant that August had spooked Moscow, which decided to end all contact with him.[153]

Shortly after leaving his White House post, Currie moved away from Washington. He set up an import/export business at 565 Fifth Avenue in New York and found a house in the northern suburb of Scarsdale. Summoned before a federal grand jury in Manhattan on August 1, 1948, Currie testified that he had never known Elizabeth Bentley.[154] (Of this, there was little doubt, since Bentley herself had said that she had only "suspected" Currie as a probable source in the Silvermaster ring.[155]) Thirteen days later, at his own request, Currie appeared in Washington before HUAC itself. Again he denied knowing Bentley and further denied being, knowing, or abetting a Communist of any stripe. "Among the thousands of loyal Americans who have been my colleagues during my 11 years of Government service," Currie said, his voice echoing through the chamber, "I challenge anyone to find one person who ever doubted my loyalty to this country."[156]

It was a strident, confident showing and differed bravely from that of others (including Gregory Silvermaster) whose words before HUAC's terrifying inquisitors strayed no further from evoking the Fifth Amendment.[157] But Currie's eloquence made little difference. Nourished by HUAC's sensationalism, the press—getting its first taste of the blood that would color the water for many years—cranked out incendiary stories from the testimony. The drama reached its peak (or depth) with items such as "How Red Agents Operated Inside the White House," published in the March 1954 issue of the *National Police Gazette* and brimming with phrases like "the Currie circle of spy-tainted and Soviet-sympathizing friends."[158]

In the end, Currie's self-professed loyalty to his country would not be enough to stop him from leaving it. In 1950, he accepted an invitation from the government of Colombia to become an economic advisor in Bogotá and elected to make Colombia his home. Contrary to reports that he renounced his citizenship, the former FDR aide actually allowed it to be forfeited—which happens automatically when an American lives outside the country for more than five years.[159] In Currie's view, given the climate of fear and suspicion in the United States, there was little reason to return. "You never live down guilt by association," he said.[160] Currie was long gone from the United States before *new* documents would surface—ones that would leave little doubt of his culpability.

For many years, the degree of Currie's spying was in dispute, largely through the lack of real proof outside the allegations raised in HUAC—a group whose definition of proof often didn't depart from hearsay. Then, in 1994, former Soviet spymaster Pavel Sudoplatov published his memoirs under the title *Special Tasks* and confirmed both the operation of what he called "the Silvermaster spy cell" and Lauchlin Currie's membership in it.[161]

Still, the extent of Currie's involvement would never be known were it not for a development that began toward the end of 1946. After three years of chipping away at the notorious, double-encrypted Soviet code, the National Security Agency (NSA) finally began to unravel the cipher that had allowed pilfered intelligence to pass between the United States and Moscow during the war years with almost complete impunity. The body of decoded secret messages—nine of which mention Currie[162]—were part of what collectively became known as the Venona Project.[163]

Venona could have meant serious trouble for Lauchlin Currie—but only in theory. From its initial breakthroughs in 1946, the NSA's deencryption—slow and excruciatingly complex work—continued all the way until 1980. It remains unclear when the government code breakers translated the messages that revealed Currie's complicity. Yet even had those messages emerged prior to Currie's leaving the country in 1950, none of Venona's information could be used in a public prosecution because every translated word of it was classified as top secret and in fact would remain so until 1995.[164] (Currie died in Bogotá in 1993, aged ninety-one.)

But while Lauchlin Currie's fate was still uncertain, on the April morning in 1945 that the funeral train made its way up the banks of the

Hudson River, one fate had already been sealed: that of postwar Eastern Europe. Currie's mere presence on the same train that witnessed Harry Truman's ongoing tutelage in foreign affairs by James Byrnes was ironic indeed. In just a few weeks, Truman would travel to Potsdam to hammer out the future of a ravaged Europe with Churchill and Stalin. To his credit, Truman would take a hard line over Polish independence— but it would prove every bit as useless as the one Roosevelt had taken.[165] Stalin's troops already occupied Poland, and the Soviet leader had no intention of relinquishing it. His imperialistic intentions probably would have been the same no matter what, but Stalin had long before learned that America was willing to let him have his way, thanks to the work of the Silvermaster spy ring and the man who occupied Compartment "G" of the *Glen Lodge*, car No. 8 of the train carrying Franklin D. Roosevelt home for the final time.

The heavy Pullmans swayed as the train hugged the undulating shoreline on its way north. Back in the *Roald Amundsen*, what was perhaps funeral train's deepest and darkest secret was taking shape.

At Pullman's South Chicago Shops, Presidential car Ferdinand Magellan *receives its bulletproof sheathing in 1942.*
(Courtesy of Gold Coast Railroad Museum)

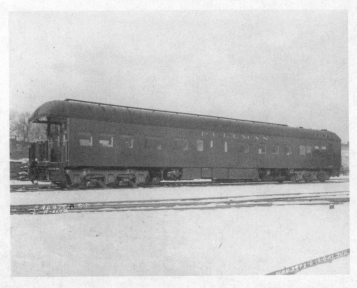

Pullman factory photo of the finished, fully-armored Magellan, *weight: 142½ tons.*
(Courtesy of Gold Coast Railroad Museum)

In the Magellan's *lounge, stately appointments included plush armchairs and sculptural ashtrays.*
(Courtesy of Gold Coast Railroad Museum)

The only known photo taken aboard the funeral train: FDR's coffin inside the Pullman Conneaut.
(AP/WIDE WORLD PHOTOS)

The funeral train pulls into Track 10 of Atlanta's Terminal Station.
(Special Collections and Archives, Georgia State University Library)

At Greenville, South Carolina, 25,000 people stand in silence as the funeral train arrives.
(Franklin D. Roosevelt Presidential Library and Museum)

Armed sentries line the platform at Charlottesville, Virginia, as the Conneaut slips slowly past.
(Albemarle Charlottesville Historical Society)

Just 23 miles from Washington, the funeral train steams through Fairfaix, Virginia, in this rare photo taken by a bystander.
(Courtesy of Lee Hubbard)

FDR confidant James Byrnes (l.), President Harry Truman, and Commerce Secretary Henry Wallace await the train's arrival at Washington's Union Station. (Abbie Rowe; Franklin D. Roosevelt Presidential Library and Museum)

President Truman exchanges a few words with Anna Roosevelt at Union Station. (Abbie Rowe, Courtesy of Harry S. Truman Library)

With the train parked on a freight track, officers prepare FDR's coffin for the procession to the White House.
(Abbie Rowe; Franklin D. Roosevelt Presidential Library and Museum)

Nearly twelve hours later, a hearse returns the casket to Union Station, where it is placed back aboard the train.
(Abbie Rowe, Courtesy of Harry S. Truman Library)

State troopers prepare the way for Elliott Roosevelt at the Hyde Park Depot shortly after the burial service's conclusion.
(E.R. Andros; Franklin D. Roosevelt Presidential Library and Museum)

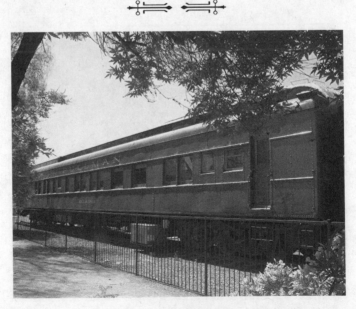

A present-day view of the Roald Amundsen, *the private Pullman car used by Truman and his entourage.*
(Photo by Bob Adler)

SEVEN

CAR NO. 3

*A*t the elegant, slate-roofed station in Garrison, New York, where the Hudson River lapped up onto stones just feet from the platform, some eighty locals had come at dawn on Sunday to wait in the cold for the funeral train to pass them. They had arrived in automobiles, some of them old Model A Fords, to which a few people returned now and then to fetch Thermoses of coffee. Distinct from the motorists was a group of Capuchin Franciscan friars, their cassocks pulled tight to their waists with white ropes. The brothers had come on foot—sandals, specifically—to the station from the Glenclyffe Monastery, one mile distant, whose Gothic turrets poked high over the trees on the hillside.

The friars positioned themselves in a row of such precision it seemed better suited to West Point, the military academy whose gray granite ramparts rose directly across the river. While the Capuchins stood in complete silence, the people around them talked, quietly, about Roosevelt. "I hope he's not in one of those old-fashioned trains. It wouldn't be proper," said one. Another expressed a lament shared by countless thousands of other Americans: "I wish to God he'd managed to hang on until Germany was licked."[1]

A father in the group turned to his young son, who had been shivering in the cold, and spoke to him. "You've got to remember everything you see today," the man said, firmly but not unkindly.[2]

A watchman's shack stood some distance from the platform, and presently a teenager in a mackinaw with blue and white stripes made a beeline to it, meaning to inquire as to the funeral train's whereabouts.

Moments later, a black engine hove into view to the south, a full head of steam driving its pistons silently in the distance. The rails registered a faint hiss that grew louder and louder, until the train pounced. Eleven cars thrummed past, the enormous heat of the locomotive giving way to the sucking tailwind of the passing Pullmans.

"That's not it," the adolescent announced, having returned from the shack and flaunting the knowledge that the watchman had obviously shared with him. The lad continued: "The President's in the next one, in a car called the *Roald Amundsen*."[3]

Usage of the term "president" was still a confusing thing for Americans on this Sunday morning, three days after the death of Franklin D. Roosevelt. Did it mean that new man from Missouri? Since Truman had been assigned the *Amundsen*, he was the one to whom the teenager must have referred. For most, though, "president" still meant the deceased squire from Hyde Park, the town 29.4 miles up the line from the Garrison platform. But of course, *he* was in the next train, too.

Minutes later, another locomotive loomed in the distance, a cottony plume of white smoke trailing from its stack. There was no mistaking the identity of this train, and now everyone joined the Franciscans in their silence. Just before engine No. 5283 reached the platform, men removed their hats. One by one, the Pullmans swayed past like drunken giants, the train's enormous weight sending a tremor through the very earth beneath everyone's feet.

There was no way to tell which dignitary was aboard which car, but it didn't matter; the reason for everyone's coming was to see the last one. A writer for the *New Yorker*, who was present in the crowd that morning, would become the lone journalist on the entire funeral story to express any sense of aesthetic appreciation for the worn but noble *Conneaut*. The magazine's sapient editorial voice pronounced it "a beautiful lounge car at the end, with its military guard of honor."[4]

In the early-morning river light, the dark-olive Pullman with the thicket of blossoms behind its windows was exactly that—beautiful—even if few thought of it in such a way. Then the lanterns on the *Conneaut*'s tail disappeared around a bend to the north, and the funeral train was gone.

As the people shuffled back to their cars, the little boy, sufficiently thawed out and excited, looked up at his father. "I saw everything," he said.

"That's good," than man answered. "Now make sure you remember it."[5]

The teenage boy in the mackinaw was excited, as well, for he had been among the few in the crowd to make out the gold lettering on the nameboard of car No. 3—*Roald Amundsen*. He knew what it meant, too. President Harry S. Truman had been aboard that one.

⁙ ⇌ ⇌ ⁙

It was a handsome old railroad car—not, perhaps, renowned like the *Ferdinand Magellan*, nor charged with the weighty task of the *Conneaut*, but dignified quarters nonetheless. Back in 1928, the *Roald Amundsen* cost the Pullman Company $205,000 to build.[6] As far as the Model A Fords in the Garrison station parking lot went, that kind of money could have purchased 532 of them. Much like the *Magellan*—with the exception of the armor plating and presidential touches like telephones in every room—the *Amundsen* was a manor house on wheels, complete with walnut paneling, plush chairs, and a mirror-backed bar.

Truman's decision to treat the *Amundsen* as his rolling study remains one of his best (and certainly least discussed) decisions of his first hundred days. Edwin Pauley—the man who had described the funeral train as a "working party" for the Truman camp[7]—was not alone in recognizing the importance of getting the new administration up and running quickly. FDR's press secretary, Jonathan Daniels, would later point out that Truman "had to accomplish a greater learning in less time than almost any other man in our history."[8] Harold Ickes believed that Roosevelt's VP was so lacking in experience that the kind of president he would make would depend entirely on the men to whom he would turn for advice.[9] And when it came to those men, even FDR's longtime confidant Harry Hopkins said that "Truman has got to have his own people around him, not Roosevelt's."[10]

Truman had indeed gathered his own people around him. From the time of the funeral train's departure from Washington the previous night until the early hours of this Sunday morning, the president had held court aboard the *Roald Amundsen* with but one brief adjournment—and that one only to allow himself a few hours of sleep.[11] Soon after he had risen and dressed, Truman resumed his meetings. He had spoken with Ickes in the privacy of Stateroom "C"—the big bedroom set aside for the first couple—and, by the time Hassett passed through on his way back to see Eleanor Roosevelt, the president had once again secluded himself with Byrnes. Now, with the funeral train closing in on Hyde Park, Harry Truman was beginning his third day as President of the United States. Two of those days had, in large part, been spent working aboard the 84- by 10-foot confines of the *Roald Amundsen*.

That Truman did his utmost in securing men to advise him is beyond question; what can possibly be regretted is that he had not sought out better men to do the advising. Until he could assemble a cabinet (and, to a degree, even afterward), Truman relied heavily on members of the "Missouri Gang," the loose agglomeration of loyalists and chums whose friendship reached back in time, geography, or both. Some, like Bob Hannegan (a detective chief's son who later became a St. Louis ward boss) and Colonel Harry Vaughan (Truman's pal since 1917 Army basic training) literally did hail from Missouri. Others, like the frumpy George Allen and DNC treasurer and California oilman Edwin Pauley, found honorary admittance—because of their loyalty, yes, but also because of an intangible that Truman seemed to value nearly as much: They were men the president called "regular guys."[12]

The regular guys had educations, if perhaps not from the Ivy Leagues. They were successful men, though they were not "born to the purple," as some had said of Roosevelt; not brought up as he had been, in the company of French tutors, sailing yachts, and Thoroughbred horses.[13] Instead, they were of the ilk who joined the Lion's Club, whose tastes ran to long jokes, stiff drinks, and ten-cent cigars.[14] Theirs were the politics of local halls and smoke-filled rooms. In many ways, they were men not unlike Truman himself[15]—which is a good part of why he'd chosen them.

"Bob, I don't know anybody," newsman Robert Nixon would recall Truman having told him well into his first term. "How can I bring *big* people into Government when I don't even know who they are, and they don't know me? They know the power of my position, but I've had no broad contacts in life. The only people I knew to bring down to the White House were those that worked in my office on the Hill. All of whom were little small town people. That's all they were."[16]

And that was the problem. Truman, as later advisor David Noyes would reflect, was "unable to overcome a preference to work and play with 'average' people."[17] During his days as a senator, perhaps that hadn't mattered much. But now, the simple truth was that a man with virtually no grooming for the presidency, who had just inherited the world's most powerful job and faced the task of ending its biggest war, could no longer afford to work and play with average people.

During those critical early weeks—which certainly included the two days spent aboard the *Roald Amundsen*—"there ought to have been some of the best talent that existed in the country [to assist Truman], and he wasn't getting it," said Edwin Locke, who would become Truman's executive assistant in 1946. "I didn't mind where the gang came from, Missouri or anywhere else," Locke went on. "What I minded was their mediocrity."[18] (Some appraisals were considerably harsher. Years later, Robert Nixon confessed that he thought "Truman brought a bunch of incompetents down to the White House."[19])

As Jonathan Daniels would later write, the main problem with "the gang" (and *Time* magazine used this very term to refer to Truman's clique[20]) was not a lack of earnestness; it was the dearth of sophistication and experience. No sooner had Truman become president, Daniels wrote, than "men who had made themselves useful in little things to Truman as a Senator . . . presumed on their relationships to move in with a show of new power."[21] Daniels referred to these figures as "precinct politician[s]"[22]—men who knew how to marshal support, votes, and cash on their local turfs. But the global stage of the presidency was simply a world too big for them. Even Truman himself probably could not have likened friends like Pauley, Hannegan, Vaughan, and Allen (his formidable speechwriting skills notwithstanding) to the polished professors, economists, and statesmen of FDR's "Brain Trust,"[23] the advisory team Roosevelt had assembled during his own first term. Indeed, Robert Hannegan had never wanted to be on the national stage at all. He'd consented to lead the Democratic National Committee only after FDR had cajoled him into it in 1944.[24] And as far as military aide Harry Vaughan went, in the words of historian David McCullough, Truman's old World War I buddy "seemed to serve no purpose beyond comic relief."[25]

Fortunately, Truman had other advisors aboard the *Amundsen*— ex-FDR men and, as such, not true members of the gang—whose value stemmed from decades of senior-level government service, not just decades of poker games. These men were Fred M. Vinson, Admiral Leahy, and, of course, James F. Byrnes. A gifted jurist and economist, Frederick Moore Vinson had served seven terms in Congress and as a justice on the U.S. Court of Appeals before becoming FDR's Economic Stabilization

Director in 1943. On April 4, 1945, in one of the final appointments made before his death, Roosevelt—rushing to fill the post that Byrnes had vacated—had named Vinson as his director of war mobilization and reconversion.[26] Still tough as granite at sixty-nine, William D. Leahy was an Annapolis graduate who'd been aboard the USS *Oregon* as she raced around Cape Horn to join the Spanish-American War in 1898. He had been Roosevelt's chief of staff since 1942 and rose to fleet admiral two years later. Byrnes, sixty-six, had served six terms in Congress and two in the Senate before joining the Supreme Court bench in 1941, only to resign a year later at Roosevelt's request to head the Office of Economic Stabilization and then the Office of War Mobilization. Not everybody liked Jimmy, but when FDR had said that Byrnes "knows more about government than anybody,"[27] few could honestly disagree.

Mismatched and varying in experience though they were, however, Truman's men were at least his own. And, savoring the *Roald Amundsen*'s baronial atmosphere as much as their newfound influence with the world's most powerful man, the advisors sunk their heels into the Pullman's thick wool carpeting, blew their smoke into the machine-chilled air, and talked their political talk. During the nearly ten hours that the funeral train took to travel from Washington to Hyde Park, it is known that all of the men aboard the *Amundsen* had something to say about domestic issues and about Monday's State of the Union Address. It is known that, privately, Truman had leaned in as Byrnes recounted all that Roosevelt had done with Churchill and Stalin at Yalta. What is not known—but for which a case can be made—is that Truman seized a few minutes during the journey to talk about the most critical topic of 1945 and, in some ways, the entire century.

He could have done so only at the exclusion of everyone except Leahy, Byrnes, and possibly Vinson, for they were the only men with the knowledge (and security clearances) suited for it. He could have done it only assured of a few minutes of privacy away from the gang. But all the ingredients were present aboard the presidential Pullman for a discussion of the biggest secret of the entire war: the atomic bomb.

The question of whether the thirty-third president deliberated over the world's first nuclear weapon while aboard the Roosevelt funeral train is one as compelling as it is ultimately frustrating. No smoking gun exists among the surviving, declassified records (at least, none that this writer has been able to uncover) to prove that the bomb was among the topics raised and pondered in the *Roald Amundsen*. Nevertheless, the evidence available—documentary and circumstantial—points, at the very least, to a fair chance that it was.

Two factors argue for the possibility. First, there was an incredibly pressing need to discuss the bomb—especially for a new president using every available minute to acquaint himself with the state of the war's conduct and its diplomatic complexities. Second, Jimmy Byrnes—a man unequivocally in favor of using the bomb as soon as it became available—not only enjoyed a near monopoly over Truman's time aboard the *Roald Amundsen* but had actively sought to influence the president from the moment he had arrived at the White House.

As to the first circumstance, in April 1945, the means of bringing the war to a swift end was a preoccupation for the country's leadership—in particular Leahy, Byrnes, and, of course, Truman. To suppose that the topic of ending the war did not come up during the hours and hours of private talks aboard the funeral train borders on the ludicrous. The issue was as urgent as it was grave. Although the fall of Berlin was imminent, so far as the men aboard the *Amundsen* knew, World War II was still nowhere close to being over. "Even after the German surrender," journalist Robert Nixon would recall, "our top military people predicted it would take another year of fierce fighting to bring about the Japanese surrender."[28] Led by Admiral Leahy, the Joint Chiefs of Staff were already planning (and just weeks from approving) the invasion of the empire. Operation "Olympic" would land 815,548 troops on the island of Kyushu; the invasion of Honshu—code named "Coronet"—was to involve 1,171,646 more. The monumental assault was to commence on November 1.[29] On the morning the funeral train made its way up the Hudson River, that date was only six months and seventeen days away.

Though casualty estimates varied, even the most sanguine advisors knew that a ground assault would amount to nothing less than a massacre of American forces. The fanaticism of the Japanese was on ferocious display at Okinawa, including the recent debut of kamikaze pilots. To the military brass, it was proof that Japan would go on fighting, and dying, even as defeat stared its people in the face. "They will continue the war," warned journalist and former Japanese prisoner Russell Brines, "until every man—perhaps every woman and child—lies face downward on the battlefield."[30] On the night of March 9, 1945, General Curtis LeMay's squadron of 325 B-29 Superfortresses had dropped 2,000 tons of bombs on a sleeping Tokyo, incinerating 100,000 people in a firestorm of phosphorus, magnesium, and napalm[31]—and still there was no hint of surrender. In recent months, the Japanese had taken up a rallying cry: "We will fight until we eat stones!"[32]

No small number of casualties would result from hurling American soldiers at an enemy like this. The Pentagon's estimate stood at 220,000,[33] but many whispered numbers that were much higher. "How many Americans will be killed in an invasion of Japan?" Curtis LeMay asked rhetorically in his writings. "Five hundred thousand seems to be the lowest estimate. Some say a million."[34]

As he traveled to Roosevelt's interment, Truman had not yet made a decision about the invasion. Nor would he have made up his mind two months hence, when he would write in his diary: "I have to decide Japanese strategy—shall we invade Japan proper or shall we bomb and blockade? That is my hardest decision to date. But I'll make it when I have all the facts."[35]

The key fact, of course, was whether the atomic bomb would work, and whether it would be ready in time to use against Japan. For Harry Truman aboard his private railroad car, neither of those pieces of information was available. The successful test of the plutonium bomb at Alamogordo, New Mexico, was three months away. But the *promise* of the bomb was present—and so was one of the weapon's staunchest proponents.

While all of the men whom Truman invited aboard car No. 3 were close to him, most had no idea that the United States was working on a nuclear weapon. Indeed, in all of Capitol Hill, only seven congressional leaders had been briefed on the bomb.[36] The War Department had insisted on the need "to maintain a secrecy beyond that of any other project,"[37] which meant that only a mere handful of even the most senior officials had been told what the theoretical physicists were up to in the New Mexico desert. Jimmy Byrnes, however, was one of them.

Byrnes had known about the atomic bomb for nearly two years. During a hot summer afternoon in 1943, when Byrnes was heading the Office of War Mobilization, he and FDR had been sitting alone and talking in the Oval Office. "Suddenly, and for no apparent reason," Byrnes recalled in his memoirs, Roosevelt "began to tell me the awesome story of the Manhattan Project."[38]

That awesome story left a deep impression on Byrnes. Though mindful of the A-bomb's promised cataclysmic power, Byrnes, being a statesman, regarded the weapon's true might not in terms of kilotons but in terms of politics. From early on, Byrnes believed that the bomb would put America in a position to dictate its own terms to the enemy once the war was over.[39]

Byrnes's favor of dropping the bomb was even more firmly rooted in domestic concerns than international ones. As director of war mobilization, he had seen the exorbitant sums secretly being funneled into the Manhattan Project in the War Department budget under the decoy line item: "Expediting Production."[40] In a memorandum he authored back on March 3, shortly before he resigned his post, Byrnes had warned FDR of the grave political consequences that would result if such a monumentally expensive armament were to go unused in the war: "Expenditures approaching two billion dollars with no definite assurance yet of production...If the project proves to be a failure," he cautioned, "it will then be subjected to relentless investigation and criticism."[41]

As March turned into April and as FDR's death gave America a new president, James Byrnes's convictions about the political urgency of justifying the bomb's enormous price tag hardened—and money was not the only reason. Should American boys start dying on Japanese soil and the public learn that a special warhead had been available that might have saved them— but was never used—political careers, the seasoned Byrnes knew, would end overnight.[42] Or worse: A president's failure to avail the country of such a powerful weapon might even result in impeachment.[43] Indeed, FDR himself had been painfully aware of those risks. "I know F.D.R. would have used [the bomb] in a minute," Admiral Leahy later stated, "to prove that he had not wasted $2 billion."[44] The simple truth was, when it came to using America's first atomic weapon, James F. Byrnes was too experienced and too skilled a politician *not* to want to use it.[45]

The possible roles of Vinson and Leahy are more ambiguous. Assuming Vinson—the new "assistant president"—did know about the atomic bomb at the time the funeral train made its run (Truman, in later years, would tell one interviewer that Vinson and Byrnes had *both* been first to tell him about the bomb[46]), Vinson nonetheless was simply not the war hawk that Byrnes had been. Indeed, War Mobilization and Reconversion Director Vinson seemed far better calibrated to the latter half of his title, wrapping his mind around the fiscal problems looming in the postwar period.[47] If Vinson did join in any conversation with Truman about the bomb, it's anyone's guess how much he had to say about it. Vinson had been supervising war mobilization for all of ten days when the funeral train left for Hyde Park that humid Saturday night in April 1945, and he would hold the post for less than four months in total. Come July, Truman would move Vinson into the job of Secretary of the Treasury, a post for which the Kentuckian's economic savvy suited him far better.[48] For his part, Admiral Leahy had learned of the atomic bomb project shortly after FDR appointed him chief of staff in July 1942. From the beginning, the old sailor was opposed to the use of a nuclear device in combat, which he likened to bacteriological weaponry—yet another secret project America was at work on, at the Edgewood Arsenal in Maryland.[49] Not only did Leahy believe tactical atomic fission to go against his war ethic by killing noncombatants, but he also was convinced that the very idea was a lark. A self-described "expert in explosives," Leahy assured Truman that the bomb would "never go off."[50] This was an opinion Leahy would hold until he saw evidence to the contrary,[51] and the one he would have had while aboard the Roosevelt funeral train.

Though Byrnes and Leahy were of opposing views when it came to the bomb's usefulness, they shared one area of agreement: It was the most sacred and profane thing in existence in the American military universe. Immediately after the Manhattan Project commenced in 1942, its fanatically secretive chief—Army colonel Leslie R. Groves—began concocting code names that would allow the relatively few officials in the know to make reference to the bomb without actually mentioning it: "the Gadget," "the Gimmick," "the Device," "the Beast," "S-1," and, simply, "It."[52] Yet even with such a rich and varied lexicon to use, it was understood that, if at all possible, any and all talk about the bomb was to be avoided. "Neither the President nor I mentioned the atomic project to each other for many months," Byrnes wrote after FDR had let him into the coterie of men in the know. "In fact, no one ever talked about it unless it was absolutely necessary."[53]

These very terms governing talk of the bomb are critical in weighing the question of whether these men spoke about the atomic project as they rode the FDR funeral train. Indeed, though Truman did not mention discussing the bomb on the train in his personal journal, the president did not mention the bomb in his journal *at all*, even in passages relating to discussions that had clearly focused on the weapon. For example, Truman's diary entry for April 12—the day Secretary of War Stimson told him about the Manhattan Project for the first time— contains no reference to that conversation. The president's personal log for the following day, when Byrnes had the first real discussion with him about what the physicists were doing in Los Alamos, says nothing specifically about the bomb, either.

The first reference to the nuclear weapon doesn't appear in Truman's diaries until the seventeenth of July, when he was at the Potsdam conference, and even then he used a euphemism—"dynamite"—to refer to it.[54] The next day's entry contains another veiled reference: "Believe Japs will fold up before Russia comes in," Truman penned. "I am sure they will when Manhattan appears over their homeland."[55] Clearly, the president was referring to the Manhattan Project. Three days after this entry, Truman would receive word of the successful atomic test at Alamogordo. Only then—on July 25, 1945—fortified by the knowledge that the United States possessed a weapon proven to work, did the president allow himself to be blunt about it: "We have discovered the most terrible bomb in the history of the world," he wrote.[56]

If indeed the atomic bomb was discussed aboard the *Roald Amundsen*, the thick and heavy curtain of secrecy hung in place during wartime would remain there to shadow the records—such as they are—left behind. Admiral Leahy kept a personal journal that was later edited into his 1950 book, *I Was There*. Neither body of work breathes a word about his talks with Truman aboard the train.[57] The personal papers of James F. Byrnes also make no specific mention of what was discussed aboard the *Roald Amundsen* on the way to and from Roosevelt's burial in Hyde Park.[58] Byrnes would go on to write two autobiographical works— *Speaking Frankly* (1947) and *All in One Lifetime* (1958); about what went on aboard the *Amundsen*, Byrnes penned one line: "the President and I discussed many matters."[59] Fred M. Vinson never wrote an autobiography, nor did he leave a personal diary among a career's worth of papers deposited with the University of Kentucky.[60] The two boxes of records from his brief term as war mobilization director make no mention of an en-route discussion about the atomic weapon.[61] Finally, as for Truman, apart from the specific mention of the work on his upcoming State of the Union address, what the president wrote about his secretive discussions aboard the FDR train amounts to all of one line: "I saw a great many people on train going up and coming back."[62] If this single sentence is meant to summarize some eighteen hours of detailed policy discussions on the funeral train—and, quite obviously, it is not—clearly much of what was deliberated aboard the Pullman *Roald Amundsen* is fated to remain a mystery.

By *the time* the train rolled past the Garrison platform, the waiter in dining car No. 4497 had arrived at one of the port-side tables with thick china plates hot from the kitchen. Attorney General Francis Biddle and his wife, poet Katherine Garrison Chapin, had made their way into the car a few minutes earlier and, finding Chief Justice Stone at one of the tables, joined him. Now the nation's top attorney and top judge quietly ate, their gazes drawn by the view outside the Pullman's windows. "We breakfasted opposite West Point," Biddle recalled, "and watched the Hudson, beautiful in the clear, cold day."[63]

Elliott Roosevelt had also noticed what a beautiful day it was, though for him the undulating route up the old river was, perhaps, too familiar to be as enchanting as it was to newcomers. "The train was winding alongside the Hudson on the curving route that Father had ridden so many times before," Elliott recalled. "The day was clear, and a spring breeze was flecking the water white."[64]

Aboard the *Roald Amundsen*, George Allen and Edwin Pauley were not admiring the weather; they were having serious difficulties with Truman's State of the Union address. The problem had become evident earlier that morning, shortly after Truman had convened a breakfast meeting with his advisors. Most of the men who had stayed up talking after the president had retired the night before made do with only a nap before rising again and returning to the *Amundsen* from their berths in the Pullmans farther ahead.[65] (Only Byrnes had been favored with one of the Pullman's five private rooms.[66]) George Allen's speechwriting partner Ed Reynolds, who had worked through the night in Drawing Room "A" in car No. 10, brought the latest draft to the table with him. Pauley began to read, and then looked at Allen. He was not pleased. "This speech is just a continuation of Roosevelt," Pauley huffed. Truman, the oilman declaimed, "is going to be President in his own right and his words have to reflect this."[67]

One can only imagine how Allen—a seasoned word slinger who had flown across the country to furnish a voice for the new president—took this advice. But once the plates were cleared and the train was winding its way along the Hudson toward Hyde Park, Pauley and Allen began reworking the speech. Their labors would continue until the funeral train pulled onto the siding at the Roosevelt estate. (Actually, if the crossed-out line in Pauley's diary is true, the two men would skip the entire funeral, staying aboard the parked train to keep working.[68])

Sixteen cars forward, high inside No. 5283's cab, Engineer Potter and Fireman T. J. Doyle stared through the forward windows on either side of the Hudson locomotive's enormous boiler, a cylinder of interlocking rings forty-two feet long. It was the length of *Tyrannosaurus rex*, of a millionaire's racing yacht. The engine was an expression of function; no attempt had been made to conceal its jagged edges, pipes, and bolts. And yet No. 5283 was also a thing of undeniable balance and grace, its axial girth regally borne aloft by the spoked pairs of driving wheels. The thrusting, turning, and retracting of its rods and crankpins was an industrial ballet. Its bell could hold its own in a cathedral carillon. Its stack vented a plume of white smoke so fat and luxurious it looked like the engine's own personal cloud, sent along as an escort.

Few men understood the beauty of such a monster in 1945, but one of those who did was currently standing two miles north of the Cold Spring Station. He was Ed Nowak, company photographer for the New York Central Railroad. No doubt, the Central had dispatched him to record the flyby for posterity, though Nowak probably would have done it on his own anyway. Franklin Roosevelt's funeral train had been an impressive sight in the South, but now, with eighteen prewar cars pulled by a Hudson class J1-d engine, it would look—for only a few miles more—the part of what it truly was: a train of state.

Knowing the Central's track like his own backyard, Nowak had picked a fine spot. He stood on the main line's southbound express track, a few feet in from the river, maneuvering carefully to get the cliffs of Breakneck Mountain in the background.[69] The funeral train hammered up the line on Track 3, and Nowak waited until the all the cars were in his frame, which could not have been easy with no time to practice the shot. With the morning sun overhead and the engine's cumulus billows of smoke like chalk marks etched into the mountain's shadow, Nowak squeezed his shutter. There is, perhaps, no better photograph ever taken of a train.

It was now a few minutes before 8:00 A.M. Many of the passengers were already awake and dressed. Had the funeral train been an express like the *20th Century Limited*, the distance remaining to Hyde Park from Cold Spring would have been a sprint of thirteen minutes. But under its speed restriction, the train still had nearly an hour to go. No doubt, there were some who were grateful for the fact; the previous night, more liquor had been put away than food.[70] For those who were up already, there was still time for a man to shave and a woman to change into a second black dress she had brought along. There was time, too, to think—about Roosevelt, about the future without Roosevelt.

Inside the Pullman *Howe*—car No. 4, a plum location near Truman's car—one man was indeed thinking about a future with no Roosevelt and what it would mean for him personally. His name was John Maragon, and he was one of the most unusual political animals of the mid-twentieth century. Before later writers settled on "Mysterious John" as a moniker, seasoned Capitol Hill reporters pressed many words into the service of describing him, among them: a "hanger-on,"[71] a "brassy little man,"[72] a "man of influence,"[73] a "weird character,"[74] a "fixer,"[75] a "bat,"[76] and an "idiot."[77]

He was a smug, smarmy, conceited man who dressed in flashy suits and reminded some of a gangster right out of the Capone era.[78] Maragon appeared to do nothing untoward while aboard the FDR funeral train; the wonder is that he was aboard the train at all. John Maragon was a rolling stone and a poseur, a man with a checkered past, a violent temper, and a rap sheet.[79] But he was also a member of the Missouri

Gang, courtesy of his friendship with Colonel Vaughan, who would later refer to him as "a lovable sort of a chap."[80] Other than Vaughan, possibly, there was no other way that this former Kansas City shoe-shine boy could ever have made it onto the funeral train to begin with— let alone deep into Roosevelt territory aboard the *Howe*. Assigned to Compartment "D," Maragon would only have had to walk back through the dining car to reach the *Roald Amundsen*, though no written record survives to prove that he did. He didn't have to; it was too soon anyway. Having come this far, Maragon was nearly within reach of the levers of power he had dreamed of grasping for years. He would watch Roosevelt be put into the ground first and then make his move.

John Maragon was born in 1893 on the Greek island of Lefkas. After emigrating to America, he started out flipping rags for change in the great marble halls of Kansas City's Union Station. Maragon, it seems clear, always wanted to be important and wasn't terribly concerned with how he accomplished it. He left Kansas City in 1916 and somehow landed on the payroll of the FBI as an undercover stooge assigned to net racketeers.[81] His career as a bluecoat was a short one; Maragon resigned under charges—ones he denied—of "certain misconduct in New Orleans with loose women," according to police records.[82]

Thus would begin a series of shadowy legal incidents that, if not exactly establishing Maragon as a criminal, surely disqualified him from teaching Sunday school. While working in D.C. for various banks as a bad-debt collector, Maragon pled guilty to illegal liquor trafficking in July 1920.[83] He was also arrested, but never prosecuted, three times for disorderly conduct[84] and was accused of trying to pinch famous slugger Lou Gehrig's jewelry at the Yankee clubhouse.[85] The most sinister development from the period, however, was Maragon's being wanted by police in connection with the murder of his friend Sergeant Detective Arthur B. Scriviner, who was found shot in the heart in an alley in D.C.'s Georgetown neighborhood on October 13, 1926.[86] Though Maragon successfully established an alibi,[87] he also refused a grand jury's request to be fingerprinted.[88] Scriviner was killed the day before he had planned to wed a nineteen-year-old Virginia woman; Maragon did no favors for his reputation when, soon after the murder, he married Scriviner's fiancée himself.[89]

In 1939, Maragon landed a job with the Baltimore & Ohio Railroad (B&O) selling tickets to senators and, as coincidence would have it, arranging their funeral trains.[90] It was during this period that Maragon was said to have met Senator Harry Truman.[91] As *Time* magazine would later put it, "when Harry Truman went to the White House, John Maragon hopped right in behind him."[92] Of course, knowing Colonel Harry Vaughan didn't hurt. The object of Maragon's desire was specific: Dewey Long's old job as White House transportation man.[93] According to one newspaper report, Maragon was in the White House less than an hour after FDR's death to ingratiate himself to the new president. Somehow he ended up with a White House pass and even a reserved parking space.[94]

Maragon would never end up getting the peach job he had been eyeing. He might have known his B&O schedules cold, but many in the West Wing during the tumultuous days following FDR's death could sense that Johnny Maragon was trouble. "In those first days," Jonathan Daniels wrote, "some of Truman's own staff gave Maragon a rebuff any more sensitive man would have understood."[95]

Maragon apparently didn't understand, and if he couldn't become Truman's transportation man, well, that didn't seem to trouble him too much, either. He was content to fashion himself as a West Wing insider—if one lacking a particular title. At first, he was just a nuisance. But Mysterious John would become far more than that. Shortly after the funeral train returned to Washington, Maragon had a plane to catch.

Apparently leveraging his in with the White House, Maragon landed a job in the summer of 1945 with a Chicago perfumer named Dave Bennett, who was quite happy to have him. In fact, Bennett quintupled the salary Maragon had made with the B&O, to $15,000.[96] Maragon wasted no time proving to his new boss that he was worth his lavish compensation package—well, almost.

On August 3, 1945, the State Department's Passport Bureau would receive a letter on White House stationery from Colonel Vaughan's office. In it, Vaughan politely but firmly pressed the State Department to issue a passport under travel code 1-D (meaning presidentially authorized) to Maragon, permitting him to travel to Italy for the purpose of procuring "essential oils" for his company.[97] The request was a big one. In those months after Germany's defeat, Europe was still officially a zone of active military operations. Ordinary Americans were prohibited from entering.[98] But Maragon breezed right in.

And what did those "essential oils" turn out to be? Perfume—specifically, Italian perfume for the Albert Verley Company,[99] the

Chicago firm owned by Bennett. As things turned out, the perfume junket to Italy was the second Maragon had made that summer; Vaughan had used the weight of the White House to clear the way for both trips.

On the night of July 31, 1945, a Boeing B-314 flying boat operated by the Army Air Transport Command (ATC) gurgled up to the pier at New York City's LaGuardia Field following a transatlantic flight from Paris. Off stepped John Maragon, hauling behind him five bags. He declared them to contain gifts "sent by the Embassy"[100] (neglecting to state which embassy), to wit: two dresses and four bottles of champagne. For good measure, Maragon had addressed one parcel to Margaret Truman and another to Secret Service man George Drescher.[101] It had been a nice try, but when the customs men opened up Maragon's parcels (ignoring the White House pass he'd angrily started waving at their faces) instead of champagne, they found 22.5 pounds of *V. Mane Fils* orange perfume oil with an estimated value of $2,225.[102] (In today's figures, it would amount to $26,400.) The customs men filled out the seizure papers, impounded Maragon's swag, and sent him on his way. Maragon later paid a $1,500 fine to get his orange oil back.[103]

The incident had been expensive and messy, but it did little to hinder Maragon's burgeoning career as a big shot. In November 1945—seven months after FDR's funeral and four months after the perfume junkets to Europe—the State Department would receive another letter. This one was from Edwin W. Pauley—whom Truman had appointed as the U.S. representative to the Allied Reparations Committee following the end of the war—addressed to Henry F. Grady, chief of the American Mission to Greece. "This will introduce Johnny Maragon," Pauley's letter chirped, "who is not only a good friend of mine, but also the President's. He is extremely anxious to accompany you to Greece on your new assignment."[104]

Grady got the hint, and Maragon ended up on the State Department payroll. His diplomatic career would last all of three months and fifteen days. Once in Greece, Maragon announced to all who would listen that he was President Truman's great friend,[105] throwing his weight around until he'd purportedly embarrassed most of the American diplomatic corps in Athens.[106] At one point, on an excursion to Rome, Maragon got into a fistfight with a man who turned out to be a brigadier general.[107]

The State Department had seen enough of "Johnny" and sent him packing for home.[108]

By then it was March 1946, and Maragon's luck was starting to run out. Before long, his White House pass and parking space would both be revoked.[109] Embarrassments like those would have chastened a more modest man, but Maragon continued to show up at the West Wing to visit his friend Colonel Vaughan, even though Truman had ordered him banned from the White House grounds. Maragon devised a way around that problem: He literally hid when he saw the president coming.[110]

Had Maragon known what was *really* coming, he might have looked for a better hiding spot. Soon his shenanigans would make for the best newspaper copy seen in Washington in years. Unfortunately, it would also signal the beginning of the most embarrassing chapter of the Truman presidency.

It was called the "Five Percenter" scandal, and it got started in May 1949 when a colonel named James V. Hunt—claiming close friendship with Truman's military aide Colonel Vaughan—demanded a 5 percent "fee" from a woodworking contractor to get him in on a job in the White House, then under renovation. Hunt had no idea that the contractor—who handed over a check for $1,000—was working undercover for the *Herald Tribune*.[111] When the influence-peddling story broke, the Senate Committee on Expenditures in the Executive Departments subpoenaed Hunt's files. Somewhere in that pile of paper, John Maragon's name turned up. It seemed that Hunt's connection to Vaughan unearthed Vaughan's connection to Chicago perfumer Dave Bennett,[112] who'd hired John Maragon to run over to Italy and France in 1945 to pick up a little perfume for him.

Maragon was finally famous. As the summer of 1949 heated up, he found himself beneath the U.S. Senate's magnifying glass—held in the fist of none other than its grand inquisitor, Senator Joseph McCarthy.[113] On July 28, 1949, when Maragon appeared on Capitol Hill to testify in closed session, he denied any wrongdoing,[114] as did Colonel Vaughan in subsequent testimony.[115] But things were not looking good for Maragon. The documents produced by the investigation showed a man whose behavior was hard to excuse—if not on legal grounds, then certainly on moral ones. Maragon's attempt to smuggle 2.5 million francs' worth of French perfume past United States Customs by claiming it was champagne bound for the White House was bad enough.[116] But when the Senate hearings uncovered the fact that Vaughan's letter securing Maragon's passport had claimed that President Truman was "personally interested" in Maragon's trip, the effect was incendiary.[117] It wasn't just the ludicrousness of it that offended. Soldiers wounded in the European theater often needed space on ATC planes bound for the States,[118] yet Maragon had booked his seat with no trouble and, apparently, no compunction. The committee, not about to settle for a string of denials, charged that Maragon had lied about specific details during his testimony. In April 1950, a jury convicted Maragon of two counts of perjury.[119] "Mysterious John" would spend the next nineteen months and eighteen days in a federal penitentiary.[120] More than any other member of the Missouri Gang, it was John Maragon who would prompt *Washington Post* reporter Drew Pearson to write in 1947: "Harry Truman will probably be known to posterity as a President having the best intentions in the world and the worst friends."[121]

The brake pipe expelled a hiss of pressurized air as the funeral train slackened its pace at milepost 72.8 and began a long, slow roll through Poughkeepsie. It was now a few minutes after 8 A.M. The redbrick station to the right nestled its lower two stories into a rocky ledge, extending a canopied walkway across the open cut so that pairs of narrow iron steps could spill down to the platforms. The embankments along the right-of-way were dappled with people. They had risen early and gone out searching for vantage points from which to see the train. Inside the station, fourteen chestnut benches stretched out beneath the high rafters. But there was no value to those seats on this morning, since the trains were not visible from there. Only the muddy banks of the Hudson or the dew-slick weeds farther up the hillside afforded a glimpse of the funeral train.

As the locomotive's side rods cranked slowly down the platform, the conductor leaned out one of the Pullman vestibules and snared a sheet of paper fluttering from an extended track arm. The typed sheet bore the news that the *Congressional* section had already pulled into the Hyde Park Station—5.7 miles up the line—and was discharging its passengers.[122]

Though the newspapers had carried many stories about the funeral train, including stations and stopping times, the press had not been furnished with all the details. As a result, many members of the public did not understand the complexities of the arrangements that had been made—that there were *two* trains heading north from Washington, that those trains were taking turns in the lead position, and that while the *Congressional's* last stop would be the Hyde Park railroad depot, the funeral train itself would be stopping at the private siding on the Roosevelt estate, a short distance south of the station. As a result, many people mistook the train packed with ordinary congressmen that ran in advance of the funeral train on the Hudson River segment of the journey for the train carrying FDR's remains. Often mourners mistakenly saluted the wrong train, only to have their deceased president pass by the spot where they'd stood thirty minutes after they had already turned and started for home.[123]

With the *Congressional* now offloading at Hyde Park, the funeral train lurched out of Poughkeepsie to cover the final few miles to Springwood on its own. Just north of the station, the tracks took a slight bend to the east so they could slip between two mammoth footings of the Poughkeepsie Railroad Bridge, whose rail deck soared over 200 feet above, lancing across the Hudson atop a black steel skeleton of trusses and cantilevers. The bridge had opened in 1889, when FDR was seven years old. For regulars on the New York Central, it was an inescapable landmark, a sign for all disembarking at Hyde Park to put on their coats and gather their things, for the stop lay just ahead. North of the bridge, the track straightened its back through a few more miles of weedy shoreline. The long, very long journey was nearly at an end.

Back in 1916, James R. Roosevelt had paid the New York Central Railroad to move a stretch of telegraph poles and construct a turnout onto his property at the shoreline of the Hudson. Workmen had piled tons of fill into the marsh in the shape of a bow that swept inland from the mainline, then laid a single track down atop it.[124] In the twenty-nine years since, the private Pullman cars of the Roosevelts and their guests had shunted off here, where they waited in the company of dragonflies and skunk cabbage while dinners up at the big house stretched late into the night. The *Ferdinand Magellan* had parked here many a time, too. Once, as FDR was down at the siding, the engineer of a passing New York Central train recognized him and pulled on his horn. Roosevelt, looking up, smiled and waved. "An old friend," the president explained to the guest who was with him. "We always wave when we see each other."[125]

At 8:39 A.M., the pilot wheels of locomotive No. 5283 rumbled across the open switch and escorted the funeral train slowly onto the private siding beneath the boughs of the property's maples and great oaks. In the rear dining car, agriculture secretary Claude Wickard had lingered at his table after breakfast, preferring to watch the river outside than return to his compartment in the *Wordsworth*. One by one, the heavy Pullmans began their wide swings into the turnout. Suddenly, Wickard's memory was awakened in surprise by the sight on the opposite shore of the Hudson River. Across the sparkling expanse of water stood a Victorian gingerbread mansion that served as a mission for a congregation based in Harlem led by sixty-five-year-old preacher George Baker, better known as Father Divine. FDR had pointed the place out to Wickard years ago, and "I remembered it well," the agriculture secretary later wrote in his diary.[126]

Beside Father Divine's mansion, a long white barn stretched up alongside the river landing. On the boards, black painted letters, each taller than a grown man, spelled out a word. "PEACE," it said.

At 8:40 A.M. on Sunday, the fifteenth day of April 1945, Engineer Potter choked off the steam and squeezed the brakes closed on the eighteen cars. After traveling 1,050 miles through nine states over three days, the interment train of Franklin Delano Roosevelt exhaled the last of the air in its cylinders, rolled a final few inches, and came to a rest. The man whom Americans had elected president four times, who had held the country's hand through its deepest economic depression and its greatest modern war, who had led the most powerful nation on earth though he could not so much as walk a single step, was home.

EIGHT

"WHERE THE SUNDIAL STANDS"

O n the private track at the foot of the estate, the funeral train lay still as a river stone. It was now close to 9 A.M. The train had been stopped for several minutes. Passengers were disembarking from the Pullmans ahead amid the din of slamming car doors and idling motors. The only other sounds were of the wind high in the elms, the occasional blackbird, and the gentle chop of the wide, gray Hudson River. Up on the heavily wooded slope rising away from the tracks, violets were in bloom beneath the canopy of oaks and pines, and the chilly air carried the scent of apple blossoms.[1] It was a flawless Sunday morning.

Engineer Potter had jockeyed the funeral train far enough up the spur to line up the *Conneaut*'s last window with a rough-hewn wooden platform below. The New York Central had just finished it the previous afternoon. The railroad's carpenters—admonished that the platform would have to bear 900 pounds—had used the heaviest timber they could find.[2] Once most of the passengers had been motored up to the estate, the uniformed men inside the *Conneaut* had their orders to begin.

The heavy copper casket—nearly seven feet long[3]—would be passed through the Pullman's window opening, down to the men on the platform, and then into the back of a waiting Army hearse. Its big engine straining under the hood, the car would begin the steep climb up the road to the estate.[4] Just before reaching the hill's crest, the hearse was to stop in the meadow below the mansion, where cadets from West Point could reposition the casket atop a black military caisson.[5] So it was that FDR's coffin would emerge from the forest behind seven horses and be recorded that way in print, on film, and for history.

That scene and every other detail of this Sunday morning ceremony had been planned out just the day before. From West Point, Colonel A. J. McGehee, the training officer charged with supervising all the cadet ceremonies, and Brigadier General George Honnen, the cadets' commandant, had driven over to Hyde Park, having been told on Friday night that they would have only one day to plan Roosevelt's interment. McGehee understood that the proceedings would have to include the obligatories of a president's burial—a caisson, an artillery salute, a trumpeter to blow "Taps." What worried him was where to put everyone. Contingents from the Navy, Army, Marines, and Coast Guard would be coming, too, and meaningful roles would have to be found for all.[6]

McGehee and Honnen had spent all of Saturday scouting Springwood's acreage, trying to envision how they could possibly deploy 2,000 servicemen, especially when the two commanders were not even sure where the funeral train would arrive. Initially, McGehee had assumed that the train would unlade FDR's coffin at the Hyde Park station, three miles distant. Only after he'd wandered down to the riverbank on Saturday afternoon and saw the New York Central's carpenters building their heavy wooden platform by the spur did he learn that the train would stop on the estate grounds instead. The railroad men were happy to fill the colonel in on the details—which was more than Washington had been willing to do. "With President Truman and the suddenly widowed Mrs. Roosevelt aboard," McGehee recalled years later, "the movement of the closely guarded funeral train was classified secret."[7]

McGehee returned to West Point on Saturday night, and by midnight, he had worked out the ceremony in his head. With so many uniformed men at his disposal, McGehee decided to line the halfmile-long road leading from the railroad spur up to the estate garden with soldiers, sailors, and Marines. To march with the cortege—and to represent West Point itself—Honnen had selected a battalion of 400 cadets, though the casket bearers themselves would be drawn from all the armed forces.[8]

At 3:00 A.M. on Sunday, the general ordered his cadets out of bed, into the mess hall for breakfast, and then into uniform.[9] In the early-morning light, the young men motored over the Mid-Hudson Bridge in buses. Inside the accompanying trucks rode the academy's funeral caisson, seven chestnut-color horses and a lone black one, along with a battery of field artillery.[10] The West Pointers wore their full-dress grays, fitted out with silver buttons, white belts, breastplates, and rifles. The other cadets had teased the boys about losing their weekend leave, but those fortunate to be chosen recognized envy when they saw it.[11] That night, several of them would write long, emotional letters home, describing the day with the most reverent words that a nineteen-year-old could conjure. "As I stood there," penned one cadet who'd marched close to Roosevelt's casket, "I felt a tear trickle down my cheek. Not more than thirty feet ahead of me was my ideal in life—perhaps the greatest man the world has ever seen."[12]

The cadets arrived at the Hyde Park estate that Sunday morning at 8:00 and immediately took the caisson and the horses down the hill. In the meadow—a beautiful, if poorly drained, plateau over the river—the men stood in mud up to their ankles for nearly two hours, none of them uttering a word.[13] The coal smoke wafting from the shoreline below signaled the funeral train's arrival about forty minutes into their vigil, but the offloading of passengers would take well over an hour, and FDR's coffin would not be passed through the *Conneaut*'s window until nearly 10:00. Minutes later, the hearse motored into the clearing, and as the sun began to burn off the morning's chill, the assembly of the procession began.

The cadets had had no time to practice their funeral step—a deliberative eighty paces a minute—but they brought it off despite their nervousness.[14] Forming a long column that started up the road, the men synchronized their footfalls to Chopin's *Funeral March*, rendered by the trumpets and drums of the cadet band in the lead. The team of brown horses drew the coffin, draped with the American flag and riding over the gun carriage's high spoked wheels. "Directly in back of the caisson," the *New York Herald Tribune* told its readers, "a Negro soldier led a riderless horse"—its stirrups reversed, head covered in a dark cowl, and a saber bouncing gently off the animal's belly.[15] The parading of a caparisoned horse (this one's symbolism heightened by its coal-black mane and coat) is a tradition dating to the empire of Genghis Khan that proclaims the passing of a great warrior.

Detachments from the Navy and Coast Guard lined the left side of the procession's path, as did a battalion of Marines that had arrived at 7:00 that morning aboard their own train. The 716th Military Police Battalion took up position along the right flank. Standing shoulder to shoulder for the entire distance from train track to grave, the men, as one reporter termed it, formed "a wall of uniforms."[16]

A fleet of Army sedans—200 olive-colored fastbacks with white stars on their doors[17]—had motored the *Congressional*'s passengers the three miles from the Hyde Park railroad station up to the estate grounds, then returned to pick up the funeral train's passengers at the estate's private siding below and do the same for them.[18]

From the start, it was clear that there weren't enough cars to serve both trains. Passengers took any seat they could find, which made for some unusual political broods: Roosevelt man William Hassett and Truman man Edwin Pauley shared a car with Mrs. Nesbitt, the White House cook.[19] Some found themselves with no ride at all. Reporter Robert Nixon was one of these luckless ones; he made the 60-degree ascent (his estimate) through the woods on foot, lugging his metal typewriter with him.[20] Black limousines had lined up alongside the *Ferdinand Magellan* to take the Roosevelts to the gravesite, but when the Trumans stepped off the *Roald Amundsen* along with Colonel Vaughan and Jimmy Byrnes, no formal cars stood at the ready for them. Instead, Truman and his company climbed into a local taxicab and trundled up the hill.[21]

The cars deposited everyone beside a garden enclosed by hedge of hemlock that, in the 134 years since its planting, had grown to the height of fifteen feet. An arched opening lay along the southern border. Inside was a quarter-acre yard with a square of clipped lawn. A tiny greenhouse indented the grass on the northwestern corner. Along the garden's eastern edge grew a thicket of roses—twenty-eight beds of them—their sepals just beginning to peel away from pink, red, and apricot buds.[22] Rose perfume mixed with the scents of pine and river air from the woods below.

FDR had made no secret of wanting to be laid to rest here. The president had pointed out the verdant, peaceful spot to Mr. Plog, the estate superintendent, five years before.[23] Roosevelt had also specified his grave's location—"Where the sundial stands in the garden"—in the burial instructions he had stashed in his bedroom safe at the White House. They were instructions that, as of this Sabbath morning, had still not been read.[24] Plog and his men had opened a rectangle in the earth on Saturday afternoon, after the special permit to bury a man in unhallowed ground had been rushed through the channels by the town health officer.[25] The ground in the caretakers' shovels had been moist and heavy for this, doubtless the saddest duty that Plog had been asked to perform in his fifty years as Springwood's caretaker. As the mourners began arriving in the garden on Sunday, William Hassett recognized Plog and moved forward to greet him. But the old man's hands were trembling, and he did not speak.[26]

By some miracle, all of the guests found a place to stand within the windbreak, though hemlock branches brushed the backs of many. The cabinet, members of Congress, and the federal agency chiefs spread out along the garden's eastern border, leaving a small nook on the north side for the Hyde Park neighbors. The Supreme Court justices stood by themselves, off to the west, below the red turrets of the old carriage house, leaving the rest of the western side to absorb the procession of West Point cadets who entered through a breach near the greenhouse. Flanking the other hedges were the enlisted men— Marines in olive drab, soldiers in white cap tops and ammunition belts, sailors in blue.[27]

Hassett estimated that some 300 mourners had managed to fit into the garden.[28] Some had traveled to Hyde Park on their own. Canadian prime minister Mackenzie King had arrived in Poughkeepsie earlier that morning. He'd come aboard *Car 100*, his private Pullman,[29] coupled to the tail of a southbound New York Central train. Hassett recognized the prime minister easily—but the man was not hard to spot. King had arrived in full morning dress, complete with waistcoat, tails, and a top hat that glinted in the sun. Realizing immediately that all the other men in the garden were dressed in business attire, King hastily withdrew. *Car 100*'s many conveniences apparently included an ample wardrobe, for the prime minister returned a short time later wearing a plain black felt hat that left him suitably less conspicuous.[30]

A good many of the guests Hassett did not immediately recognize, and he noted that many officials "had come up in the second section of the funeral train."[31] Army cars and motorbikes had kicked up dust in the lot of the Hyde Park station in the minutes following the *Congressional*'s arrival. Mourners disembarking from the train noticed that the tiny brick depot had been festooned with swags of purple bunting[32] despite the national plea from the War Production Board that all fabric was to be saved for the war effort.[33] While legislators climbed into the backs of waiting Buicks and Studebakers, workers unlatched the heavy doors of the train's baggage cars and hefted through scores of floral wreaths. Trucks hauled them up the road to the estate garden, where they formed a veritable glacier of blossoms to the north of the grave. Occasionally, a sharp gust of river wind would topple one of the floral sprays to the ground, and an usher from the Worden Funeral Home would hurry over to right it.[34]

As they stood in the garden waiting, the mourners talked quietly—or tried to. "I think most of us who were trembling and with voices quavering when we talked," White House butler Alonzo Fields remembered, "were hoping that our neighbors standing near us would assume that the chill in the spring air was the reason for the tenseness and shivering. But they, too, appeared to be having the same trouble."[35] Daisy Suckley stood near the hedge with Fala, who sat quietly in the grass at the end of his leash.

Tall and gray with his long coat and walking cane, former ambassador Leighton McCarthy approached and smiled sadly at the little dog.[36] Secretary of Commerce Henry Wallace stood nearby, crowded in near the eastern border hedge. For some reason, all he could think of was the skunk cabbage he'd seen growing in the marsh down by the railroad tracks.[37]

Most of the mourners were already up in the garden by the time FDR's remains were taken off the *Conneaut*. At 9:58 A.M., the distant boom of the howitzers, fifteen seconds apart, signaled that the coffin was on its way up from the train. The cannon's thunder tore across the Hudson, ricocheted off the hills of the opposite shore, and echoed back. Then another sound rushed among the ancient oaks of the Roosevelt forest. It was the unmistakable drone of double-wasp radial engines, and it belonged to two V-shape formations of P-47s. The Thunderbolts swung in low over the estate grounds, blessed the spectators with their vapor trails, and disappeared.[38] For these few moments, with the sounds of warplanes and artillery fire splitting the air, upstate New York sounded exactly like the battle zones of Europe and the Pacific.

The opening in the hedge's south flank had been too small for the cortege to enter with FDR's coffin at shoulder height, so the previous day Plog had ordered his gardeners to cut back several feet of branches to make way for them.[39] When the bearers appeared, shuffling with apparent effort, "the heavy burden of the great bronze coffin [seemed like] all they could carry," Hassett noted.[40] Behind them walked Eleanor Roosevelt, tall and regal but "her face showing strain,"[41] according to one reporter. Elliott had offered his arm for support, and she had taken it.[42] Anna kept a matching gait alongside her mother and brother. The Trumans followed the family into the garden at a respectful distance. Later, as befits a general, Elliott would recall the military details: The matching heights of the eight casket bearers, the "lines of soldiers, sailors and marines whose ribbons testified to battles won across the world."[43]

FDR's body had come over a thousand miles; The Reverend Dr. W. George W. Anthony had come from the other side of the Albany Post Road. The rector of St. James Protestant Episcopal Church stood over the open grave, his craggy hands clutching the Book of Common Prayer. In his white surplice and black cassock billowing in the wind, the goateed, seventy-eight-year-old cleric, who wore a black-velvet skullcap atop his head of chalk-white hair, radiated the authority of heaven itself. Staring at Dr. Anthony, Hassett was convinced he was seeing the portrait of Cardinal Richelieu in London's National Gallery come to life.[44]

No outfit like the United States military knows better how to meld pomp and efficiency, with the possible exception of the Episcopal Church. A reverend of Dr. Anthony's polish could not have failed to understand that Americans had been following the slow progress of Roosevelt's funeral train for three days; that to this man every conceivable tribute both big and small had already been paid; that countless speeches had already been uttered, tears already shed, and the largest state funeral in history already held. The time had come now simply to lay the man to rest.

Slipping his skullcap off his head, the reverend began the committal rite. As the coffin was slowly lowered into the ground, the clergyman lifted his hand in benediction and uttered the verse penned by Vicar John Ellerton in 1871[45]:

> *Now the laborer's task is o'er,*
> *Now the battle day is past.*
> *Now upon the farther shore,*
> *Lands the voyager at last.*

The cadets raised their rifles 40 degrees into the azure blue sky. Suckley held tight onto Fala's leash.[46] When the rifle volley sounded—once, twice, and again—the Scottie barked after each. "An unconscious salute of his own," Suckley wrote in her diary, "to his master."[47]

NINE

HOMEWARD

For all the service's pageantry and pomp—and these would not be equaled until another president would die in office eighteen years later—none of the tributes would exceed the fact of the funeral train itself: that hundreds of the nation's most powerful and influential people dropped every piece of business to make a 22-hour, 656-mile U-turn for the sake of one man. For that, in essence, was what the entire endeavor was. At Hyde Park, while Roosevelt was gently lain in the earth, the conductors of the waiting trains regarded their pocket watches with hawk eyes. The firemen kept a head of steam on the boilers. Porters swept the sleeper carpets. The dining-car cooks prepared to serve lunch as soon as everyone was back on board. In all, the funeral train and its counterpart paused for only three hours.

On the return run, the train would maintain—literally—its funereal pace, even though there were compelling reasons to quicken it. Most of the passengers aboard (not the least of whom was President Truman himself) had left pressing business back in Washington. The logistical arguments for restricting the train's speed—including the safety of the civilians gathered near the tracks—were relatively few; most likely, the headway was kept down simply as a show of respect; the funeral train's return journey to Washington would prove but fifty minutes faster than the running time to Hyde Park.[1] Indeed, for some who were directly involved in the war, the train's leisurely schedule of just under nine hours was altogether too leisurely. Though Navy secretary James V. Forrestal had taken the funeral train to Hyde Park, he decided to join Stimson and Stettinius, secretaries of war and state, in a car that drove to the airfield at East Hackensack, New Jersey, where the three boarded a plane for Washington.[2]

The funeral service itself had taken all of seventeen minutes, ending at 10:51 A.M., when the Army trumpeter blew "Taps."[3] There followed the heavy slam of car doors and the crunch of tires on gravel. Within half an hour, the garden was all but deserted. Still carrying his heavy typewriter, Robert Nixon of the International News Service was among the few who lingered. He stood at the opening of the hedge as the chilly breeze rushed up from the river below. The desolation of the scene struck him. "Here was Roosevelt in his grave, completely, and utterly alone," Nixon would recall many years later. "No one at hand—the world had passed on."[4] Then Nixon turned and left for the train himself.

At the moment Nixon had been contemplating the deserted green, Eleanor Roosevelt was in the Big House.[5] Its white portico and broad flagstone terrace stood 400 feet to the garden's southwest. Following the interment, Mrs. Roosevelt made a brief visit to Sara Delano's former domain—but only long enough to change her clothes and search for a brooch she wanted to wear.[6] She had never felt welcome in the magisterial house of her husband and his mother. "For over 40 years," Eleanor would later be heard to say, "I was only a visitor there."[7] A few minutes afterward, Eleanor turned her back on the mansion and returned to the grave. She regarded it in silence for a moment, and then took her leave.[8]

Truman had decamped for the train as soon as the service was over. The same Marine detachment that had stood at attention at FDR's grave rushed down to the New York Central's tracks to assemble in formation at the *Amundsen*'s vestibule steps before the president got there. As he emerged from the back of an Army sedan, the Marines shifted to present arms, their rifles locked at perfect vertical. President Truman walked past and clambered aboard.[9]

Though earlier that morning the funeral train and the *Congressional* had disembarked their passengers at different points—the estate's private siding and the Hyde Park station, respectively—both would be departing for Washington from the depot.[10] The proximity of the two parked trains made it easy for many of the *Congressional*'s passengers to detour briefly to the *Roald Amundsen*, where they could exchange a few words with the new president. "I saw a great many Senators and members of the House who were at the funeral," Truman recalled in his brief diary entry for the fifteenth of April. "They came to the train to pay their respects."[11]

That Truman chose that particular terminology—assuming he meant it to denote expressing sympathy—gives pause. After all, he was not exactly a man bereaved, at least not to the degree that the Roosevelt family was. At the same time, however, Truman had done little to conceal the genuine fear he had felt upon assuming the nation's highest office. On Friday, when he had paid a visit to Capitol Hill during his first full day as president, Truman had run into a group of reporters and young Senate pages. He told them: "Boys, if you ever pray, pray for me now."[12] Perhaps, this Sunday, for the men who came to the *Roald Amundsen* to shake the hand of a man whom fate had selected for such enormous burdens, condolences were indeed in order.

The *Congressional* was under way as soon as its passengers had re-boarded. But the funeral train—and Truman on it—would wait until Eleanor Roosevelt arrived.[13] It is possible that, initially, she had planned to stay in Hyde Park and let the train leave without her. Val-Kill, her lakeside cottage nestled in the woods just across the Albany Post Road, was a simple, rustic hideaway she preferred to both her rented apartment in Manhattan and the White House itself. Though Eleanor was plenty fond of Apartment 15A at 29 Washington Square West—covering its walls with Turner watercolors and photos from her and Franklin's 1905 honeymoon in Venice[14]—Val-Kill's fieldstone foundations had been sunk, on FDR's orders, expressly for her. Perhaps he had not been as oblivious to Sara's withering effect on Eleanor's spirits as it had seemed. From the day she had first set foot inside Val-Kill's doorway in 1924, Eleanor Roosevelt considered the cottage the first home she could truly call her own.[15] As for the executive mansion, she had long disdained the stultifying hostess duties and loss of privacy that accompanied the move to Pennsylvania Avenue. "I doubt," Eleanor had once observed of life behind the storied white walls, "if the public realizes the price that the whole family pays in curtailment of opportunity to live a close family life."[16] Whether on purpose or out of indifference, she had essentially ignored the dwelling. Eleanor spent not a dime of the Congressionally appropriated $50,000 stipend for the White House's upkeep,[17] which in due course had yellowed the plaster and turned the carpets threadbare. By the end of the Roosevelts' stay, the mansion resembled, in the words of usher J. B. West, "an abandoned hotel."[18] Eleanor would also feel compelled to warn President Truman that the house was infested with rats.[19] [20]

It was no wonder, then, that the former First Lady had no desire to return to an abode so impersonal and ragged—and one now dispossessed of her husband. "She could not be finished with the White House soon enough for her personal satisfaction," Elliott wrote. But, for whatever reason, his mother had accepted the Trumans' invitation to go back to Washington on the train.[21] Assuming Elliott's recollection was correct, Truman never said why he had invited Eleanor back aboard. Perhaps it was because, since the funeral train had left Washington, the Trumans and the Roosevelts had yet to spend any time together in privacy, and the new president saw the return journey as offering that opportunity.

After the limousine deposited them at the Hyde Park station, the Roosevelt family stepped aboard the *Ferdinand Magellan*. Before long, Eleanor would notice that the car had been restored to its customary place at the rear of the train, its observation platform again open to the sun.[22] During the funeral, the railroad men had cut the *Conneaut* off the tail end. Where it ended up remains something of a mystery. Possibly, the road crew coupled the car ahead of the *Roald Amundsen* so it could act as a security buffer for the two private Pullmans. But the *Conneaut*'s location was academic. What mattered far more was the apparent desire of the White House transportation men to remove what had been the hearse car from Eleanor Roosevelt's sight.[23]

Henry Morgenthau had been aboard for some minutes already. Up at the rose garden, his twenty-three-year-old daughter, Joan, had sobbed so violently that the secretary of the treasury grew worried enough to remove her from the view of FDR's coffin. The pretty, dark-haired young lady had adored Roosevelt—five years before, he had thrown a debutante ball for her at the White House. Morgenthau took Joan back to the train and fetched her a sandwich from the dining car. "Then," he wrote, "she felt better."[24]

Morgenthau, fifty-four, had been a close friend of Roosevelt's since 1913, when he had purchased Fishkill Farms, a Hudson Valley apple orchard not far from FDR's estate. Both men were what were then called gentleman farmers. In his journal, Morgenthau recalled very little of the funeral train's journey from Washington to Hyde Park. But when it came to the return trip, his recollections filled eight single-spaced, typed pages. The funeral of his president and his friend had affected him profoundly.

The funeral train was scheduled to leave at 11:50 A.M., but things had moved along more quickly than expected. The Army cars returned the mourners to the station plaza, and the Pullmans filled. At forty minutes after eleven, the conductor gave the signal to the enginemen, high up in the cab behind the boiler.[25] Potter cracked his throttle open. The train bucked under the first tug from the locomotive, its wheels inching forward along the gleaming rail head. With another nudge to the lever, Potter's engine exhaled a brume of smoke into the sky, and the train was off.

Aboard the Wordsworth, the porter had already stowed all the bedding and made up the compartments in preparation for his passengers' return. Inside "D," Attorney General Francis Biddle and his wife were settling in. Biddle's drooping mustache and the furrow to his brow had always given him something of a hangdog look, but after a night of lost sleep there were few happy faces to be found aboard this train. Biddle glanced up to see the round glasses and gruff, gray features of Harold Ickes filling the door frame. Jane Ickes hovered at his shoulder. The Ickeses' compartment was only three doors down, but it was clear that they wanted company. Biddle invited them inside. The secretary of the interior asked if anyone had a drink. Postmaster General Frank Walker, sitting next door in Compartment "E," overheard and rose to produce an unopened quart of whiskey, the amber liquid inside the bottle sloshing to the sway of the train.[26] The men smiled, relieved.

Labor secretary Frances Perkins joined the group and, as the trees and rock face swept past the windows in a greenish blur, Roosevelt's intimates did the only thing possible at that moment: They talked about the Boss. "Perkins spoke of his good looks as a young man, of his arrogance, of his solemnity as a youthful reformer, and how all that changed after his paralysis," Biddle remembered.[27] Before long, FDR's press secretary Jonathan Daniels came down the corridor, accompanied by Josephus Daniels, his octogenarian firecracker of a father. Both had adjacent compartments three cars forward in the *Glen Doll*.

The elder Daniels had been Woodrow Wilson's Navy secretary during World War I and had appointed a young Franklin Delano Roosevelt to serve as his deputy. Josephus had raged against alcohol since his days as a teenage newspaper editor in North Carolina, and the Navy remembered him best for forcing the fleet to go dry in 1914.[28] (When, because of Josephus, coffee was the only beverage of choice left on the ships, the contemptuous sailors in the canteen would ask for a "cup of Joe."[29]) Now, crinkling his nose at the whiskey-laced air in Biddle's compartment, the old man declared that he did not mind everyone's drinking if they "liked to poison" themselves. At this, the assembled group, no doubt familiar with Josephus's tireless moralizing about booze, erupted in laughter.[30] Chances are, the senior Daniels had only been kidding. Even if he hadn't, his cantankerousness had succeeded in breaking the lock of grief that had imprisoned everyone for days. Finally, Biddle noted, everyone "felt more normal."[31]

The sturdy *Wordsworth* rumbled down the line, its tonnage bobbing gently behind the pull of the locomotive. Voices and cigarette smoke mingled in the air as the car gradually shook off the tensions of the previous night. In Compartment "I," Commerce Secretary Henry Wallace had fallen into conversation with Bill Hassett. FDR's long-serving man of letters had left his quarters in the *Glen Brook* in search of company. Hassett had said little to anyone about what had happened down in Warm Springs three days earlier. But now, either because FDR was finally buried or because watching the burial had shaken the bookish Vermonter from his customary reserve, he wanted to talk. Hassett unburdened himself to the pensive Wallace, recounting the memories that had haunted him—the doctors whispering among themselves, the dreadful rasping sounds coming from the bedroom where FDR lay mortally stricken. Then Hassett paused. "He said that in all the 10 years of intimate daily associations the President had never once spoken crossly to him," Wallace recalled. Later it occurred to Wallace that, in some ways, there was no finer tribute than could be paid a man than that.[32]

Claude Wickard and his wife Louise had been resting in Compartment "H" of the *Wordsworth* since the train steamed out of Hyde Park. Not long afterward, the sad-eyed and jowly Fred M. Vinson lumbered down the car's aisle along with his wife, Roberta, and the Wickards invited them into their compartment. Though Fred Vinson had spent much of the northbound trip with Truman aboard the *Roald Amundsen,* the Vinsons had slumbered in Drawing Room "C" up in the *Glen Doll* further ahead. The war mobilization director's very presence in the Pullman assigned to the Roosevelt cabinet said much about the sort of man Fred Vinson was. Having been welcomed into Truman's inner circle, he could count on a political future far brighter than that of many of the *Wordsworth*'s denizens, and yet Vinson obviously did not see that as a reason to avoid a visit. The genuine warmth and respect with which Vinson treated people had won him many friends in Washington[33]— and kept him many friends aboard this Pullman. Wickard and Vinson talked for an hour.[34]

In Compartment "E" of the *Howe*, William D. Leahy sat by himself. Though, like Vinson, the admiral was welcome to spend as much time as he wished aboard the *Roald Amundsen*, Leahy had decided that he wanted to be alone. "A thousand memories crowded my mind as I sat in the compartment," he recalled later.[35] The old sailor had been shaken by the scene in the rose garden; it had plunged him into a contemplative mood that would last the remainder of the day.[36]

Sometime during the afternoon, Leahy noticed a figure at his doorway. He turned to see the grandmotherly face of Frances Perkins staring at him sadly. She was in her mourning attire—a caplet with a fishnet veil, a black dress, a simple string of pearls. Leahy invited her in, and she sat. Just why Perkins choose the querulous admiral as sympathetic company is hard to say, but she stayed a long while with him, reminiscing about FDR.[37]

Henry Morgenthau was on his way through the train, poking his head into the open compartments in search of Grace Tully. He found her in the *Glen Brook*, one car behind his, and invited her back to the *Wordsworth*. His drawing room, which he had to himself, was more comfortable. Tully told Morgenthau that she had no idea what she was going to do now, with no president to be a secretary for, but all she wanted was to go away and take a long rest. The Pullman bounced and swayed gently, and Tully— weary from crying yet bearing up with the sort of emotional iron that is the backbone of Irish Catholic women—allowed her mind to wander back into the darkness of the past three days. She told Morgenthau about the final hours in Warm Springs—how the doctors had resorted to pulling the president's tongue out of his mouth to help him breathe.[38]

Inwardly, Morgenthau's anger smoldered, but not at Grace Tully. He had long ago been told by several people that FDR had serious heart problems. He had also heard that Admiral McIntire—Roosevelt's own physician—was collaring people aboard the funeral train and telling them that the hemorrhage had been a complete surprise. That, Morgenthau later told his journal, "is just sheer damned nonsense."[39]

Now that Roosevelt's remains were no longer aboard, attention shifted naturally to the new president. In a train filled with seasoned politicians, few failed to grasp that the return journey was an opportunity to make an impression. Wishing Truman luck might have seemed uncouth on the way to the burial; now it was appropriate. And for every FDR Democrat on board uncertain of his standing with the new administration, the gesture was obligatory. So it was that the private clubhouse that the *Roald Amundsen* had been for the northward journey now became a kind of reception hall.

Claude and Louise Wickard were among the first callers, making the pilgrimage down from the *Wordsworth*. Keenly observant, Wickard looked around the Pullman's walnut-paneled dining room and noted the faces at the table, its surface set with china, silver, and cut crystal. There was the president, along with Bess and Margaret, and the young and handsome Bob Hannegan, seated by his wife, Irma. Colonel Harry Vaughan's jaunty manner and rotund body could not have cut a sharper contrast to the tall, mortician-like Edwin Pauley—a man whom Truman would describe as "a tough, mean so-and-so" (and intend it as a compliment, no less).[40] Finally, Wickard spotted Jimmy Byrnes, a man whom Ickes had already concluded was in seclusion in the *Amundsen*, for he was nowhere else to be glimpsed aboard the train.[41] Wickard could see that his timing had not been the best; the group was just sitting down to lunch. Wickard shook Truman's hand while he had the chance, then he and Louise turned to leave. Bess Truman asked, "Won't you sit down and eat with us?" The agriculture secretary demurred. "No," he said politely. "There is plenty of space in the dining car."[42]

The Wickards had made a wise call. The *Amundsen*'s diminutive dining parlor had already filled to its comfortable seating capacity of eight and could not easily have accommodated two more. The waiter began serving. At the center of the heavy walnut table stood a vase of fresh-cut spring flowers, their petals fluttering as the Pullman's tonnage rumbled down the rails. After a while, the president put down his napkin, stood, and walked down the long corridor toward the rear of the car. He was going to check on George Allen, who was at work in the observation lounge on Monday's still-unfinished speech to Congress.[43]

The lounge at the tail end of the *Roald Amundsen* was tiny but private, a useful distance from the babble of the dining room. Through the Pullman's rear windows, Truman could see the forward end panel of the *Ferdinand Magellan*—a riveted stump of armor plating so dark and imposing it might as well have been the hull of a battleship. At its center was an accordion diaphragm framing a narrow door. With its foreboding appearance alone, the *Magellan* discouraged the uninvited visitor better than its own guards did. Suddenly, the Secret Service men were on the move. A gust of wind and noise rushed into the observation lounge as the rear door swung open. Truman looked up. There, clad all in black, her shoes planted on the *Amundsen*'s carpeting, stood Eleanor Roosevelt.[44]

Only two days before, as she'd broken the news of FDR's death to Truman, Eleanor's affectionate dollop—"*You* are the one in trouble now"—had kindled what would soon grow into an unlikely but genuine friendship. Harry Truman had not always liked FDR's wife, initially believing (as many Americans did) that a First Lady's place was beside her husband, preferably with her knitting basket, and not on the road making speeches.[45] But shortly after feeling the weight of FDR's mantle on his shoulders, Truman realized that Eleanor was not only a knowing and empathetic presence but a savvy political animal in her own right. Truman would later tell Byrnes that Eleanor Roosevelt was an ally he "had to have," especially if he harbored any hopes of carrying the black vote.[46] (Eleanor counted NAACP [National Association for the Advancement of Colored People] leader Walter White and civil rights activist Mary McLeod Bethune among her close personal friends.[47]) All political considerations notwithstanding, however, Harry Truman had found that he simply liked her.

Eleanor had chosen this moment to leave the solitude of the *Ferdinand Magellan* and, taking Elliott with her, step across the gap between the two private Pullmans in order to formally express her best wishes to the new president. Bess Truman walked down the *Roald Amundsen*'s corridor to join her husband, and the two did what they could to comfort Eleanor, not realizing that she did not require their help. In fact, it was

Eleanor who, in Truman's words, "broke the tension" in the *Amundsen*'s lounge by joking about the travails that the Roosevelts had faced as residents of the White House. Elliott confessed that supervising cook Mrs. Nesbitt—striving to stay within the food budget—had prepared meals so spare and flavorless that he had nearly starved.[48]

Truman saw the anecdote as his cue. "Now don't you be in any hurry to leave the White House," he said to Eleanor in his no-frills, heartland twang. "Take all the time you need in the world."[49] Bess agreed in earnest. The Trumans would be moving to Blair House on Monday evening, and they would be quite content to stay there, Bess assured Eleanor, for a month or even longer if it came to that. Eleanor Roosevelt expressed her gratitude. In private, however, she knew that if she could have fled the White House that very night, she would have. Sometime during the past few days—and quite possibly aboard the funeral train itself—Eleanor had already begun a detailed set of instructions for the White House movers on the proper tagging and crating of the family's belongings. "She was possessed," Elliott was to write later, "with the idea of putting life as First Lady behind her."[50]

Nine minutes behind schedule, the train crossed the invisible border into New York City at the College of Mount Saint Vincent in the Bronx, hugging the industrial shoreline along the Harlem River through Morris Heights and High Bridge until Engineer Potter slipped below the white ramparts of Yankee Stadium, eased the throttle off, and rolled the train into the rusty gullet of the Mott Haven yards. It was just shy of 2:00 P.M. Yardmen in overalls descended on the train, preparing to sever the steam locomotive. The Hudson-class engines were the thoroughbreds of open-air track, but with the clots of smoke and fumes they spat from their stacks, they became death machines if allowed into long tunnels—two of which lay ahead beneath the East and Hudson rivers. The old steamers had been banned from Manhattan since 1908 for this reason.[51] Just up the track, a New Haven electric engine stood fast, waiting to take the funeral train in hand for its zigzag through the city. On the surrounding streets, high over the yards, hundreds of New Yorkers perched along the fencing, peering down into the parked train in the hopes of catching a glimpse of the new president.

They would not get one. The spectators had no idea where in the long train to look for him. With Truman finishing his lunch at that very moment inside the unarmored *Roald Amundsen*—separated, in theory, from a would-be assassin by nothing more than a window and a canvas shade—the Secret Service was not about to divulge which car he (or anyone else, for that matter) was in.

True, the New York Central's watchman at the Garrison depot had revealed the identity of the *Amundsen's* famous occupant to the teen-age boy in the mackinaw coat that morning—but the railroader probably would have paid dearly had the Secret Service learned of his loose lips. Now, on the streets and avenues framing the Mott Haven train yards, a hundred military police and the same number of New York City cops paced the asphalt, and all were armed.[52] The hour-plus lay-over was tense—perhaps even more so than it had been when the train had passed through earlier that morning, for more New Yorkers were awake and out of their apartments. By 3:10 P.M., the new locomotive was hitched up. The train snaked its way clear of the yards and headed for Penn Station.

Henry Wallace decided to take a walk down to the *Ferdinand Magellan* to pay his respects to Eleanor Roosevelt. For the past two days, newspapers had described her as gaunt and pale. But that was not the countenance that rose to meet the secretary of commerce as he entered the presidential Pullman. Despite the tired eyes and care-worn lines, "her face was the most beautiful I had ever seen,"[53] Wallace would write later. Suffering, he added, had imbued her with a kind of spirituality. The effect was mesmerizing. Wallace gave her his best and took his leave.

After lunch, Henry Morgenthau, too, decided it was a good time to walk down to visit Eleanor. After clearing the Secret Service detail and slipping through the door of the *Ferdinand Magellan*, Morgenthau walked the length of the car. He found an intimate gathering back in the observation lounge—Elliott Roosevelt and his wife, Mrs. John Roosevelt, Eleanor's friend Trude Lash, and Eleanor herself. "I didn't see either John [Boettiger] or Anna around," Morgenthau recorded. "I don't know where they were." Morgenthau's appraisal of Eleanor's appearance differed from that of the decidedly chivalrous Wallace. The treasury secretary found her to be "sweet and calm, but she looked rather drawn."[54]

After the two settled down to speak, Eleanor told her husband's old friend that she was worried. There was no way she or the children could pay for the upkeep of the Hyde Park estate, she said, and it would be a while before probate. Morgenthau listened thoughtfully as Eleanor confided that she'd have no choice but to approach a bank for a loan to tide them over. He wasted no time in telling her that under no circumstances should she go to a bank; he would lend her the money, and keep the matter private.[55]

Then Morgenthau decided to impart another piece of advice. The sixty-year-old woman seated beside him was, Morgenthau knew, already the most public First Lady in the history of the republic. Some 300,000 letters had arrived for her at the White House during FDR's first year alone,[56] and her "My Day" column reached millions of readers six days a week. But Eleanor Roosevelt's preeminence had always been rooted in the fact that she was the president's wife; that she had his ear at the dinner table and could induce him to act. Now that FDR was gone, Morgenthau was concerned that Eleanor would assume that her public role would vanish along with him, and the world would be deprived of a voice that had already spoken up so eloquently for everything from civil rights to the asylum of Jewish refugees.[57] Morgenthau had thought about what he was about to say to Eleanor for some time, and now, as the afternoon sunlight spilled into the *Magellan*'s lounge through the window blinds, he told her he felt it would soon be time for her to "speak to the world as Eleanor Roosevelt."[58] At first, Eleanor did not understand. "Do you mean I should say, 'This is what the President thought?'" she asked.

Morgenthau shook his head. "No," he said, explaining that, in the days ahead, Americans would want to know what *she* thought. Eleanor mulled the point and said she doubted whether anyone would want to hear what the president's widow had to say. "I assured her," Morgenthau recalled later, "that they would want to hear her."[59]

He rose to leave. On his way out, Elliott took him aside and the two talked for several minutes. Morgenthau asked the Roosevelt boy how the war was going. "Well," the bomber pilot said, "the Eighth Air Force has notice to be alerted in 30 days to go to the Pacific."[60]

It was bitter news. As things stood, Elliott Roosevelt was, in his own words, "lucky to be alive."[61] To fly in Roosevelt's unit was an honor an airman could not expect to hold for long; it lost a quarter of its men each month.[62] Somehow this pilot had come home standing. Now his squadron would be off to Japan, where the old odds would, if anything, get worse.

Just one car forward in the *Roald Amundsen*, there rode a new president who during this same trip would quite possibly discuss a bomb that could bring the war to a swift close—as likely as not to save the life of Elliott Roosevelt, who had no inklings, as he rode on the *Ferdinand Magellan*, that such a weapon even existed. War hosts incredible coincidences; so, it must be said, do trains.

Morgenthau let the Roald Amundsen's heavy door shut behind him and walked up through the president's car. Finding Democratic party chair Robert Hannegan, one of the Truman advisors who'd stayed up late at the Pullman's dining-room table the previous night, Morgenthau asked if the two could talk in private. They found an unoccupied stateroom, and the Pullman's door closed with a solid *click* of the bolt. At forty-two, blessed with a boyish face and an Irish wit, Hannegan was the youngest member of Truman's circle. He was also a stalwart New Dealer, which is probably why Morgenthau felt some kinship with him. A trusted ear was just what he needed. Like many aboard, Morgenthau had heard rumors wafting up the train from the *Roald Amundsen*, and one of them frightened him.

"Maybe I will be cutting my own throat with what I am going to say now," he confided to Hannegan. He paused, then continued: "Truman would make a great mistake if he made Byrnes Secretary of State... on the Hill, they think he has a swelled head. I don't think he would do Truman any good because he just can't play on anybody's team." There. He'd come out with it. Hannegan looked thoughtfully at the secretary. "I agree with you completely," he said.[63]

By now there could be no doubt that James F. Byrnes had officially thrown his lot in with the new administration. Though Byrnes owed most of his political career to FDR, the South Carolinian had not stood with the Roosevelt men at the burial. Instead, Ickes spotted him sheltering behind Bess and Margaret Truman.[64] Byrnes had followed Harry Truman like his personal footman, much to the dismay and offense of the Roosevelt camp. "He never left Truman's side," Eleanor's friend Trude Lash wrote, "and after the funeral went immediately back with the President and his family—in their car to the train."[65]

Once at the train, Jimmy Byrnes had followed Truman right into the *Amundsen* and there, shielded from the judging stares of his former Roosevelt colleagues, he stayed put. The *New York Times* would report that Truman was "in constant consultation" with Byrnes for the whole trip back to Washington.[66] When Attorney General Francis Biddle appeared in the *Amundsen* sometime after lunch to give his regards to Truman, he found the new president ensconced with Byrnes, "who clung to him as if [Byrnes] were afraid that he might be captured by someone else."[67]

As a cabinet officer whose days under Truman were numbered, Biddle had a right to his sardonic quip. Nonetheless, Byrnes had good reasons of his own for sticking close to the new president. Up until Friday afternoon, two days earlier, when Truman had told Byrnes of his intention to make him secretary of state, a retired Jimmy Byrnes had had little to look forward to but sitting at home in Spartanburg, snacking on his wife's preserves and walking Whiskers, his wire fox terrier. If Byrnes "clung" to the president, who had put him back on the political map—indeed, put him on a road that might even lead to his own eventual presidency—could anyone have blamed him?

Not, surely, the fidgety callers awaiting their few moments with the new president in his Pullman. In a literal heartbeat, FDR's passing had changed a political status quo that had been in place for well over a decade. Though Truman was a Democrat and had vowed to hold the wheel to the course Roosevelt had set, he had also made it clear—by using these very words just minutes after his swearing in—that he intended to be "President in my own right."[68] It meant that the old bets were off; good impressions had to be remade, the flesh pressed all over again. Fittingly, the handful of people who did not have to play these political games were the ones who could see it being played most clearly.

"On the return trip, politics began to buzz," wrote Supreme Court Justice Robert H. Jackson—secure in a lifetime appointment. "There was much rushing about by those who had political axes to grind. Conferences were numerous and prolonged....The subdued tone of the train changed considerably on the return trip. The loyalties of politicians shift quickly."[69]

Margaret Truman, a twenty-one-year-old undergrad with no aspira-
tions to public office, noticed the same thing: "Now the real politicking
began. Every congressman and senator on the train was trying to get to
see the President. He was working on the speech he had to give tomorrow,
and it must have been maddening to be interrupted so often."[70]

For Henry Wallace, who had been one of liberalism's most eloquent
voices before and during his years as FDR's vice president, the walk through
the *Roald Amundsen* following FDR's burial was nothing short of a visit to
another graveyard. Wallace "knew that an era of experimental liberalism
had come to an end and that trouble lay ahead," he wrote. "I was overcome
with sadness as I thought of what the Pauleys would do to the putty which
is Truman...I fear the Pauleys and Allens are in the saddle."[71]

Indeed, they were—and Pauley especially. At one point during the
afternoon, Admiral Leahy made Truman aware that FDR had kept a
secret "black book" of notes taken during talks with Stalin in Tehran
and Yalta. It was a scroll of immense diplomatic value, one that belonged
in the hands of the secretary of state at the very least. Instead, Truman
turned to Pauley and said, "Ed, you look through this for me."[72]

Having stayed up all night giving Truman his advice and now being
charged with custody of FDR's secret papers, Edwin Pauley was no
doubt buzzing from his first few intoxicating sips of political power.
If so, it might explain the next thing that was to transpire aboard the
Roald Amundsen. The trouble began when Harold Ickes made the obligatory visit to the car to congratulate Truman.

Having regaled the occupants of the *Wordsworth* with his anti-
Truman oratory just the night before, Ickes had been in no mood to
wish the man well. Jane, Ickes's wife, had put him up to it.[73]

Ickes entered the Pullman and found Hannegan, Colonel Vaughan,
and Pauley at the rear, in the observation lounge. Truman was taking a
nap. Deciding it would be ill-mannered to turn on his heel and leave,
Ickes sat down. In the next few moments, the other men drifted into
the *Amundsen*'s corridor, leaving Pauley and Ickes alone. It was then,
Ickes later claimed, that Pauley asked point blank what Ickes "proposed
to do about offshore oil."[74] Pauley was referring to plans then under consideration by the Department of Justice to have California tidelands—
where oil had recently been discovered—declared federal property.

To understand the import of Pauley's remark, it is important to
recognize that, though he was the Democratic National Committee's

treasurer, Edwin Pauley was foremost an extraordinarily wealthy and powerful California oil man. In 1928, though he was only twenty-five, Pauley founded Petrol Corporation, an independent petroleum producer that he later sold to John D. Rockefeller's Standard Oil.[75] Pauley would later evince a knack for locating offshore oil deposits, which is why he was apparently so concerned about the tidelands—where untold fortunes lay beneath the silt—being taken over by Uncle Sam.[76] Though Ickes was not a Justice official, he ran the Department of the Interior, which had traditionally taken the position that these oil finds belonged to California.[77] Whether Pauley expected (assuming he expected anything) Ickes to exert his influence to have the suit dropped was not clear. It was also never proven that Pauley, as Ickes would later allege publicly, dangled $300,000 in the form of a donation to the DNC if the government's suit were to conveniently disappear.[78] But in Ickes's view, the very fact that Pauley would raise such a matter aboard the train that had just taken FDR to his grave was treacherous.[79]

Ickes frostily informed Pauley that the matter was in the hands of the Justice Department. The conversation might have devolved further had Truman himself not cut it short, inadvertently, by waking from his nap and wandering down into the observation lounge. Pauley left the two men alone.

⊨ ⊨

At noon, as the train was threading its way southward along the Hudson's east shore, the silvery skin of a Naval Air Transport Service plane glinted in the skies over Brooklyn as the mammoth, twin-engine bird banked on its final approach to Floyd Bennett Field. Five minutes later, the tires were on the cement and the pilot cut the engines down to idle. The hatchway door opened. A tall man in a khaki Marines uniform stepped out into the propeller wash and made his way toward the terminal. After 10,000 miles and sixty hours aloft, Marine colonel James Roosevelt had finally arrived.

He was too late, and he knew it. The flight was supposed to have landed at 8:00 that morning. The night before, countervailing headwinds had hit the airframe like a stone wall, pinning the plane in the sky over Nebraska while the props spun, at full throttle, for nothing.[80]

James had then radioed a message to Hyde Park, telling them not to wait for him.[81]

It took a long time to get into Manhattan, but Roosevelt was now no longer in a hurry. In Midtown, he wandered up and down Fifth Avenue, attempting to kill at least some of the four hours that remained until the funeral train, with his mother, sister, and brother aboard, would roll into Pennsylvania Station on its return to Washington.

At first, nobody recognized the eldest Roosevelt boy. Then James noticed a blur of yellow as a fat Checker cab roared to a halt at the curbstone. The front door opened, and out bounded the taxi's driver wearing a stunned look. "My God," he blurted, fixing his gaze on the officer whom nature had imbued with a precise copy of his father's nose and chin. "Aren't you Jimmy Roosevelt?"[82] James said that he was, and the driver—who had left the engine running and his passenger waiting in the backseat—fell over himself attempting to express everything FDR had meant to him, all the while holding Roosevelt's hand as if it were a mystical amulet.

But the tribute was not to end well. Leaning out of the cab and yelling over the din of Midtown traffic, the passenger sneered that he had paid for a ride, not to listen to talk about "that_____Roosevelt!"[83] James, in his memoirs, was too polite to repeat the exact profanity. But whatever the modifier was, it had its effect immediately.

The driver lunged at the passenger. James, holding him back, suddenly found himself protecting a man who had just hurled invective at his deceased father. Furious to the point of incoherence, the cabbie kicked his passenger out onto the street, losing the fare. Then the driver spun around, tears streaming down his face, and looked helplessly at James Roosevelt. The president's son slowly walked away. There were tears steaming down his face, too.[84]

In the echoing concourse of Pennsylvania Station, James located the stationmaster's office, went inside, and introduced himself. Thomas L. Hawkes came out an immediately gave James a place to rest until the train arrived. Then he asked the thirty-eight-year-old Marine if the newspaper reporters—who had already assembled outside, waiting for the train to come through—could come in. Roosevelt told Hawkes it would be all right with him.

The newsmen found the colonel to be friendly but obviously exhausted. Roosevelt confessed that he had not seen much of his father for the past two years, but that "each time I saw him I could see changes. He lost a lot of weight. At the last inauguration I noticed how tired he looked... We used to try to get him to eat more to get back what he had lost, but he wouldn't do it."[85] Just as White House doorman John Mays had done, James Roosevelt had assumed that his father's health problems could not have been too serious, seeing that his personal physician, Admiral McIntire, chose not to accompany the president on his March 29 departure for Warm Springs. James had been under the impression that his father was in "good shape."[86]

At about 4:00 P.M., James left the stationmaster's office and went downstairs to the concourse. A phalanx of Secret Service and FBI men, New York City cops and military police were guarding the gate and stairs. The wall of agents and police parted to let James Roosevelt slip through, and the Marine walked slowly down the ornate, brass-railed steps to the platform. Hundreds of New Yorkers watched him silently from above. Hissing quietly beneath the high-voltage catenary wire, the electric locomotive slipped down Track 12 at 4:10, pulling the funeral train behind it.[87]

Fifteen minutes remained until departure time. The porters unlatched the dutch doors of the Pullmans, and some of the passengers stepped out to breathe the cool, subterranean air. Claude Wickard found Henry Wallace on the platform and exchanged pleasantries.[88] Military police in their olive drab stood watch nearby. New York was the first major stop since Hyde Park, and a number of passengers would be leaving the funeral train here, including Eleanor Roosevelt's friend Trude Lash. Pauley would remember thinking, as the train emptied out at various stops on its way southward, that "it was as though the Roosevelt Administration had got off the train and the Truman Administration had continued on back to Washington."[89]

If Pauley felt any envy of those who could simply leave the train behind, he could be forgiven it. Aboard the *Roald Amundsen*, he, Byrnes, Allen, and the president were laboring under the increasingly alarming fact that Monday's address to Congress was still not finished. "I spent a good portion of the return journey working on the speech," Truman would recall in his memoirs.[90] Concerned about setting just the right tone, the president had even gone over some of its parts with the FDR officials who had come to give their regards to him aboard the *Amundsen*. The newspapers—anticipating the importance of the State of the Union address promised for Monday—would make much of the frantic work that went on aboard the train during the journey home: How the president "toiled"[91] while his assistants "smoothed some of the rough edges off."[92] How, in these few hours remaining before the funeral train pulled into Washington, Truman "discussed the speech with Justice Byrnes, and, with his assistance, drafted it in its final form."[93]

That the press had picked Jimmy Byrnes to receive most of the credit for the address did not appear to bother George Allen very much[94]— but by the time the train had reached New York, Allen was fuming at Byrnes for more personal reasons. At some point during the slow trek south from Hyde Park, Allen had shown the president his latest draft. Truman "liked the material," Allen recalled, but had suggested he go over everything with Byrnes. Jimmy Byrnes took Allen's work in hand, read it, and then spat out the patronizing condolence that he, too, had trouble expressing his thoughts on paper. The remark had "outraged my pride of authorship," Allen said later.[95] But George Allen was not the first man whom Jimmy Byrnes had belittled, and Allen endured it as he had Pauley's skewering of his prose earlier in the day.

Fortunately, the funeral train's pause at Penn Station would afford George Allen a measure of justice. As Allen stepped off the *Roald Amundsen* to take a few gulps of platform air, some newspaper reporters spotted him with the triple-spaced draft of the presidential address in his hand.[96] "As a result," Allen would recollect, "I was soon reading newspaper stories to the effect that I was Mr. Truman's speech writer."[97] But that, of course, was precisely what George Allen deserved the credit for being.

Meanwhile, from the vestibule of the *Howe*, just ahead of the train's aft dining car, Robert Sherwood—one of FDR's erstwhile speechwriters—stepped out onto the platform along with his wife. They lived at 1545 Broadway, only twelve blocks north, and would be returning home straightaway. Sherwood was at the peak of a vigorous career as a playwright and author in New York City; now that Truman had recruited his own scribes to pen his speeches for him, Sherwood had few reasons for returning to Washington. Three cars ahead, Supreme Court justice Frank Murphy left the *Glen Canyon*, bound for the gilded ballroom of the Hotel Biltmore across town, where he would be accepting the American Hebrew

Medal for promoting better understanding between Jews and Christians. The honor could not be turned down, of course, though Murphy did tell a reporter he regretted that he would not be on hand for President Truman's much-anticipated address the following day. "It's his first speech to Congress, and I don't like to miss it," the justice lamented.[98]

James Roosevelt walked down to the eastern end of Track 12, following the hand-painted name boards of the funeral train's idling Pullmans—*Wordsworth, Glen Brook, Howe* . . . In the shadows, framed by the support columns holding up Seventh Avenue, waited the *Ferdinand Magellan,* the colored-glass lenses of its vestibule lanterns glimmering like gargantuan rubies and sapphires. The lounge's glowing windows beckoned. James stepped inside. Eleanor Roosevelt had been expecting her son—and had worried, too, no doubt, that James might miss this narrow slice of time to rendezvous with the train. But he had made it. He looked exhausted, but the other Roosevelts looked no better. Eleanor wrapped her arms around her eldest, holding him gently but not permitting her emotions to spill over.[99] James embraced Anna, too, then Elliott. And there, inside a bulletproof sleeping car concealed in the iron caverns beneath Pennsylvania Station, the Roosevelt family—such as it could muster itself, for the two youngest Roosevelt boys were still somewhere in the Pacific war—was reunited.

At 4:26 P.M., the *Magellan* bucked as a GG-1 engine—coupled to the front of the train just minutes earlier—doused its rotors with voltage and lurched ahead. Soon the train was slipping into the open cut of Ninth Avenue, on its course for home.

⊶⇌ ⇌⊷

Except for the low rumble beneath the carpeted floor as the Pullman's wheels scuttled across the switches, the *Ferdinand Magellan* was quiet. Moments later, the car would be nodding like a porpoise as the GG-1 broke a sweat inside the Hudson River Tube, tugging the train up the 1.3 percent grade. Eleanor approached James and motioned him to a quiet corner of the car where their conversation would not be overheard. In the amber light of the wall sconce, she produced an envelope, and James took it from her hands. He noticed his own name written on the front. The back remained sealed. The propriety was very much his mother's way; the letter had not been addressed to her, and so she had not felt entitled to open it.[100]

James separated the flap and eased out four sheets of paper. The writing, in pencil, was in his father's hand. The first sheet bore the date of 1937; it had been written the day after Christmas. James stared at the unbelievable document in his hands. These were FDR's funeral instructions.[101]

It would never be clear how Eleanor had come into possession of it, for FDR, James later wrote, "never had told Mother of the document in the safe."[102] Subsequent accounts would say only that the papers had been discovered—but not by whom.[103] Somehow, however, the envelope had found its way to Eleanor's hands. Suddenly the blackness outside the windows vanished as the train clattered out of the Bergen Portal and hissed onto the high embankment over the Secaucus Meadowlands. As the late-afternoon sun cut thick slivers of orange light through the *Magellan*'s starboard windows, James and Eleanor read the papers together in silence.

Though it would be later said, not untruthfully, that the last twenty-seven years of the Roosevelt marriage had been a legal partnership more than an intimate one, the handwritten pages that James held in his hands would leave no doubt that Eleanor had known her husband more intimately than anyone. She had chosen his postmortem rituals with nothing more than instinct and memory—and now, it was clear, she had hardly made a mistake.

The majority of FDR's final wishes had been carried out—from a simple service in the East Room, to the use of a gun carriage, to the prohibition of lying in state.[104] Of the orders not observed, some would have simply been impossible. Prayers over FDR's remains could not, as he had wanted, have been conducted by Endicott Peabody, FDR's old headmaster at the Groton School for Boys. The reverend had died on January 20, 1944, the day of FDR's fourth inauguration. And though FDR had wished not to be embalmed, he had also probably not expected to die well over a thousand miles from the final resting place he had chosen.

Eleanor and her son's eyes moved down to paragraph four, where they found yet another last request that had been fulfilled. Franklin D. Roosevelt had specified that a special funeral train be assembled to carry his remains, and those mourning him, to Hyde Park.[105]

Exactly 77.2 miles south of Penn Station, switch tower "Holmes" stretched its thin neck beside the main line. Up on the model board, the tiny indicator bulbs were slowly tracking the train's movement through the block. The wall clock stood at 5:41 P.M. when the GG-1's headlamp emerged from the web of catenary wire outside on the main line and the Pullmans swayed past below. The train had entered the Pennsylvania Terminal Division now, a rust-streaked realm where the tracks skirted the peeling backsides of factories as they crept through the slums of North Philly. At 5:56, the train plunged into the tomb-like bowels of the 30th Street Station and screeched to a stop. A few breaths of air were all that passengers would be allowed before the conductor shooed them back aboard. At 5:59, the GG-1's traction motors took a quick sip of 11,000 volts from the wire overhead and led the train away again.

For the final time, William Hassett pushed open the heavy door of the *Ferdinand Magellan* and stepped into the cool air inside. When he found Eleanor Roosevelt, he asked her if she required anything. This time, she did. The funeral train was due into Union Station just before 8:30 P.M. Eleanor told Hassett to wire the White House and instruct the kitchen to have dinner ready for 9:00.[106] Hassett turned and left the Pullman.

South of Philadelphia, the shadows beneath the catenary poles began to lengthen. Though the work of state continued among the men aboard Truman's car, other passengers slipped into a contemplative silence as, it seems, near the end of railroad journeys, passengers often do. Perhaps it was nothing more than the toll of heartbreak and exhaustion, those twin demons of loss that can be held at arm's length only for so long. Or maybe it was the simple realization that an era had ended, that change was at hand, and that here were a few precious hours remaining on a train before everyone would have come to terms with it. Many of those aboard would soon be leaving the White House, leaving Washington altogether. And there was still a war to be fought and won. Perhaps, some thought, their grief over the loss of one great man was nothing more than a public magnification of thousands—millions—of smaller, more private griefs that the newspapers never covered, griefs for which there were no artillery salutes and horse-drawn caissons and expensive caskets hammered from copper. Nearly everyone in the country had lost someone in the war—or knew someone who had. It was as if the United States itself was like one huge funeral train, its compartments full of muffled sobs, its cold iron wheels rolling inexorably toward a future of unknowns.

Inside his compartment, Admiral Leahy tried to get some sleep but found he couldn't. Leahy, a man of deep religious faith, had differed with Roosevelt on many matters, social issues especially. But now all he could think was that the president had been the same kind of Christian that Leahy himself tried to be. The admiral thought, too, of the long years of their friendship. The memories, he wrote, "pressed upon me" in a "confused fashion." Leahy's eyes would not close.[107]

At 7:34 P.M., as the train rolled through the quiet Maryland town of Odenton, the sun slipped behind the canopy of white pines, hemlocks, and sugar maples on the western tract of the right-of-way and abandoned the land to nightfall. Now the GG-1's headlight, glinting off the pair of silvery ribbons ahead of the train, would be the way finder for the journey's final hour. The *Ferdinand Magellan*'s lounge, comfortable as ever, basked in the cinnamon glow of its cove lights. In the darkness outside the windows, signal lights streaked past like tiny yellow comets. The armor-plated skin of the car kept its interior eerily quiet, but every so often, clanging crossing bells trailed into the night, their pitch dropping and then slowly disappearing into the steady *clickety-clack*—the dialog between wheel and rail, the heartbeat of any train.

Somewhere along this final stretch of track, Eleanor Roosevelt found she could fend off sleep no longer and closed her eyes. Relieved of the weight of FDR's coffin, the train almost seemed to make better time; the whole journey had seemed to Eleanor like a dream, and it surprised her for passing so quickly.[108] Elliott would later reflect that, though the ruse constructed to hide the presence of Lucy Rutherfurd did not work, an even bigger ruse had—this one Eleanor's own. Her outer appearance of equanimity and peace had concealed the inner agonies perfectly. Her countless well-wishers had been fooled. "Not one of them," Elliott wrote, "sensed what she had endured."[109]

At exactly 8:27 P.M., the funeral train rolled up beneath the white granite walls of Union Station and was still. A liveried chauffeur fetched Eleanor and the other Roosevelts from the *Ferdinand Magellan* and led them to the waiting White House limousine. As Eleanor arranged her long black coat around her shoulders, a tawny glint flashed from a place just below the neckline of her blouse.[110] It was the pearl-encrusted gold brooch she'd found among her things up at the Big House earlier that afternoon—a tiny *fleur de lis*, the one Franklin had given her for their wedding in 1905.[111]

Truman, his wife, and daughter repaired quickly to another official car that would drive the family home to their Connecticut Avenue apartment. Though the hour was early, the new president needed his sleep.[112] Tomorrow there was a speech to deliver.

TEN

"WE DO NOT FEAR THE FUTURE"

The Washington sun cast its first auburn rays over the Capitol dome at 6:16 A.M. on the morning of Monday, April 16, 1945. While the chieftains of the United States government had occupied themselves with a railroad journey that had removed them from the city's marble corridors for nearly twenty-two hours, the events of a burning world had dragged onward.

British soldiers had liberated the German concentration camp of Bergen-Belsen near Hanover. In London, broadcasting from Studio B-4 of the British Broadcasting Company, Edward R. Murrow recalled his walk through the barracks at the Buchenwald death camp three days earlier, having first advised listeners to turn off their radios if they happened to be eating lunch. On this Monday, as Washington awoke beneath a blanket of humidity, U.S. Seventh Army units in Europe were reaching the smoky outskirts of Nuremberg while the Red Army commenced its final artillery assault on what remained of Berlin. These actions would prompt Hitler to order his officers to fight to the death or face execution if they did not. The substantive difference between the two choices was anyone's guess. In the Pacific, U.S. Marines had entered their sixteenth day of fighting on a rocky reef of carnage known as Okinawa.

In Apartment 209 at 4701 Connecticut Avenue in Washington, Harry Truman rose early and dressed. The Trumans had loved their spacious apartment in the quiet courtyard building. Margaret, who studied voice at nearby George Washington University, enjoyed the luxury of her own bedroom. But this would be the last day the family would call the stately old apartment house their home. The security of a vice president was not the same thing as that of a commander in chief; it was literally the difference between a single guard and a ubiquitous, dark-suited entourage. Having pitched camp in the building's lobby several days earlier, the Secret Service had created a hardship for the Trumans' neighbors, who endured the embarrassment of explaining to grim-faced agents that they were simply on their way up to supper. The building's residents had thus far taken it all in stride, but it was clear that the first family could no longer stay. Blair House, the 121-year-old mansion across the street from the White House, would be ready to receive the Trumans that very afternoon.[1]

Truman reached the Oval Office before 9:00 A.M. with one order of business on his mind: the speech. In the quiet of the elliptical room, where FDR's heavy green-velvet draperies still hung from the windows overlooking the South Lawn, Truman rehearsed his lines. When he finished, he was palpably satisfied. "Yes," he said aloud. "This sounds like me."[2]

The Washington police had closed off the route from the White House to the Capitol at noon, and by the time Truman's eight-car motorcade set off, the misty streets were clear of traffic. The trip took only six minutes.[3] Margaret Truman, her sandy curls brushing the neck of her yellow coat, was waiting at the Capitol as the cars drew up. Emerging from the presidential limousine, Mrs. Truman was all in blue, a lighter-blue feather jutting from the hat she had placed level as a mantelpiece atop her head. Footmen took the family to the President's Gallery above the well of the House chamber. Truman made straight for Speaker Sam Rayburn's office, where he would wait until it was time.[4]

At 12:45 P.M. the House was called to order, and members waited while the senators, the Supreme Court, foreign diplomats, and the cabinet that Truman had inherited from FDR filed slowly to their seats. Every chair in the room was taken. Men stood with their backs to the walls. Up in the gallery, which was also full, an unthinking usher had put Margaret Truman in a seat behind one of the support columns, and she craned her neck for a clear view.[5]

On the top tier of the white-marble rostrum, with his bald pate and studied, dark eyes, Speaker Sam Rayburn of Texas occupied the center chair. One tier below was a wooden podium where the president would speak. It was barely visible behind the knot of wires and circular carbon microphones set up by the press. All but the house mikes flew different metal station flags: NBC, Mutual, the Blue Network, and six other broadcasters. According to CBS, 32 percent of the homes in the United States had stopped to listen to the radio, some 16,850,000 people in total.[6] For a workweek afternoon, the figure was staggering.

Truman appeared in the chamber at two minutes after 1:00. In the coming years, the onetime clothier would be known for his natty attire—the two-tone wingtips, the bright bow ties, and even the Hawaiian shirts that appeared during fishing trips.[7] But this afternoon, Truman was a study in pure authority, fitted out in a tie of diagonal white-and-black stripes, a dark suit, and a peak of white kerchief jutting from his breast pocket.[8] The chamber rose to applause as the president made his way down the carpeted aisle, and the approbation continued until he stepped up to the dais and shook hands with Rayburn and then with Kenneth McKellar, president *pro tem* of the Senate.

Truman turned to face the microphones, cutting the applause short with a smile and a quick nod.[9] For a split second, he glanced up at the gallery and saw his wife and daughter. At that moment, Margaret Truman knew her father was nervous ("he was always nervous before a speech," she later wrote),[10] but the new president's bearing was confident enough that his daughter was among the very few who could see beneath it.

At the podium, Truman opened a large black loose-leaf binder and stared down at the speech that had taken so much time, arguing, and energy to compose. The work had begun on Saturday afternoon as soon as George Allen had arrived at the West Wing and continued unabated aboard Franklin Roosevelt's funeral train. The speech had gradually taken shape in Compartment "I" of the *Glen Doll*, in Drawing Room "A" of the *Glen Gordon*, and at the dining table and the observation lounge of the *Roald Amundsen*. Its structure and tone had evolved as the train rocked down the main line, as it paused on guarded platforms, and even as it sat parked during the interment itself. The speech had been read and reread, drafted and drafted again; it had been added to, deleted from, torn up, crossed out, and marked with the inks of various fountain pens over the course of two days and 656 miles of railroad track.

And now here it was: a composition of 1,886 words, neatly typed on crisp white paper and opened flat before the gaze of a nearsighted president, who stared through his thick, circular glasses at the momentary wonder of its even being there. The newspapers had made clear that the world was waiting to hear what this man—the one who presumed to replace Franklin Delano Roosevelt—had to say. It was 1:04 P.M., and the time had come to say it. In a clear, steady voice, President Truman began: "Mr. Speaker..."

"Just a moment, Harry," Sam Rayburn said gently from his seat on the predella behind him. "Let me present you."

"Sure," Truman answered. Rayburn introduced the president who needed no introduction, and Truman commenced his speech again.[11] The procedural glitch had been minor, and it would be the only one. Harry Truman stood straight and began to speak.

"It is with a heavy heart that I stand before you," Truman said, the five house microphones wiring his voice to speakers in the far corners of the chamber. "Only yesterday, we laid to rest the mortal remains of our beloved President, Franklin Delano Roosevelt."[12]

It was the first time most Americans were hearing the voice of their new president. Truman was not blessed with the rhetorical grace and aristocratic cadences of FDR. His pitch was unusually high, almost tinny. A hollow, midwestern twang flattened his words. On balance, it did not matter. The largely unknown man whose voice crackled through the speaker cloth of their Zenith, Crosley, and Emerson radios across America sounded confident.

"At a time like this, words are inadequate," Truman continued. "The most eloquent tribute would be a reverent silence. Yet, in this decisive hour, when world events are moving so rapidly, our silence might be misunderstood and might give comfort to our enemies."

It was a shrewd setup. In a few lines, not only had Truman paid homage to the leader mourned by millions, he foreshadowed his coming retort to those millions' greatest fear: that this president would alter the course that his predecessor had steered or lack the spine even to grasp the wheel. Knowing that Americans harbored doubts about Truman was what had driven Allen, Reynolds, Pauley, and Byrnes through so many drafts of the speech aboard the *Amundsen*.

Fate, Truman told the crowd, had left him with a grave responsibility. FDR had never looked back, the Missourian said; he had always insisted on looking forward. And now that FDR was gone, Truman said, the only choice before the country was to unite. "We *must* carry on," Truman declared, raising his voice for the first time. "That is what he would want us to do. That is what America *will* do."

A wave of applause broke the silence of the chamber. The polite restraint of Truman's tone had been fractured at the words "must" and "will"; Truman's sudden punching of the rhetorical accelerator had been effective. He was only warming up. Harnessing the energy of the round of hands, Truman moved quickly to his next point. FDR, the president said, had fashioned ideals for this country—ideals that now had to be defended.

"I will support and defend those ideals with all my strength and all my heart," Truman pledged, all but echoing the oath of office he had taken just four days earlier. "That is my duty," he said as another wave of applause rose to meet him, "and I shall not shirk it."

Now the stage was set. Having positioned himself—somehow both humbly and confidently—as the country's new leader, Truman moved on to confront the war itself. Three days before, when the speech was a mere collection of thoughts on paper in the West Wing conference room, Allen had buttonholed Truman over the sticky matter of unconditional surrender. Since Roosevelt's death, murmurs had grown louder about the possibility that the Allies might make partial peace terms in order to quell the suicidal fanaticism of the Germans and Japanese and thereby reduce American bloodshed. Truman had dismissed the idea in front of Allen; now the time had come to dismiss it before the rest of the world.

"So that there can be no possible misunderstanding," Truman intoned, savoring the punch he was about to deliver, "both Germany and Japan can be certain, beyond any shadow of a doubt"—and here his voice hardened suddenly as it rose to an electrified pitch—"that America will continue the fight for freedom until no vestige of resistance remains!"

This time, the cheering was lusty, the stuff of blood and gritted teeth. Truman had the crowd, and he allowed the applause only a few seconds of life before jabbing the ferment with his next declaration. The Allies, he said, had already made a heavy down payment (in American lives, it was clear; it did not have to be stated) on the goal of complete victory. Negotiated terms with the Axis, Truman said, amounted to nothing more than a "plan for partial victory."

"To settle for merely another temporary respite would surely jeopardize the future security of all the world," Truman announced. Then the president raised his palms, as if he were halting something in midair. Those close to Truman knew the gesture well; he used it in conversation when he wanted to emphasize a point.[13]

"Our demand has been," Truman said, keeping his open hands aloft, "and it remains"—and here the palms closed suddenly into fists—"*unconditional surrender!*" A boom ricocheted from the hollow lectern as the president brought his fists down, hard, onto the wood. This time the House chamber shook in a caterwaul of cheering.

Truman had been speaking for all of four minutes and forty-three seconds. Americans accustomed to the velvety intonations and gilded prose of Roosevelt's speeches were no doubt startled by this entirely new style—equal parts schoolteacher and newsreel narrator, punctuated (but only when necessary) by the lightning-quick fury of a tent preacher. That Truman's outbursts were meted out with precision, retracting quickly into his calm, agrarian plainspeak, conveyed a confidence and authority unseen until this moment. His style—an improvised blend of the patriotic, the fatherly, and the righteously severe—felt fresh and wholly American.

Truman had moved on to the topic of victory, where there remained one further point to be made. For days, the newspapers had been rife with rumors of the replacements that Truman was likely to make in his cabinet. And indeed, sweeping changes were on the way. As commander in chief of the armed forces, Truman possessed considerable latitude when it came to the military command as well. But for the moment, the president planned to do precisely the opposite—namely, nothing—and wanted the public to know that he intended to leave these hard-bitten, effective men in their commands.

The "grand strategy" of the war, Truman said to the microphones, had been carried forth under the "able direction" of Generals Marshall, Eisenhower, Arnold, and MacArthur and Admirals Leahy, King, and Nimitz. Truman's eyes then moved down to a line in the speech where he had directed the typists to put two words in solid capital letters[14]—not so he would forget to emphasize them but so the press (which had all been given copies) would not fail to understand.

"I want the entire world to know," Truman uttered, "that this direction must and will remain"—a split-second pause hung in the air, and again his voice suddenly flared—"UNCHANGED and UNHAMPERED!"

This time the applause was thunderous, and Truman allowed it to saturate the chamber. Barely nine minutes into his delivery, Truman had left no doubt that the war would be pursued to triumph and that he, along with FDR's handpicked military brass, was the man who would lead that pursuit. Truman was credible, the consummate man of the moment—and the moment would be a defining one of his presidency.

He would spend another ten minutes at the rostrum, devoting the time mainly to the subject of peace. Specifically, he made clear his support for the nascent United Nations—set to conduct its inaugural session in San Francisco in just nine days—using the analogy that no good can be sustained without the active participation of all involved. "It is not enough to yearn for peace," the president said. "We must work, and if necessary, fight for it...If wars in the future are to be prevented the nations must be united in their determination to keep the peace under law."

It would have been enough to stop there, and no doubt the speech would have been considered a success had he done so. Instead, as he neared the end of his printed text, the president made one final, calculated move—one that risked undermining the authority he had so methodically constructed for his entire delivery: He confronted the fear gripping him as he assumed the role of the most powerful leader in the world.

"You, the Members of the Congress, surely know how I feel," Truman said, his voice assuming a deferential, nearly plaintive, tone. "Only with your help can I hope to complete one of the greatest tasks ever assigned to a public servant."

Truman was doing what Americans were not accustomed to their presidents doing: He was behaving with genuine humility. Coming on the heels of nearly fifteen minutes of oratorical hardball, the sudden expression of diffidence was potentially jeopardous. Instead, Truman turned it into a masterful setup for his conclusion. Although most of the speech had been written aboard the funeral train, the ending, here and now, was wholly of his own crafting.[15]

"At this moment, I have in my heart a prayer," Truman said. "As I have assumed my heavy duties, I humbly pray Almighty God, in the words of King Solomon: Give therefore thy servant an understanding heart to judge thy people, that I may discern between good and bad; for who is able to judge this thy so great a people?"

The chamber was as quiet as a tomb. Truman's voice crackled into the microphones for the last time.

"I ask only," he said, "to be a good and faithful servant of my Lord and my people."

Blinking through his glasses, Truman watched as the entire assembly rose to its feet in a tumultuous ovation. The president stood on the rostrum with his hands in his pockets; he was visibly moved.[16] It took only another smile and quick nod for him to recover himself. Then Truman stepped down and left the chamber. While the crowd remained standing and shouting, a reporter from the *New York Times* looked over to the Presidential Gallery and noticed Bess Truman standing, too. Her eyes were filled with tears.[17]

Not since the first days of the Roosevelt administration had the Congress so overwhelmingly embraced a presidential address.[18] In the course of an eighteen-minute delivery, the assembled senators, representatives, judges, and cabinet officers had interrupted the president with applause thirteen times. Now, as the reporters threaded their way through the audience, none could find an elected official who had not been impressed. "President Truman picked up the torch where President Roosevelt dropped it," said Democrat Sol Bloom of New York.[19] Robert Ramspeck, Democratic representative from Georgia, called the speech "a statement from the heart and soul of a sincere man."[20]

Even conservative Republicans conceded that the address had won their confidence. "I have only commendation," said Wallace H. White, Republican from Maine and minority leader in the Senate.[21] "I have been listening to speeches of Presidents for twenty-six years and it is the first time I have heard no comment of criticism by Congressmen," added Senator Arthur Capper, Republican from Kansas.[22] A reporter from the *New York Herald Tribune* readied his pencil when he spotted Soviet ambassador Andrei Gromyko—a man not given to forms of idle flattery. The Russian uttered only three words about the speech: "It was wonderful."[23]

And yet, to the American populous—the truly intended, if invisible, recipient of the president's message—the speech was not political; its themes did not concern policy. For the average American tuned in to the radio, Truman's speech was about something more personal. It was about holding on, keeping faith—and winning. "His address deals with all the essentials of a fateful hour," editorialized the *New York Times*. "It sounds a call to duty."[24]

Truman's address had been devoid of fancy rhetoric and grandstanding; no single line could be drawn out and called eloquent. The speech's power, rather, was entirely in the whole. With a combination of humility, simplicity, and frankness, Truman had set out to win the confidence of the country, and—thanks in large part to his speechwriters, but owing as much to his own powers of delivery—he had known exactly how to do it. "Harry Truman said little that was new, used few phrases which have not been used before," editorialized *Time* magazine a week later. "But he said what the country and its allies wanted him to say, and he said it in a clear, firm voice."[25]

And, in short order, the country rewarded him for saying it. In the days to follow, editorial pages to the right and to the left lined up behind the man from Missouri. "Mr. Truman has risen to the occasion of a great moment in history with a straightforward statement which carries deep sincerity," intoned the *New York Times* on April 17.[26] "Whatever hopes were kindled in our enemies by the death of Mr. Roosevelt must have died when our foes read President Truman's address to Congress," added the *Washington Post* on the same day.[27] "Our new President has begun well," observed the *Los Angeles Times*. "With the help of Congress and the support of the public, there need be no doubt he will succeed."[28] *Newsweek*'s editorial writers said simply: "Thus, in this fateful April, the nation set a new course."[29]

The big-city editorial writers could say what they wanted, of course, but perhaps the most reliable appraisal of Truman's speech came from the woman who had known him for his entire life of nearly sixty-one years. In Grandview, Missouri, Martha E. Truman, the president's ninety-two-year-old mother, had barely left her radio since FDR's death had been announced on Thursday—and she was faithfully tuned in for the speech on this Monday afternoon after his burial. Later, the diminutive, white-haired lady told an Associated Press reporter she was confident everything with the country and the war would be all right with her son in charge. "Everyone who heard him talk this morning," Mrs. Truman said, "will know he's sincere and will do what's best."[30]

⊹⊱ ⊰⊹

In the coming years, though support for the thirty-third president would ebb and flow, it would prove difficult even for Truman's critics not to concede that he was a man of sincerity and that he had—at least in his own view—tried to do what was best. He had done it for a country that, at first, he had doubts that he *could* lead but ended up leading nonetheless with a no-nonsense vigor. This spirit would be embodied by a gift received in the White House mailroom on October 2, 1945, from Fred Canfil, U.S. Marshal for the Western District of Missouri. Inside the package was a wooden sign that read: "The Buck Stops Here."[31] Truman promptly placed it on his desk.

In the ensuing months and years, Truman's mettle would be tested repeatedly—through the allegations of cronyism that surfaced as some of his Missouri Gang functionaries could no longer conceal their ineptitudes; to accusations that the Soviets might have been brought to heel "if Roosevelt had lived"[32]; and, of course, to the charges of those who argued that Truman had ignored viable alternatives to dropping the atomic bombs on Japan.

Truman had taken pains to issue a final warning to the Japanese empire on July 26 to surrender or else "expect a rain of ruin from the air, the like of which has never been seen on this earth."[33] Although the unusually graphic wording made it clear that a weapon both terrible and new waited under wraps, Tokyo once again refused to capitulate. The president had also considered the suggestion that a staged demonstration of the atomic bomb—say, on an uninhabited Pacific island—would be sufficient to frighten Japan into surrender. But Truman's key advisors—including Manhattan Project director J. Robert Oppenheimer and Secretary of War Henry Stimson—were dubious of the idea.[34] "To expect a genuine surrender from the Emperor and his military advisors," Stimson wrote, "they must be administered a tremendous shock which would carry convincing proof of our power to destroy the Empire."[35] Ultimately, Truman agreed. Flattening a small island of coconut trees would not, in his view, achieve such an effect. "The only language [the Japanese] seem to understand is the one we have been using to bombard them," he would later say. "When you have to deal with a beast, you have to treat him as a beast."[36]

It was not lost on Harry S. Truman that the bomb would inflict "casualties beyond imagination,"[37] and no small measure of his character can be found in the fact that he assumed full and sole responsibility for the decision to use it.[38] His reasoning, much like his first address to Congress the day after FDR's burial, was linear and succinct: "We were at war," he wrote. "We were trying to end it in order to save the lives of our soldiers and sailors. The new bomb was a powerful new weapon of war. In my opinion it had to be used to end the unnecessary slaughter on both sides."[39]

There were those who disagreed. There were many more who, by 1947, had had enough of Harry Truman, with his brusque, unrefined manner. His too-slow domestic reconversion had stalled the economy, grumbled some.[40] His withdrawal of American troops from Berlin had hastened the start of the Cold War, shouted others.[41] Yet Truman would win reelection in 1948 despite the most informed predictions—one of which belonged to the *Chicago Tribune*, which sent its "Dewey Defeats Truman" front page to the presses before all the polls had reported in. Later Truman would recapture some of his earlier political élan while shaking the laughable front page in triumph before the news photographers. He did so while standing in the open vestibule of the *Ferdinand Magellan*.

But with the sole exception of the end of the war itself, no moment during Truman's two terms would equal the rush of popular support and national pride generated by his first major speech—the one he had been discouraged from giving but had the foresight to give regardless. The magic of Truman's homespun style was its ability to rouse emotions in a way that gilded oratory could not have. Truman had harnessed the raw feeling of the country and turned it to his favor with little more than an honest voice and a direct message. Perhaps the very haste and sorrow from which the words were forged—aboard a night train chuffing toward its date with an open grave—was what made the delivery so believable.

Although the power of the speech did not last indefinitely, it was startling and immediate enough to galvanize the public and to shake American morale from the dangerous torpor induced by the death of Roosevelt. Its power endured long enough to buoy a weary citizenry through the remaining months of a war whose end was, as Truman privately foresaw, closer than anyone had expected.

The address contained perhaps just one phrase of quotable caliber. It came precisely seven minutes and four seconds into the discourse. "In the difficult days ahead," Truman had begun, "unquestionably we shall face problems of staggering proportions. However, with the faith of our fathers in our hearts," he said, "we do not fear the future."

Across the country, as millions of Americans listened to the broadcast on factory floors and car radios, at soda-fountain counters, kitchen tables, and firesides, many no doubt felt a sudden surge of familiarity in that line. They did not have to think too hard in order to recall it. It had been uttered on March 4, 1933, exactly twelve years, one month, and twelve days before, when another great president had faced a battery of microphones at another time of great national crisis, this one the Great Depression. And indeed, many could probably quote that line verbatim, as it is quoted still:

"This great Nation will endure as it has endured, will revive and will prosper," FDR had told the country. "So, first of all, let me assert my firm belief that the only thing we have to fear is fear itself."[42]

EPILOGUE

Eleanor Roosevelt became a columnist, author, lecturer, United Nations delegate, and one of the greatest humanitarians in the history of the United States. Her strength began to ebb in early 1962 and, following a hospitalization for a lung infection later confirmed as tuberculosis, she died peacefully in her townhouse at 55 East 74th Street in Manhattan on November 8, at the age of seventy-eight.[1]

Harry S. Truman became a president in his own right, witnessing the signing of the United Nations Charter, instituting the Marshall Plan for the rebuilding of Europe, and creating the heroic Berlin airlift—all of which helped him win reelection in 1948. At the end of his term, in 1953, Truman moved back to Missouri and enjoyed a quiet life as a private citizen until he died two days after Christmas of 1972, at the age of eighty-eight.[2]

Anna Roosevelt was granted a divorce from her husband, John Boettiger, in 1949 (he committed suicide the following year) and married Dr. James Halsted in 1952. She enjoyed a long career in medical public relations, dying in 1975 at the age of sixty-nine.[3]

Elliott Roosevelt went on to practice a remarkable variety of professions, including advertising, public relations, sales, real estate, finance, journalism, ranching, radio-station management, politics (he served two years as mayor of Miami Beach in 1965), and writing (his memoirs and mystery novels were both well received). He finally settled in Scottsdale, Arizona, where he died of congestive heart failure in 1990 at eighty.[4]

John Roosevelt became a Republican—heading up a citizens' group for Eisenhower—and a successful investment banker with homes in

Manhattan and Tuxedo Park, New York. He died of heart failure in 1981 at the age of sixty-five.[5]

Margaret Truman went on to become a concert vocalist, TV and radio personality, biographer, and mystery-novel writer (her bestselling "Capital Crime" series topped out at twenty-three books). In 1956, she married *New York Times* editor Clifton Daniel, and the two lived on Manhattan's Upper East Side for many years prior to her death in 2008 at the age of eighty-three.[6]

Margaret "Daisy" Suckley continued to raise Scottish terriers at her Rhinebeck, New York, mansion—including the descendants of Fala, whom she had given to FDR in 1940. She worked as archivist at the Franklin D. Roosevelt Presidential Library until 1963 and died in 1991, having lived ninety-nine years.[7]

Fala lived another seven years, keeping Eleanor Roosevelt company at her Hyde Park cottage. The "the elder statesman of dogs," as one obituary called him,[8] was buried in the rose garden of the Springwood estate in 1952, a few feet away from FDR.

Laura "Polly" Delano spent the next twenty-seven years much as she'd spent the ones that preceded it—living in her Tudor-style mansion in Hyde Park and going to dog shows. Her Irish setters and long-haired dachshunds—bearing names like Thiro of Knocknagree—won many ribbons before Delano passed away at her home on January 28, 1972, at the age of eighty-six.[9]

Elizabeth Shoumatoff continued to paint until the very month she died, in December of 1980, at ninety-two years. Her 3,000 portraits would include one of President Johnson, which was used on a U.S. Postal stamp.[10]

Lucy Mercer Rutherfurd survived FDR by only three years. At age fifty-seven, she died of leukemia at Memorial Hospital in New Jersey, near her Allamuchy estate.[11]

Grace Tully stayed in Washington, D.C., after the war, becoming the executive secretary of the F.D.R. Foundation. On June 15, 1984, at the age of 83, she died of cancer at George Washington University Hospital near her home in the capital city.[12]

Arthur Prettyman stayed at the White House nearly eight more years, retaining his post as presidential valet under Harry Truman. He died at his home in Washington in 1957, aged fifty-seven years.[13]

Fred Fair, at age eighty-five, finally received public recognition for his two decades of service aboard the *Ferdinand Magellan* in a 1983 feature that appeared in the *Washington Post*, "Memoirs of Porter Aboard the Presidential Pullman."[14]

William D. Hassett decided to go to work for Harry Truman, doing the same job he had done so inimitably for FDR: penning charming letters for the president to sign. He retired in 1952 and returned to Northfield, Vermont, where he died in the summer of 1965, age eighty-five.[15]

Jonathan Daniels, having served as FDR's press secretary for just a few weeks, immediately moved back to Raleigh, North Carolina, to lead the family newspaper business as editor of the *News and Observer.* He retired to Hilton Head Island, where he died in 1981, at the age of seventy-nine.[16]

Josephus Daniels, who was just weeks shy of his eighty-third birthday as he rode the FDR funeral train, returned to his home in Raleigh, where he lived another two years and nine months. In his honor, the Navy commissioned the cruiser USS *Josephus Daniels* in 1965.[17]

Dr. Howard G. Bruenn, the man who very likely added a year to FDR's life by diagnosing his cardiac condition, opened a private practice after the war and treated heart patients for another three decades. Together with his wife, he made his home in the Bronx, and lived to be ninety years old.[18]

Admiral Ross T. McIntire continued, for the rest of his life, to insist that FDR had showed no signs of the impending hemorrhage that killed him in 1945 and that his shocking physical decline the year prior to his death was due only to influenza and bronchitis.[19] In 1959, at age seventy, Dr. McIntire died in Chicago—of a heart attack.[20]

Dr. James Paullin, who valiantly tried to save FDR in his final seven minutes of life, lost his own life only six years later, at age sixty-nine. Paullin suffered a fatal heart attack while treating a patient at his Atlanta office.[21]

Fred Patterson stayed in the funeral business into his late eighties. He died in December of 1972, age ninety.[22]

James F. Byrnes lasted as secretary of state less than two years, having angered the president by negotiating with the Soviets without troubling to seek Truman's advice or approval.[23] Though he was elected South

Carolina's governor in 1950, his political career had peaked, and he died peacefully at home in 1972, having lived ninety-two years.[24]

Edwin W. Pauley would be nominated by Truman in 1946 to be undersecretary of the Navy—until Harold Ickes went public before Congress, relating the "proposition" the oil tycoon had made to him aboard the *Roald Amundsen*.[25] Nothing was proven, but the taint was enough to end Pauley's political career.[26] Pauley went on to found Pauley Petroleum in 1958 and died at his house in Beverly Hills in 1981, age seventy-eight.[27]

Harold Ickes led a life of semiretirement after resigning as interior secretary following the stormy Pauley affair, though his poison pen scratched incessantly in the form of op-eds in the *New Republic* and the *New York Post*. When he died in 1952 at age seventy-seven, President Truman stated that "although he was often irascible . . . his sharpest critics never doubted his integrity."[28]

Henry Wallace was forced from the cabinet in 1946 following a speech that criticized Truman's policy toward the Soviet Union.[29] After an unsuccessful 1948 run for the presidency as a Progressive party candidate, Wallace retired to his 115-acre Connecticut farm, where he lived and worked as an agricultural geneticist until Lou Gehrig's disease took his life in 1965.[30]

Claude Wickard went on to serve under Truman has head of the Rural Electrification Administration, bringing electricity to over 88 percent of American farms by the end of his tenure. In 1967, Wickard, seventy-four, was killed when his car was hit by a truck in Delphi, Indiana.[31]

Henry Morgenthau resigned from the cabinet in July 1945 after Truman rejected the "Morgenthau Plan"—a punitive postwar economic policy that advocated reducing Germany to a country of peasant farmers. Morgenthau devoted the remainder of his life to Jewish philanthropic causes, dying in Poughkeepsie in 1967 at the age of seventy-five.[32]

Fleet Admiral William D. Leahy, as close a military advisor to Truman as he had been to Roosevelt, attended the Potsdam Conference in 1945 and retired in 1949. He later moved into a seventeenth-floor suite at Bethesda Naval Hospital where, refusing the admittance of either a TV or a radio, he lived a life cut off from the outside world until his death, at age eighty-four, in 1959.[33]

Robert Hannegan was rewarded by Truman with the job of postmaster general but extreme high blood pressure forced him out of public life just two years later. With earnings from his lucrative law practice, Hannegan purchased a majority stake in the St. Louis Cardinals but died soon afterward, in 1949, having lived to be only forty-six years old.[34]

George E. Allen, famed for his ability to ease presidential tensions with his quick wit, stayed in Truman's inner circle and built an even closer friendship with Dwight D. Eisenhower. When Allen died in 1973 at the age of seventy-seven, the *New York Times* ran a three-column obituary that termed him a presidential "crony" while failing to mention his talent as a speechwriter.[35]

Merriman Smith enjoyed a thirty-year career as a journalist, covering six presidents including John Fitzgerald Kennedy, in whose motorcade Smith was riding in Dallas the day the president was assassinated in 1963. (Smith won a Pulitzer for his reporting that day.) On the evening of April 13, 1970, Smith's wife found him in the bathroom of the couple's Alexandra, Virginia, home, dead at age fifty-seven of a self-inflicted gunshot wound.[36]

Lauchlin Currie set up a dairy farm in Colombia shortly after moving there in 1950, becoming a citizen in 1958. In 1993 at the age ninety-one, Currie died of a heart attack in Bogotá, having maintained his innocence of spying charges to the last.[37]

"Mysterious" John Maragon finally vanished from the public spotlight in 1959, when the House Patronage Committee dismissed him from his job in the mailroom of the House of Representatives. Maragon was sixty-five at the time.[38]

The *Pullman sleepers* **Wordsworth** and **Glen Willow** were the first cars of the FDR funeral train to be scrapped (1958), and most of the other cars met the same fate not long after: the **Howe** (1962), the **Glen Doll** (1962), the **Glen Brook** (1964), the **Glen Canyon** (1964), the **Glen Gordon** (1966), and the **Glen Lodge** (ca. 1972).[39] The crew dormitory car **Crusader Rose** spent its final years as a work car for the Great Northern Railway.[40] The Pullman **Treonta** (quarters for journalism's

"Three Musketeers," on the Washington-to-Hyde Park segment of the trip) rolled on the American rails until July 1959, when it was sold to the National Railways of Mexico.[41]

The *Conneaut,* the Pullman sleeper/lounge that carried FDR's remains, returned to passenger service and operated until October 1956, when it was sold to Strates Shows, a Florida-based operator of carnival midways.[42] In 1972, the car was heavily damaged in a major flood while in Wilkes-Barre, Pennsylvania, and was scrapped soon afterward.[43]

The *Glengyle* (which had quartered the *Philadelphia Inquirer*'s William Murphy) was retired in 1957 and sold to the Lone Star Steel Company in Texas, which used the car as a dormitory for its workers. The Dallas-based Southwest Railroad Historical Society purchased the *Glengyle* in 1961 and fully restored it. The car remains in Texas, on display at the Museum of the American Railroad.[44]

Southern Locomotive No. 1401, which hauled the funeral train 150 miles between Greenville, South Carolina, and Salisbury, North Carolina, ended its days pulling local trains and was retired in 1952. In 1953, the Southern Railway gave the 189-ton steam engine as a gift (complete with tender) to the Smithsonian Institution.[45] Now fully restored, the locomotive is the centerpiece of the America on the Move collection at the National Museum of American History in Washington, D.C.

The *Roald Amundsen,* after carrying Truman's party on the funeral train, returned to Pullman's charter fleet, where it served until 1948. The New York Central Railroad then purchased the *Amundsen,* remodeling it as a business car and renaming it *Car No. 17.* After a period of private ownership, the Pullman was donated to the McCormick-Stillman Railroad Park in Scottsdale, Arizona, in 1971, where it can be visited today.[46]

The *Ferdinand Magellan* faithfully served Presidents Truman and, for a handful of trips, Eisenhower, before being listed as government surplus in April of 1958 and mothballed in a Maryland Army base.[47] In 1959, the then-nascent Gold Coast Railroad Museum gained ownership of the *Magellan* (which, incredibly, was not granted National Historic Landmark Status until 1985[48]) and the car remains on display on its grounds in Miami, Florida, restored to its appearance during the FDR era.

DRAMATIS PERSONAE

George E. Allen—Political fixer, speechwriter for Harry Truman

Reverend Dr. W. George W. Anthony—Rector of St. James' Church, Hyde Park, New York

Toinette "Toi" Bachelder—Clerical assistant at the White House

Elizabeth Bentley—KGB spy turned FBI informer who implicated Lauchlin Currie

Francis Biddle—U.S. Attorney General during FDR's final term

Claude E. Blackinon—Engineer who took over the funeral train in Atlanta

Col. John Boettiger—Husband of FDR's daughter Anna Roosevelt

Daisy Bonner—Cook at FDR's cabin at Warm Springs, Georgia

Dorothy Brady—White House typist; assistant to FDR's secretary Grace Tully

Dr. Howard G. Bruenn—Heart specialist who cared for FDR in his final year

James F. "Jimmy" Byrnes—D.C. insider and FDR's powerful "assistant president"

Lauchlin Currie—Economic assistant to FDR; member of the Silvermaster spy ring

Jonathan Daniels—FDR's assistant and press secretary who replaced Steve Early

Laura "Polly" Delano—FDR's flamboyant and ignoble cousin from Hyde Park

George Drescher—Secret Service agent assigned exclusively to Harry Truman

Rev. Angus Dun—Episcopal bishop of Washington, D.C.

Steve Early—FDR's long-serving press secretary

Faye Emerson—Hollywood actress and wife of FDR's son Elliott Roosevelt

Fred Fair—Porter assigned to the *Ferdinand Magellan*, FDR's private Pullman car

Fala—FDR's beloved Scottish terrier, a gift from Margaret ("Daisy") Suckley

Edwin Fauver—White House transportation man under Dewey Long

Alonzo Fields—Chief butler at the White House

William A. Gawler—Mortician who supervised funeral proceedings in Washington

Louise "Hacky" Hackmeister—Telephone switchboard operator; traveled with FDR

Robert Hannegan—Chairman of the Democratic National Committee

William D. Hassett—FDR's letter-writer, assistant, and occasional press secretary

Edith Helm—Social secretary to Eleanor Roosevelt

Harry Hopkins—Intimate advisor to FDR; gravely ill at time of Roosevelt's death

Harold Ickes—FDR's proudly cantankerous secretary of the interior

Jane Ickes—Young wife of Harold Ickes

Robert H. Jackson—Supreme Court justice, appointed by FDR in 1941

Mackenzie King—Prime minister of Canada

Trude Lash—Wife of Joseph P. Lash, both young friends of Eleanor Roosevelt

Admiral William D. Leahy—FDR's military advisor; chairman of the joint chiefs

Dewey Long—White House transportation chief during FDR's presidency

John "Mysterious John" Maragon—B&O ticket agent with big political dreams

Leighton McCarthy—U.S. Ambassador to Canada and FDR's old friend

Lizzie McDuffie—Housekeeper; traveled with FDR to Warm Springs

Colonel A. J. McGehee—Officer who supervised West Point cadet ceremonies

Admiral Ross T. McIntire—FDR's personal doctor; denied the president had any serious ailments

Henry Morgenthau, Jr.—FDR's treasury secretary and old Hudson Valley friend

William C. Murphy, Jr.—White House correspondent for the *Philadelphia Inquirer.*

Robert Nixon—White House correspondent for the International News Service

Ed Nowak—Official photographer for the New York Central Railroad

Harold Oliver—White House correspondent for the Associated Press

Col. Richard Park—FDR's military aide, later the planner of much of the funeral

Fred Patterson—Atlanta funeral director called to attend to FDR's body

Edwin W. Pauley—Democratic National Committee treasurer; wealthy oilman

Dr. James E. Paullin—Heart specialist from Atlanta who attended a dying FDR

Frances Perkins—Secretary of labor; the lone female appointee in the FDR cabinet

C. A. Pless—The Southern Railway's station agent at Warm Springs, Georgia

Mr. Plog—Superintendent of Springwood, the Roosevelt estate in Hyde Park

C. J. Potter—Engineer of the funeral train between the Bronx and Hyde Park

Arthur Prettyman—FDR's longtime personal valet; traveled with the president

Michael F. Reilly—Secret Service guard assigned exclusively to protect FDR

Ed Reynolds—Assistant to speechwriter George E. Allen

Nicholas Robbins—Assistant to portraitist Elizabeth Shoumatoff

Anna Roosevelt—Eleanor and Franklin's only daughter

Eleanor Roosevelt—First lady; wife of FDR

Elliott Roosevelt—Bomber pilot; only Roosevelt son to make it to the funeral

Franklin Delano Roosevelt—President of the United States, 1933–1945

James "Jimmy" Roosevelt—FDR's oldest son; a Marine colonel in the Pacific

Lucy Mercer Rutherfurd—FDR's onetime mistress and ongoing soulmate

Robert E. Sherwood—Author, playwright, and occasional speechwriter for FDR

Elizabeth Shoumatoff—Russian-born portraitist commissioned to paint FDR

Gregory Silvermaster—Operator of the Washington spy ring that fed intelligence to the KGB

Merriman Smith—White House correspondent for the United Press

Dave Snell—Reporter for the *Atlanta Constitution* assigned to the Warm Springs story

Henry Stimson—FDR's aging secretary of war

Harlan Stone—Chief Justice of the Supreme Court; administered oath to Truman

Margaret "Daisy" Suckley—FDR's favorite cousin and stalwart companion

George Summerlin—Chief of protocol at the White House

Edward R. Stettinius, Jr.—Secretary of state during FDR's fourth term

Malvina Thompson—Personal secretary to Eleanor Roosevelt

A. B. Tolley—White House calligrapher and social bureau administrator

Bess Truman—Wife of Harry S. Truman

Harry S. Truman—FDR's vice president, later thirty-third president of the United States

Margaret Truman—Only child of Harry and Bess Truman

Grace Tully—Longtime, trusted secretary to FDR; traveled with the president

Col. Harry Vaughan—Harry Truman's WWI buddy, later his military aide

Fred M. Vinson—War mobilization director at time of Truman's taking office

Frank Walker—Roosevelt's old friend; postmaster general at time of FDR's death

Henry Wallace—FDR's vice president from 1941–45, then commerce secretary

J. B. West—Assistant chief usher at the White House

Ferman White—Roundhouse foreman at Atlanta's North Avenue railroad yards

Claude R. Wickard—Secretary of agriculture under FDR

C. R. Yowell—Engineer who drove the funeral train into Washington, D.C.

ACKNOWLEDGMENTS

efore I began writing this book, I chanced upon a small, hand-tinted portrait of FDR taken in 1933 and paid the antiques dealer eight dollars for it. Sealed in shellac and mounted on a piece of wood, the commemorative relic of Roosevelt's first term in office had been meant for hanging, and I did hang it—directly across from my laptop, so I could have FDR with me while I wrote. Time and again over the next year, I would pause to look at the friendly, appeasing visage on the wall and ask: "Am I getting this right?"

FDR never answered me. I was, however, incredibly fortunate to meet so many individuals in the course of researching and writing this book who could—and did—respond to that question. I only regret that this space will not permit me to name and thank all of them individually.

First, I owe my deepest gratitude to my agent, Gary Heidt, who saw potential in the book idea I pitched in his office on West 35th Street during a wet, snowy day in December 2007. Without his encouragement, humor, and unfailing savvy, this undertaking would never have made it to a printing press.

To Robert Clark of the Franklin D. Roosevelt Presidential Library, Randy Sowell of the Harry S. Truman Library, and their colleagues too numerous to name, I owe my heartfelt thanks—not only for their encyclopedic knowledge of their holdings but for their patience in dealing with a researcher whose requests for documents and photographs seemingly knew no end. I would also like to thank Michael Kohl, head of special collections for the Clemson University Libraries, for scouring the personal papers of James F. Byrnes when I could not go to South Carolina to do so; and Matthew A. Harris, who did me the same courtesy with the papers of Fred M. Vinson at the University of Kentucky. Adriane Hanson of the Princeton University Library and Harold L. Miller of the Wisconsin Historical Society went out of their way to locate, dust off, and send me copies of the long-forgotten journals of James V. Forrestal and Admiral William D. Leahy, respectively. All of these dedicated archivists have my deepest gratitude.

My special thanks goes to David Smith of the New York Public Library, who, among his countless services and personal favors, opened the door to the privacy of the Frederick Lewis Allen Room, where parts of this book were written.

I also wish to acknowledge J. Scott Chafin, attorney for the United States Army, who helped me decipher a mysterious picture shot at Union Station by an Army photographer, and Mr. Lee Hubbard, retired policeman from Fairfax, Virginia, who was nine years old when he watched the funeral train pass his grandmother's house and who gave me a copy of the photograph that captured a moment he has never forgotten. For his e-mails and enthusiasm, I would also like to thank Jack Allen, grandson of Fred Patterson—the mortician who embalmed Franklin D. Roosevelt.

For all the years I have studied and written about railroading, I still find myself continuously impressed by men whose knowledge of, and dedication to, trains humble my own efforts. Those men include Bob Adler of the McCormick-Stillman Railroad Park, the *Roald Amundsen*'s tireless keeper and champion; and Michael Hall, executive director of the Gold Coast Railroad Museum in Miami, refuge of the *Ferdinand Magellan*.

For her sharp eye and deft hand, Alessandra Bastagli, my editor at Palgrave Macmillan, has my sincere gratitude. I would also like to thank her colleague Colleen Lawrie for her unflagging sense of humor and a martyr's patience.

Finally, I am wholeheartedly grateful to those family members, friends, and colleagues who sustained me with an inexhaustible reserve of support and encouragement. I am in debt to my parents, not just for their faith in me, but for taking me as a child to visit the FDR estate in Hyde Park, New York. Obviously, something of the experience rubbed off. Author Lorraine B. Diehl—whose book *The Late, Great Pennsylvania Station* is one of the finest tributes ever paid to a railroad—always reached for the dinner check and never wearied of quelling my anxieties. Biographer Hazel Rowley, whom I met while attending an authors' function at the Algonquin Hotel, buoyed me with a knowledge of Eleanor and Franklin Roosevelt so intuitive that the first couple began to feel like relatives. To my sister, Maria, and my beau, David, thank you for never letting me give up on this project and myself.

At length, I would be remiss in not giving a nod to professor, author, and historian John R. Stilgoe of Harvard, who sent me a note after reading one of my magazine pieces about Pullman cars. He told me I needed to write a book instead. He was right.

ROBERT KLARA
NEW YORK, NEW YORK
SEPTEMBER 12, 2009

NOTES

FOREWORD

1. *History of the Bureau of Engraving and Printing* (Washington, D.C.: U.S. Treasury Department, 1964), 129.
2. Grace Tully, *F.D.R., My Boss* (New York: Charles Scribner's Sons, 1949), 203.
3. Ibid., 204.
4. Herbert Monroe, "President's Special," *Railroad* (November 1945): 19.
5. Ibid.
6. Ibid.
7. Tully, *F.D.R., My Boss,* 204.
8. Fred B. Wrixon, "FDR's Wartime Train Travels," *Railroads and World War II,* Special Edition No. 6 of *Classic Trains* (2008): 21.
9. Alden Hatch, *Franklin D. Roosevelt: An Informal Biography* (New York: Henry Holt and Co., 1947), 376.
10. Robert H. Ferrell, *The Dying President* (Columbia: University of Missouri Press, 1998), 35.
11. Ibid., 39.
12. Ibid., 46.
13. Alonzo Fields, *My 21 Years in the White House* (New York: Coward-McCann, 1961), 114.
14. *Step by Step through the Little White House* (Warm Springs, GA: The Franklin D. Roosevelt Warm Springs Memorial Commission, 1950), 2.
15. Hugh Gregory Gallagher, *FDR's Splendid Deception* (New York: Dodd, Mead and Co., 1985), 174.
16. Tully, *F.D.R., My Boss,* 359.
17. Ibid.
18. Doris Kearns Goodwin, *No Ordinary Time* (New York: Simon & Schuster, 1994), 598.
19. Tully, *F.D.R., My Boss,* 358.
20. Ibid., 206.
21. "The Gold Cost Railroad Museum's Famous U.S. Presidential Car No. 1," Miami, undated, 2.
22. Crispin Y. Campbell, "Memoirs of a Porter Aboard the Presidential Pullman," *Washington Post,* March 2, 1983, D.C.3.
23. Ibid.
24. Fred B. Wrixon, "Staying in Touch via the 1401," *Railroads and World War II,* Special Edition No. 6, *Classic Trains* (2008): 24.

25. David Wayner, *Passenger Train Consists, 1923–1973* (New York: Wayner Publications, 1971), 31.
26. Tully, *F.D.R., My Boss*, 358.
27. Fred B. Wrixon and Michael Hall, "The Heaviest Pullman Ever," *Railroads and World War II*, Special Edition No. 6 of *Classic Trains*, 2008, 26.
28. Gallagher, *FDR's Splendid Deception*, 174.
29. Monroe, "President's Special," 24.
30. "The Gold Coast Railroad Museum's Famous U.S. Presidential Car No. 1," Fact sheet, undated.
31. William D. Hassett, *Off the Record with F.D.R.* (New Brunswick, NJ: Rutgers University Press, 1958), 146.
32. Margaret Suckley, *Closest Companion: The Unknown Story of the Intimate Relationship Between Franklin Roosevelt and Margaret Suckley*, ed. Geoffrey C. Ward (Boston: Houghton Mifflin, 1995), 189.
33. Campbell, "Memoirs of a Porter aboard the Presidential Pullman," D.C.3.
34. Hatch, *Franklin D. Roosevelt*, 374.
35. Fala's collar, displayed at the Franklin D. Roosevelt Presidential Library and Museum, Hyde Park, New York.

ONE PINE MOUNTAIN

1. Bernard Asbell, *When F.D.R. Died* (New York: Holt, Rinehart and Winston, 1961), 134.
2. "This Was His Georgia," Georgia Department of Natural Resources, Marker 072–7, 1984.
3. Jim Bishop, *FDR's Last Year* (New York: William Morrow & Company, 1974), 530.
4. James MacGregor Burns, *Roosevelt: The Soldier of Freedom* (New York: Harcourt Brace Jovanovich, 1970), 595.
5. Robert H. Ferrell, *The Dying President* (Columbia: University of Missouri Press, 1998), 115.
6. William D. Siuru and Andrea Stewart, *Presidential Cars & Transportation* (Iola, WI: Krause Publications, 1995), 51.
7. Burns, *Roosevelt*, 595.
8. Robert D. Graff and Robert Emmett Ginna, *FDR* (New York: Harper & Row, 1963), 235.
9. Ibid., 232–33.
10. "The Week's Census," *Jet* (May 8, 1959): 49.
11. Turnley Walker, *Roosevelt and the Warm Springs Story* (New York: A. A. Wyn, 1953), 291.
12. Elizabeth Shoumatoff, *FDR's Unfinished Portrait* (Pittsburgh: University of Pittsburgh Press, 1990), 101.
13. Ibid., 98.
14. Doris Kearns Goodwin, *No Ordinary Time* (New York: Simon & Schuster, 1994), 19.
15. Ibid.
16. Ibid., 20.
17. John Whitcomb and Claire Whitcomb, *Real Life at the White House* (New York: Routledge, 2000), 314.
18. Shoumatoff, *FDR's Unfinished Portrait*, 80.
19. Ibid., 98.

20. Ibid., 99–100.
21. Elliott Roosevelt and James Brough, *Mother R: Eleanor Roosevelt's Untold Story* (New York: G. P. Putnam's Sons, 1977), 19.
22. Ibid.
23. Asbell, *When F.D.R. Died*, 34.
24. Shoumatoff, *FDR's Unfinished Portrait*, 116.
25. Margaret Suckley, *Closest Companion: The Unknown Story of the Intimate Relationship Between Franklin Roosevelt and Margaret Suckley*, ed. Geoffrey C. Ward (Boston: Houghton Mifflin, 1995), 418.
26. Ibid.
27. Roosevelt and Brough, *Mother R.*, 18.
28. William D. Hassett, *Off the Record with F.D.R.* (New Brunswick, NJ: Rutgers University Press, 1958), 335.
29. Roosevelt and Brough, *Mother R.*, 23–24.
30. Ibid., 19.
31. Certificate of Death for F.D.R., Georgia Department of Public Health, certified copy dated April 18, 1945. In 1945, documents and newspaper reports filed in Georgia frequently used Central War Time; seaboard states to the north were on Eastern War Time—one hour ahead. Times given herein are local.
32. Roosevelt and Brough, *Mother R.*, 24.
33. Bishop, *FDR's Last Year*, 593.
34. Asbell, *When F.D.R. Died*, 71.
35. *The Associated Press News Annual: 1945* (New York: Rinehart & Company, 1946), 159.
36. Asbell, *When F.D.R. Died*, 73.
37. Clark Kinnaird, ed., *The Real F.D.R.* (New York: Citadel Press, 1945), 114.
38. Ibid.
39. Donald Porter Geddes, ed., *Franklin Delano Roosevelt: A Memorial* (New York: Pocket Books, 1945), I.
40. Kinnaird, *The Real F.D.R.*, 115.
41. Grace Tully, *F.D.R., My Boss* (New York: Charles Scribner's Sons, 1949), 364.
42. Ibid.
43. Asbell, *When F.D.R. Died*, 74.
44. "Woman Artist Sketched F.D.R.," *The Philadelphia Inquirer*, April 14, 1945, 3.
45. Bishop, *FDR's Last Year*, 611.
46. Eleanor Roosevelt, *This I Remember* (New York: Harper & Brothers, 1949), 344.
47. Ibid.
48. Joseph P. Lash, *Eleanor & Franklin* (New York: W. W. Norton & Co., 1984), 721.
49. Margaret Truman, *Harry S. Truman* (New York: William Morrow & Company, 1973), 209.
50. Harry S. Truman, *Memoirs by Harry S. Truman, Volume One: Year of Decisions* (Garden City, NY: Doubleday & Company, 1955), 5.
51. Ibid.
52. Herbert G. Monroe, "President's Special," *Railroad* (November 1945): 30.
53. Fred W. Patterson, "Details Described by Fred Patterson," *The American Funeral Director* (May 1945): 36.
54. Gordon Thomas and Max Morgan Witts, *Enola Gay* (New York: Stein and Day Publishers, 1977), 107.
55. Jonathan Daniels, *The Man of Independence* (Philadelphia: J. B. Lippincott Company, 1950), 264.

56. James F. Byrnes, *Speaking Frankly* (New York: Harper & Brothers, 1947), 48.
57. Edwin W. Pauley, "The Life and Times of Edwin W. Pauley," manuscript in the holdings of the Harry S. Truman Library, V-1, Independence, MO.
58. George E. Allen, *Presidents Who Have Known Me* (New York: Simon and Schuster, 1960), 162–3.
59. David McCullough, *Truman* (New York: Simon and Schuster, 1992), 159.
60. Allen, *Presidents Who Have Known Me*, 162.
61. "The Regular Guys," *Time* (August 12, 1946): 17.
62. James Roosevelt and Sidney Shalett, *Affectionately, F.D.R.: A Son's Story of a Lonely Man* (New York: Harcourt, Brace, 1959), 361.
63. E. Roosevelt, *This I Remember*, 344.
64. Tom McGann, "Funerals of the Famous: Franklin Delano Roosevelt," *American Funeral Director* (August 1992): 65.
65. Advertisements in *American Funeral Director* (April–November 1945).
66. Patterson, "Details Described by Fred Patterson," 44.
67. McGann, "Funerals of the Famous," 65.
68. Monroe, "President's Special," 30.
69. Ibid., 31.
70. William Webb, *The Southern Railway System: An Illustrated History* (Boston: Boston Mills Press, 1986), 299.
71. Monroe, "President's Special," 29.
72. Ibid., 32.
73. Ibid.
74. Ibid.
75. Ibid.
76. Harry S. Truman, *Off the Record: The Private Papers of Harry S. Truman*, ed. Robert H. Ferrell (New York: Harper & Row, 1980), 16.
77. Lash, *Eleanor & Franklin*, 722.
78. Tully, *F.D.R., My Boss*, 366.
79. Jonathan Daniels, "Romantic Footnote to an Era," *Life* (September 2, 1966): 44.
80. Shoumatoff, *FDR's Unfinished Portrait*, 119.
81. Ibid., 118.
82. Ibid., 119.
83. Ibid., 120.
84. A. Merriman Smith. *Thank You, Mr. President: A White House Notebook* (New York: Harper & Brothers, 1946), 189.
85. Merriman Smith, "President Roosevelt Dies at Home in Warm Springs," *The Atlanta Constitution*, April 13, 1945, 1.
86. Smith, *Thank You, Mr. President*, 189.
87. Bishop, *FDR's Last Year*, 623.
88. Dave Snell, "Warm Springs Weeps Over Its Biggest Loss," *The Atlanta Constitution*, April 14, 1945, 2.
89. Ibid.
90. Monroe, "President's Special," 32.
91. Bishop, *FDR's Last Year*, 624.
92. Asbell, *When F.D.R. Died*, 127.
93. Ibid., 126.
94. Ibid., 130.
95. Patterson, "Details Described by Fred Patterson," 44.
96. Bishop, *FDR's Last Year*, 621.

97. "Roosevelt Bier of Georgia Pine," *The Atlanta Constitution*, April 14, 1945, 5.

98. Bishop, *FDR's Last Year*, 622.

99. Jonathan Daniels, *White House Witness* (Garden City, NY: Doubleday & Company, 1975), 282.

100. Patterson, "Details Described by Fred Patterson," 44.

101. Ibid.

102. Snell, "Warm Springs Weeps Over Its Biggest Loss," 2.

TWO "RUN SLOW, RUN SILENT"

1. Robert H. Ferrell, *The Dying President* (Columbia: University of Missouri Press, 1998), 17.

2. A. Merriman Smith, *Thank You, Mr. President: A White House Notebook* (New York: Harper & Brothers, 1946), 189.

3. Smith, *Thank You, Mr. President*, 190.

4. Ibid.

5. Lee Fuhrman, "Warm Springs Hushed as 'Loved One' Departs," *The Atlanta Constitution*, April 14, 1945, 1.

6. Turnley Walker, *Roosevelt and the Warm Springs Story* (New York: A. A. Wyn, 1953), 301.

7. Beth J. Herzog, "President Roosevelt's Funeral Service," *Southern Funeral Director* (May 1945): 18.

8. "The Funeral of President Franklin D. Roosevelt," *American Funeral Director* (May 1945): 44.

9. Walter McCall, e-mail message to author, August 23, 2008.

10. Frank Kluckhohn, "Crowds in Tears at Rail Stations Watch Funeral Train Roll North," *New York Times*, April 14, 1945, 4.

11. Rexford Tugwell, *FDR: Architect of an Era* (New York: Macmillan, 1967), 258.

12. Merriman Smith, "Funeral Train Seen on Way by Silent Crowds," *New York Herald Tribune*, April 14, 1945, 1.

13. Tom McGann, "Funerals of the Famous: Franklin Delano Roosevelt," *American Funeral Director* (August 1992): 68.

14. Fred W. Patterson, "Details Described by Fred Patterson," *American Funeral Director* (May 1945): 44.

15. Jim Bishop, *FDR's Last Year* (New York: William Morrow & Company, 1974), 629.

16. Smith, *Thank You, Mr. President*, 193.

17. David Wayner, *Passenger Train Consists, 1923–1973* (New York: Wayner Publications, 1971), 31.

18. Smith, *Thank You, Mr. President*, 193.

19. Herbert G. Monroe, "President's Special," *Railroad* (November 1945): 33.

20. Bernard Asbell, *When FDR Died* (New York: Holt, Rinehart and Winston, 1961), 151.

21. Ibid., 153.

22. Thomas Reynolds, "Thousands Watch FDR Train," *Philadelphia Record*, April 14, 1945, 1.

23. William Webb, *The Southern Railway System: An Illustrated History* (Boston: Boston Mills Press, 1986), 81.

24. McGann, "Funerals of the Famous," 69.

25. Grace Tully, *F.D.R., My Boss* (New York: Charles Scribner's Sons, 1949), 370.
26. "Going Home: The Trip North," *Life* (April 23, 1945): 20.
27. Monroe, "President's Special," 33.
28. Martha Gellhorn, introduction to *Eleanor Roosevelt's 'My Day': Her Acclaimed Columns, 1936–1945*, ed. Rochelle Chadakoff (Jupiter, FL: Pharos Books, 1989), 389.
29. Harold Oliver, "Roosevelt's Body Begins Last Journey," *Washington Post*, April 14, 1945, 1.
30. Ted Morgan, *FDR: A Biography* (New York: Simon and Schuster, 1985), 767.
31. Doris Kearns Goodwin, *No Ordinary Time* (New York: Simon & Schuster, 1994), 612.
32. William D. Hassett, *Off the Record with F.D.R.* (New Brunswick, NJ: Rutgers University Press, 1958), 340.
33. Jonathan Daniels, *White House Witness: 1942–1945* (Garden City, NY: Doubleday & Company, 1975), 13.
34. Hassett, *Off the Record with F.D.R.*, 327.
35. Ibid., 339.
36. Ibid., 1.
37. Ibid., 340.
38. Margaret Suckley, *Closest Companion: The Unknown Story of the Intimate Relationship Between Franklin Roosevelt and Margaret Suckley*, ed. Geoffrey C. Ward (Boston: Houghton Mifflin, 1995), 421.
39. Ibid.
40. Reynolds, "Thousands Watch FDR Train," 1.
41. Bishop, *FDR's Last Year*, 637.
42. An example of this error can be seen in Robert Nixon's April 13 dispatch for the International News Service, in which he wrote that a "W. Robbins" was the artist painting the president. Nixon's account also related that FDR's cousin Laura Delano was in the cabin, but does not specify if she was in the same room. Presumably, the haste and hectic nature of a breaking story was the cause of details such as these being rendered incorrectly.
43. "Woman Artist Sketched F.D.R.," *Philadelphia Inquirer*, April 14, 1945, 3.
44. Asbell, *When F.D.R. Died*, 74.
45. Tully, *F.D.R., My Boss*, 115.
46. "Woman Artist Sketched F.D.R.," 3.
47. Tully, *F.D.R., My Boss*, 360.
48. Jonathan Daniels, "Romantic Footnote to an Era," *Life* (September 2, 1966): 44.
49. Asbell, *When F.D.R. Died*, 31.
50. Daniels, "Romantic Footnote to an Era." 44.
51. Tully, *F.D.R., My Boss*, 366.
52. Elliott Roosevelt and James Brough, *Mother R.* (New York: G.P. Putnam's Sons, 1977), 27.
53. Ibid., 28.
54. Goodwin, *No Ordinary Time*, 611.
55. Elliott Roosevelt and Brough, *Mother R.*, 30.
56. Southern Railway System passenger timetables, May 1, 1946, 18–19.
57. John Whitcomb and Claire Whitcomb, *Real Life at the White House* (New York: Routledge, 2000), 314.
58. Ibid.
59. Daniels, "Romantic Footnote to an Era," 47.

60. Asbell, *When FDR Died*, 155.
61. Elliott Roosevelt and Brough, *Mother R.*, 29.
62. Cecile Davis, "Saddened Atlantans View Funeral Train en Route to Capital," *Atlanta Constitution*, April 14, 1945, 1.
63. Kluckhohn, "Crowds in Tears Watch Funeral Train Roll North," 4.
64. "Fala Strolls Station Platform," *Atlanta Constitution*, April 14, 1945, 10.
65. Davis, "Saddened Atlantans View Funeral Train En Route to Capital," 1.
66. "The Last Train," *Time* (April 23, 1945): 19.
67. "Roosevelt Body Begins Journey to Washington," *Los Angeles Times*, April 14, 1945, 1.

THREE THE FISH ROOM

1. Jim Bishop, *FDR's Last Year* (New York: William Morrow & Company, 1974), 615.
2. Jonathan Daniels, *White House Witness, 1942–1945* (Garden City, NY: Doubleday & Company, 1975), 282.
3. Ibid., 283–85.
4. Joseph Alsop, *F.D.R.: A Centenary Remembrance* (New York: The Viking Press, 1982), 170.
5. Daniels, *White House Witness*, photo plate 10.
6. James MacGregor Burns, *Roosevelt: The Soldier of Freedom* (New York: Harcourt Brace Jovanovich, 1970), 498.
7. Ibid., 503.
8. Bernard Asbell, *When F.D.R. Died* (New York: Holt, Rinehart and Winston, 1961), 114–115.
9. Margaret Truman, *Harry S. Truman* (New York: William Morrow & Company, 1973), 209.
10. Donald Porter Geddes, ed., *Franklin Delano Roosevelt: A Memorial* (New York: Pocket Books, 1945), I.
11. Asbell, *When F.D.R. Died*, 104–108.
12. Harry S. Truman, *Off the Record: The Private Papers of Harry S. Truman*, ed. Robert H. Ferrell (New York: Harper & Row, 1980), 15.
13. Conrad Black, *Franklin Delano Roosevelt: Champion of Freedom* (New York: Public Affairs, 2005), 901.
14. "Details in Connection with the President's Funeral, as Recollected by Mrs. Helm and Mr. Tolley," Office of Social Entertainments file, Franklin D. Roosevelt Presidential Library and Museum, Hyde Park, New York.
15. *Chronicle of America* (Mount Kisco, NY: Chronicle Publications, 1988), 622.
16. Asbell, *When F.D.R. Died*, 155.
17. "Details in Connection with the President's Funeral." Only later did Helm learn that the files she had upended the White House to locate had long before been given to First Lady Florence Harding—who herself had passed on a year after her husband.
18. Ibid.
19. Notes and telegrams requesting admittance to F.D.R. funeral, Office of Social Entertainments file, Franklin D. Roosevelt Presidential Library and Museum.
20. Ibid.
21. Ibid.

22. Edith Helm, Memorandum concerning groups to be admitted, April 13, 1945. Office of Social Entertainments file, Franklin D. Roosevelt Presidential Library and Museum.

23. Edith Helm, standard telegram sent to those denied White House admittance, April 13, 1945. Office of Social Entertainments file, Franklin D. Roosevelt Presidential Library and Museum.

24. Tom McGann, "Funerals of the Famous: F.D.R.," *American Funeral Director* (August 1992): 70.

25. "Details in Connection with the President's Funeral."

26. Robert H. Jackson, *That Man: An Insider's Portrait of Franklin D. Roosevelt* (New York: Oxford University Press, 2003), 166.

27. The White House Museum, Oval Office History, www.whitehousemuseum.org.

28. Harry S. Truman, *Memoirs by Harry S. Truman, Volume One: Year of Decisions* (Garden City, NY: Doubleday & Company, 1955), 13.

29. Ibid.

30. Ibid.

31. Ibid.

32. The White House Museum, Roosevelt Room, www.whitehousemuseum.org.

33. "Details in Connection with the President's Funeral."

34. Daniels, *White House Witness*, 285.

35. Report of Michael F. Reilly, Supervising Agent, United States Secret Service, April 12, 1945, 2–3.

36. "Details in Connection with the President's Funeral."

37. The author was able to identify at least four separate passenger lists during various stages of development. Yet the number is somewhat misleading because, for example, the earliest list—wired to the White House from the funeral train as it stopped in Greenville, South Carolina—was almost immediately corrected and augmented and hence became, in effect, an entirely new list. The records preserved from this effort also include myriad memos from Edith Helm (most dated April 14) to Mike Reilly and Colonel Park, adding individual passenger names as they were chosen and approved; as well as a wholly separate list drafted for Fauver and Reilly (dated April 13) that was limited to the names of the press corps. Finally, many of the notes regarding passengers to be added to the manifest appear on undated sheets of paper that were covered with handwriting that, absent corroborating documents, lacked context. The only reasonable inference that can be drawn was that the drafting of the passenger manifest was a near-continuous effort—one that involved numerous officials, and one that continued until virtually the last possible hour.

38. Telegram from funeral train to White House, Greenville, SC, April 13, 1945, 7:17 P.M. Office of Social Entertainments file, Franklin D. Roosevelt Presidential Library and Museum.

39. Ibid.

40. "List of Those to Go on Train from Washington to Hyde Park," Revised guest list, Office of Social Entertainments file, Franklin D. Roosevelt Presidential Library and Museum.

41. "Members of the Party," Passenger list and Western Union telegram from Dewey Long to Agent Robert H. Lowery dated April 14, 6:28 P.M., Office of Social Entertainments file, Franklin D. Roosevelt Presidential Library and Museum.

42. Invitation to Hon. Edward R. Stettinius, Jr., April 13, 1945, Office of Social Entertainments file, Franklin D. Roosevelt Presidential Library and Museum.

43. William Manchester, *The Glory and the Dream* (Boston: Little, Brown & Co., 1974), 440. Though the name *Congressional* was apt for the occasion, it probably caused some degree of confusion among trainmen. During those years, the Pennsylvania Railroad had a regularly scheduled passenger train that was also called the *Congressional*. It made a daily run in each direction between Washington and New York—along the same tracks the funeral train would be using.

44. Lucius Beebe, *Mansions on Rails* (Berkeley, CA: Howell-North, 1959), 380.

45. *The Complete Roster of Heavyweight Pullman Cars* (New York: Wayner Publications, 1985), 185.

46. Bob Adler, McCormick-Stilllman Railroad Park, e-mail message to author, October 14, 2008.

47. Ibid.

48. Herbert Monroe, "President's Special," *Railroad* (November 1945): 23.

49. Handwritten meeting notes on Secret Service letterhead, Office of Social Entertainments file, Franklin D. Roosevelt Presidential Library and Museum.

50. Thomas F. Reynolds, *Franklin Delano Roosevelt, 1882–1945: Reprint of the* Chicago Sun's *Distinguished Stories Covering the Death and Burial of our Late Beloved President Roosevelt* (Chicago: The Chicago Sun, 1945), 5.

51. Margaret Truman, *Harry S. Truman* (New York: William Morrow & Co., 1973), 223.

52. Barrington Boardman, *Flappers, Bootleggers, "Typhoid Mary" and The Bomb: An Anecdotal History of the United States from 1923–1945* (New York: Harper Perennial, 1989), 271.

53. Peter Hoffman, *Hitler's Personal Security: Protecting the Fuhrer, 1921–1945* (New York: Da Capo Press, 2000), 66–72.

54. Monroe, "President's Special," 15.

55. Doris Kearns Goodwin, *No Ordinary Time* (New York: Simon & Schuster, 1994), 72.

56. Jonathan Daniels, Introduction to *Off the Record with F.D.R.*, by William D. Hassett (New Brunswick, NY: Rutgers University Press, 1958), vi.

57. "Washington Hyde Park Schedule of President's Funeral Train," Syndicated AP wire story, April 14, 1945.

58. "Trip of the President, Washington to Hyde Park, N.Y., and Return. April 14–15, 1945," original funeral train itinerary of April 14, 1945, Secret Service file, Franklin D. Roosevelt Presidential Library and Museum. The times given here were those listed in the itinerary finalized shortly before the funeral train's scheduled departure from Union Station. However, because the train would end up leaving an hour late, the schedule was adjusted one last time and then labeled as the "Corrected Itinerary." Newspapers, of course, had already printed the earlier schedule, part of which was in error, though the train did eventually make up the lost hour en route.

59. Bishop, *FDR's Last Year*, 660–61.

60. "Hundreds Rise Early to View Funeral Train," *New York Herald Tribune*, April 16, 1945, 4.

61. "15,000 View Train Halted in Greenville," *Greenville News*, April 14, 1945, 1.

62. Bishop, *FDR's Last Year*, 660.

63. Ibid.

64. "Funeral Train Starts the Last Journey Home," *New York Herald Tribune*, April 15, 1945, 1.

65. "The Funeral of President Franklin D. Roosevelt," *American Funeral Director* (May 1945): 35.

66. Asbell, *When F.D.R. Died*, 186. Asbell was in error concerning the viaduct's location, stating it to be 156th Street. According to a 1942 Bromley atlas of the Bronx, the viaduct stood at 153rd Street.

67. Report of Michael F. Reilly, Supervising Agent, United States Secret Service, April 12, 1945, 2–3.

68. Department of Homeland Security, letter to author, January 7, 2009.

FOUR   THE MAIN LINE

1. Bernard Asbell, *When F.D.R. Died* (New York: Holt, Rinehart and Winston, 1961), 153.

2. Ibid.

3. Drafts of condolence-acknowledgment card, Office of Social Entertainments file, Franklin D. Roosevelt Presidential Library and Museum, Hyde Park, New York. The first draft of the condolence message ended with "your kind thought." Apparently, the women noticed the repetition of the word "your" and dropped the second mention.

4. Grace Tully, Telegram to B. Tolley, April 13, 1945. Office of Social Entertainments file, Franklin D. Roosevelt Presidential Library and Museum, Hyde Park, NY.

5. Doris Kearns Goodwin, *No Ordinary Time* (New York: Simon & Schuster, 1994), 612.

6. Ibid.

7. Grace Tully, *F.D.R., My Boss* (New York: Charles Scribner's Sons, 1949), 366–67.

8. Ibid., 367.

9. Asbell, *When F.D.R. Died*, 197.

10. Eleanor Roosevelt, *This I Remember* (New York: Harper & Brothers, 1949), 345.

11. Tully, *F.D.R., My Boss*, 370.

12. Ibid., 371.

13. Jim Bishop, *FDR's Last Year* (New York: William Morrow & Company, 1974), 623.

14. Telegram from funeral train to White House, Greenville, SC, April 13, 1945, 7:17 PM, Office of Social Entertainments file, Franklin D. Roosevelt Presidential Library and Museum.

15. A. Merriman Smith, *Thank You, Mr. President: A White House Notebook* (New York: Harper & Brothers, 1946), 194.

16. Gallery 2: FDR Funeral Train, City of Clemson, South Carolina, www.cityofclemson.org.

17. Merriman Smith, "Funeral Train Seen on Way by Silent Crowds," *New York Herald Tribune*, April 14, 1945, 2.

18. Smith, *Thank You, Mr. President*, 195.

19. Thomas F. Reynolds, "Body to Arrive in Washington This Morning," *Philadelphia Record*, April 14, 1945, 1.

20. Asbell, *When F.D.R. Died*, 157.

21. "15,000 View Train Halted in Greenville," *Greenville News*, April 14, 1945, 1.

22. Herbert G. Monroe, "President's Special," *Railroad* (November 1945): 34.

23. Smithsonian Institution, "Steam Locomotive, Southern Railway No. 1401," http://americanhistory.si.edu.

24. Ibid.

25. Monroe, "President's Special," 33.

26. Smithsonian Institution, "Steam Locomotive, Southern Railway No. 1401." http://americanhistory.si.edu.

27. Telegram from funeral train to White House, Greenville, SC, April 13, 1945, 7:17 P.M. Office of Social Entertainments file, Franklin D. Roosevelt Presidential Library and Museum.

28. James Roosevelt, *Affectionately, FDR: A Son's Story of a Lonely Man* (New York: Harcourt Brace, 1959), 364.

29. Smith, *Thank You, Mr. President*, 194.

30. James MacGregor Burns, *Roosevelt: The Soldier of Freedom* (New York: Harcourt Brace Jovanovich, 1970), 603.

31. "President's Body Is Borne from Southern Home," *Chicago Daily Tribune*, April 14, 1945, 3.

32. Asbell, *When FDR Died*, 25.

33. Robert G. Nixon "Roosevelt Is Borne Home," International News Service syndicated item, April 13, 1945.

34. "President's Body Is Borne from Southern Home," 3.

35. "11,000 Spartans Out," *Greenville News*, April 14, 1945, 8.

36. Bishop, *FDR's Last Year*, 643.

37. Though Eleanor Roosevelt had been given her own private quarters aboard the *Ferdinand Magellan*—Stateroom "B," decorated in beige and peach—most of the accounts of FDR's trips aboard the car make clear that the First Lady was not present. Even for the inaugural journey of the *Ferdinand Magellan* in December of 1942, Eleanor left FDR to take the trip to Hyde Park by himself, according to Daisy Suckley's diary entry: "Mrs. R. very nice and very busy —About 10 she went off to her train to somewhere." Though Eleanor Roosevelt was a heavily traveled First Lady, she preferred to take planes whenever possible, believing the presidential train (indeed, trains in general) to be too slow.

38. Rexford Tugwell, *FDR: Architect of an Era* (New York: Macmillan, 1967), 259.

39. Burns, *Roosevelt: The Soldier of Freedom*, 604.

40. Smith, *Thank You, Mr. President*, 195.

41. Asbell, *When F.D.R. Died*, 158.

42. "Goin' Home," *Newsweek* (April 23, 1945): 29.

43. Beth J. Herzog, "President Roosevelt's Funeral Service," *Southern Funeral Director* (May 1945): 16.

44. Incredibly, such a thing would be overlooked twenty-three years later on the funeral train of the slain Robert F. Kennedy, when, in order to allow spectators a similar view, Penn Central Railroad officials would be forced to place the casket on ordinary chairs in the rear observation car. Relatives took shifts in the Pullman to make sure the casket didn't fall from its makeshift perch. Jules Witcover, *85 Days: The Last Campaign of Robert Kennedy* (New York: G. P. Putnam's Sons, 1969), 308.

45. "Goin' Home," 29.

46. Elizabeth Shoumatoff, *FDR's Unfinished Portrait* (Pittsburgh: University of Pittsburgh Press, 1991), 99.

47. Ibid., 122.

48. Ibid., 94–96.

49. Ibid., 122.

50. The *Imperator* was the only Pullman on the train that was not made up of private staterooms. Listed as a "dormitory car," it had one enclosed room and twelve open sections—an older sleeping arrangement that consisted of upper and lower bunks assembled from the daytime seating benches and separated from the center aisle by a heavy curtain. It is likely that the *Imperator* was used to berth

members of the train crew, but it was quite likely used as an accommodation for the domestic help, too—which would have included staffers of color such as McDuffie.

51. Asbell, *When F.D.R. Died*, 159–160.
52. Ibid., 160.
53. Jonathan Daniels, *White House Witness* (Garden City, NY: Doubleday & Company, 1975), caption of photo plate no. 5.
54. Ibid., 255.
55. Asbell, *When F.D.R. Died*, 161.
56. Jim Bishop, "FDR's Final Ride," uncited vertical file clipping, Franklin D. Roosevelt Presidential Library and Museum.
57. Ibid.
58. Ibid.
59. Smith, *Thank You, Mr. President*, 196.
60. Ibid.
61. Ibid.
62. Ibid., 186.
63. Ibid., 196.
64. "Crowds Line Route of Funeral Train in Old Dominion," *Washington Post*, April 15, 1945, M5.
65. Bishop, *FDR's Last Year*, 646–647.
66. Smith, *Thank You, Mr. President*, 197.
67. Bishop, *FDR's Last Year*, 647. The inscription would never end up on the stone. It bears only the president's name and the years of his birth and death.
68. Ibid.
69. "Along the Line," uncited vertical file clipping, Franklin D. Roosevelt Presidential Library and Museum.

FIVE   TWELVE HOURS

1. Tom McGann, "Funerals of the Famous: F.D.R.," *American Funeral Director* (August 1992): 70.
2. Invitation, Office of Social Entertainments file, Franklin D. Roosevelt Presidential Library and Museum, Hyde Park, New York.
3. Carol M. Highsmith and Ted Landphair, *Union Station: A History of Washington's Grand Terminal* (Washington, D.C.: Chelsea Publishing, 1998), 59.
4. Invitation, Office of Social Entertainments file, Franklin D. Roosevelt Presidential Library and Museum.
5. Union Station, "History of Union Station DC," www.unionstationdc.com/history.aspx.
6. Though a close examination of most any of the surviving photographs of the funeral train's arrival will indicate that it was parked on the freight siding and not on Track 1, conclusive proof rests with the Secret Service's "Schedule of Ceremonies" dated April 13, 1945, which clearly states that "the train will arrive...at the yards on the extreme right (east) of the station facing the main entrance."
7. "Roosevelt Begins His Last Journey," *The Atlanta Constitution*, April 15, 1945, 1.
8. Ray Cooney, National Railway Historical Society, e-mail message to author, February 4, 2009.
9. Author's collection of period photographs and station blueprints.

10. Paul Tobenkin, "Capital Throng, Sad and Silent, Views Cortege," *New York Herald Tribune*, April 15, 1945, 1.

11. Because the police prevented automobiles from driving any closer than three blocks from Union Station, passengers bound for regularly scheduled departing trains were forced to carry their luggage for that distance.

12. Jim Bishop, *FDR's Last Year* (New York: William Morrow & Co., 1974), 648.

13. Robert H. Jackson, *That Man: An Insider's Portrait of Franklin D. Roosevelt* (New York: Oxford University Press, 2003), 166.

14. Fleet Admiral William D. Leahy, *I Was There* (New York: Whittlesey House, 1950), 343.

15. Beth J. Herzog, "President Roosevelt's Funeral Service," *Southern Funeral Director* (May 1945): 18.

16. Robert E. Gilbert, *The Mortal Presidency* (New York: Fordham University Press, 1998), 72.

17. Bishop, *FDR's Last Year*, 626.

18. Harold Ickes, personal diary entry of April 29, 1945, collection of Franklin D. Roosevelt Presidential Library and Museum.

19. Bishop, *FDR's Last Year*, 645.

20. "Military Chiefs Meet Roosevelt Train," Associated Press Wirephoto, April 14, 1945, author's collection.

21. Leahy, *I Was There*, 345.

22. Bishop, *FDR's Last Year*, 648.

23. "Funeral Crowds Break Thru Line," *Washington Daily News*, April 14, 1945, 3.

24. Bishop, *FDR's Last Year*, 646.

25. Ibid., 648.

26. Harry S. Truman, *Memoirs by Harry S. Truman, Volume One: Year of Decisions* (Garden City, NY: Doubleday & Company, 1955), 29.

27. Bishop, *FDR's Last Year*, 648.

28. David McCullough, *Truman* (New York: Simon & Schuster, 1992), 293.

29. Elliott Roosevelt and James Brough, *Mother R: Eleanor Roosevelt's Untold Story* (New York: G. P. Putnam's Sons, 1977), 32.

30. Ted Morgan, *FDR: A Biography* (New York: Simon and Schuster, 1985), 762.

31. Grace Tully, *F.D.R., My Boss* (New York: Charles Scribner's Sons, 1949), 167.

32. Alden Hatch, *Franklin D. Roosevelt: An Informal Biography* (New York: Henry Holt & Co., 1947), 338.

33. Bishop, *FDR's Last Year*, 646.

34. Claude Wickard, personal papers, recollection of the death of F.D.R., 7–8. Collection of Franklin D. Roosevelt Presidential Library and Museum.

35. Tobenkin, "Capital Throng," 1.

36. "Patient Throng Waits to Bid Last Farewell," *Washington Post*, April 15, 1945, 1.

37. Walter Trohan, "Body Taken to Hyde Park After Simple Services in White House," *Chicago Daily Tribune*, April 15, 1945, 1.

38. Ibid.

39. Clark Kinnaird, ed., *The Real FDR* (New York: Citadel Press, 1945), 119–20.

40. "Washington in Wartime," *Life*, January 4, 1943, 47.

41. A. Merriman Smith, *Thank You, Mr. President: A White House Notebook* (New York: Harper & Brothers, 1946), 197.

42. Frances Perkins, *The Roosevelt I Knew* (New York: Viking Press, 1946), 6.

43. Tom McGann, "Funerals of the Famous: Franklin Delano Roosevelt—Part II," *American Funeral Director* (September 1992): 27.

44. "Along the Line," unidentified newspaper clip, vertical file, Franklin D. Roosevelt Presidential Library and Museum.
45. Floral condolence cards, Office of Social Entertainments file, Franklin D. Roosevelt Presidential Library and Museum.
46. Ibid.
47. Frank Kluckhohn, "Nation Pays Final Tribute to Roosevelt," *New York Times*, April 15, 1945, 1.
48. Joseph H. Short, "Funeral Train Bound for Hyde Park After Rites at White House," *Baltimore Sun*, April 15, 1945, 1.
49. William D. Hassett, *Off the Record with F.D.R.* (New Brunswick, NJ: Rutgers University Press, 1958), 341.
50. "Roosevelt Begins His Last Journey," 1.
51. "Funeral Crowds Break Thru Line," 3.
52. H. S. Truman, *Memoirs by Harry S. Truman, Volume One: Year of Decisions*, 10.
53. H. S. Truman, *Off the Record*,16.
54. Jonathan Daniels, *The Man of Independence* (Philadelphia: J. B. Lippincott Company, 1950), 255.
55. Robert E. Sherwood, *Roosevelt and Hopkins* (New York: Harper & Brothers, 1948), 882.
56. Margaret Truman, *Harry S. Truman* (New York: William Morrow & Company, 1973), 199.
57. Robert H. Ferrell, *Truman: A Centenary Remembrance* (New York: Viking Press, 1984), 110.
58. Robert H. Ferrell, *The Dying President* (Columbia: University of Missouri Press, 1998), 89.
59. Daniels, *The Man of Independence*, 259.
60. Ibid.
61. Ibid., 258.
62. Robert G. Nixon, Harry S. Truman Library "Oral History" series interview, October 19, 1970, Harry S. Truman Library and Museum, Independence, Missouri.
63. Bishop, *FDR's Last Year*, 638.
64. M. Truman, *Harry S. Truman*, 216.
65. Daniels, *The Man of Independence*, 263.
66. David Robertson, *Sly and Able: A Political Biography of James F. Byrnes* (New York: W. W. Norton & Co. 1994), 388.
67. M. Truman, *Harry S. Truman*, 218.
68. Bishop, *FDR's Last Year*, 646.
69. McCullough, *Truman*, 300–301.
70. Hatch, *Franklin D. Roosevelt: An Informal Biography*, 338.
71. Clayton Sinyai, *Schools of Democracy: A Political History of the American Labor Movement* (Ithaca, NY: ILR Press, 2006), 165–66.
72. Hatch, *Franklin D. Roosevelt: An Informal Biography*, 338.
73. H. S. Truman, *Off the Record*, 17.
74. Richard Rhodes, *The Making of the Atomic Bomb* (New York: Simon & Schuster, 1986), 628.
75. H. S. Truman, *Memoirs by Harry S. Truman, Volume One: Year of Decisions*, 23.
76. Gordon Thomas and Max Morgan Witts, *Enola Gay* (New York: Stein and Day Publishers, 1977), 108.
77. H. S. Truman, *Memoirs by Harry S. Truman, Volume One: Year of Decisions*, 10.
78. M. Truman, *Harry S. Truman*, 216.
79. James F. Byrnes, *All in One Lifetime* (New York: Harper & Brothers, 1958), 280.

80. H. S. Truman, *Memoirs by Harry S. Truman, Volume One: Year of Decisions*, 32.
81. Daniels, *The Man of Independence*, 247.
82. H. S. Truman, *Memoirs by Harry S. Truman, Volume One: Year of Decisions*, 17.
83. H. S. Truman, *Off the Record*, 17.
84. Edwin W. Pauley, "The Life and Times of Edwin W. Pauley," manuscript in the holdings of the Harry S. Truman Library and Museum, V-3.
85. Ibid.
86. "The Right Rev. Angus Dun," *Time* (August 23, 1971): 39.
87. Kluckhohn, "Nation Pays Final Tribute to Roosevelt," 1.
88. M. Truman, *Harry S. Truman*, 223.
89. Kluckhohn, "Nation Pays Final Tribute to Roosevelt," 1.
90. Eleanor Roosevelt, *This I Remember* (New York: Harper, 1949), 345.
91. Martin Gilbert, *Churchill: A Life* (New York: Henry Holt and Company, 1991), 835–36.
92. Doris Kearns Goodwin, *No Ordinary Time* (New York: Simon & Schuster, 1994), 150.
93. "Roosevelt Begins His Last Journey," *Atlanta Constitution*, April 15, 1945, 1.
94. Short, "Funeral Train Bound for Hyde Park," 1.
95. Ibid.
96. Harold Ickes, personal diary entry of April 29, 1945, Collection of Franklin D. Roosevelt Presidential Library and Museum.
97. Short, "Funeral Train Bound for Hyde Park," 1.
98. George E. Allen, *Presidents Who Have Known Me* (New York: Simon & Schuster, 1960), 164.
99. Ibid., 163.
100. Robert L. Messer, *The End of An Alliance: James F. Byrnes, Roosevelt, Truman, and the Origins of the Cold War* (Chapel Hill: University of North Carolina Press, 1982), 17.
101. "The Regular Guys," *Time* (August 12, 1946): 17.
102. Bishop, *FDR's Last Year*, 645.
103. H. S. Truman, *Memoirs by Harry S. Truman, Volume One: Year of Decisions*, 33.
104. Allen, *Presidents Who Have Known Me*, 164.
105. Michael Beschloss, *The Conquerers* (New York: Simon & Schuster, 2002), 14.
106. Allen, *Presidents Who Have Known Me*, 165.
107. Elliott Roosevelt and Brough, *Mother R.*, 31.
108. Bishop, *FDR's Last Year*, 657–58.
109. Ibid.
110. Elliott Roosevelt and Brough, *Mother R.*, 31.
111. Ibid.
112. Fred W. Patterson, "Details Described by Fred Patterson," *American Funeral Director* (May 1945): 44.
113. Eleanor Roosevelt, *This I Remember*, 345.
114. Goodwin, *No Ordinary Time*, 613.
115. David Wayner, *Passenger Train Consists, 1923–1973* (New York: Wayner Publications, 1971), 31.
116. Dewey Long, Telegram to Agent Robert H. Lowery, April 14, 1945, 6:28 P.M., Office of Social Entertainments file, Franklin D. Roosevelt Presidential Library and Museum.
117. Colonel Richard Park, Memorandum dated April 14 and accompanying "Trip of the President, Washington to Hyde Park, N.Y., and Return. April 14–15, 1945," Secret Service file, Franklin D. Roosevelt Presidential Library and Museum. Park's memo accompanied a passenger list and operating schedule finalized just prior to

the funeral train's departure. The document was soon after revised and labeled "Corrected Itinerary" to reflect the train's hour-late departure from Washington Union Station and various minor adjustments to the berth assignments. Though the actual title "Trip of the President..." appears only on the Corrected Itinerary, that title has been used generally herein to refer to the final schedule that Park approved. In addition, all berth assignments used in this book reflect the latest ones found on the Corrected Itinerary.

118. *The Complete Roster of Heavyweight Pullman Cars* (New York: Wayner Publications, 1985), 259.

119. The heavyweight Pullman car was designed to be a luxury hotel on wheels, which included the understanding that the porter would acquiesce to most any legal request to make passengers comfortable. A Pullman *Instructions to Porters* manual from this period states that "the porter is required to wait upon passengers, assist them with their baggage, shine shoes...and attend to all other duties requiring his attention." It was common for passengers to request ice, telegrams, playing cards, and even warm milk for baby bottles—all in the course of treating their compartments like their own living rooms. The journals of at least two passengers aboard the funeral train reference drinking parties that took place within car No. 6, the sleeper *Wordsworth*.

120. Herzog, "President Roosevelt's Funeral Service," 18.

121. Thomas A. McPherson, *Superior: The Complete History* (Ontario: Specialty Vehicle Press, 1995), 160. The author used the preceding work to confirm the year and make of Gawler's hearse, which was pictured in the *Baltimore Sun* of April 15, 1945.

122. William C. Murphy, "Roosevelt Starts Final Trip Home," *Philadelphia Inquirer*, April 15, 1945, 1.

123. Colonel Richard Park, Memorandum dated April 14, and accompanying "Trip of the President, Washington to Hyde Park, N.Y., and Return. April 14–15, 1945," Secret Service file, Franklin D. Roosevelt Presidential Library and Museum.

124. Ibid.

125. Lela Stiles, *The Man Behind Roosevelt* (Cleveland: The World Publishing Company, 1954), 80.

126. Ibid., 81.

127. Leahy, *I Was There*, 345.

128. William Manchester, *The Glory and the Dream* (New York: Little, Brown & Co., 1974), 440.

129. Miscellaneous undated notes of funeral committee, Office of Social Entertainments file, Franklin D. Roosevelt Presidential Library and Museum.

130. Tully, *F.D.R., My Boss*, 372.

SIX THE TRAIN OF SECRETS

1. American Society of Mechanical Engineers, *Pullman Sleeping Car Glengyle* (Dallas: The Age of Steam Railroad Museum, 1987), 7–8.

2. Jim Bishop, *FDR's Last Year* (New York: William Morrow & Company, 1974), 660.

3. Elliott Roosevelt and James Brough, *Mother R.* (New York: G. P. Putnam's Sons, 1977), 32.

4. "Trip of the President, Washington to Hyde Park, N.Y., and Return. April 14–15, 1945 (Corrected Itinerary)," Secret Service file, Franklin D. Roosevelt Presidential Library and Museum, Hyde Park, New York.

5. Robert E. Sherwood, *Roosevelt and Hopkins* (New York: Harper & Brothers, 1948), 882.

6. "When Harry Hopkins Was a Presidential Aide," *New York Times*, September 25, 1986, A30.

7. Harold Ickes, personal diary entry of April 29, 1945, The Franklin D. Roosevelt Presidential Library and Museum.

8. Bernard Asbell, *When F.D.R. Died* (New York: Holt, Rinehart and Winston, 1961), 185.

9. A. Merriman Smith, *Thank You, Mr. President* (New York: Harper & Brothers, 1946), 199.

10. A read of the surviving record suggests that passengers were free to use either dining car on the train—No. 4478 on the forward end or No. 4497 toward the rear—and mostly likely they used whichever was closer to their sleeping quarters. Neither the Truman nor Roosevelt party would be relegated to eat in an ordinary dining car, however, as both the *Roald Amundsen* and the *Ferdinand Magellan* had their own galleys, dining rooms, and serving staff.

11. Karl R. Zimmerman, *The Remarkable GG-1* (New York: Quadrant Press, 1977), 16.

12. William C. Murphy Jr., "Roosevelt Starts Final Trip Home," *Philadelphia Inquirer*, April 15, 1945, 1.

13. "Funeral Train Starts the Last Journey Home," *New York Herald Tribune*, April 15, 1945, 2.

14. Asbell, *When F.D.R. Died*, 184.

15. Ibid.

16. Smith, *Thank You, Mr. President*, 202.

17. Margaret Truman, *Harry S. Truman* (New York: William Morrow & Company, 1973), 201.

18. "Unwelcome Secret," *Time* (April 23, 1945): 20.

19. Smith, *Thank You, Mr. President*, 202.

20. Ibid., 201.

21. Ibid.

22. Elliott Roosevelt and Brough, *Mother R.*, 27.

23. Mr. X, *The Roosevelt Death: A Super Mystery* (Copyright by G. L. K. Smith, 1947), 10.

24. Ibid., 14.

25. Ibid., 16.

26. Emanuel M. Josephson, *The Strange Death of Franklin D. Roosevelt* (New York: Chedney Press, 1948), 243.

27. The Open Library, "Emanuel Mann Josephson, 1895–," http://openlibrary.org.

28. Josephson, *The Strange Death of Franklin D. Roosevelt*, 246.

29. Ross T. McIntire, *White House Physician* (New York: G. P. Putnam's Sons, 1946), 243.

30. Elliott Roosevelt and Brough, *Mother R.*, 27.

31. Asbell, *When F.D.R. Died*, 130.

32. William J. Eaton, president of Newmark of Colorado, wholesale casket distributors, e-mail correspondence with author, January 21, 2009.

33. "The Funeral of President Franklin D. Roosevelt," *American Funeral Director* (May 1945): 44.

34. Walter Trohan, "Body Taken to Hyde Park After Simple Services in White House," *Chicago Daily Tribune*, April 15, 1945, 1.

35. Eleanor Roosevelt, *This I Remember* (New York: Harper & Brothers, 1949), 345.
36. Elliott Roosevelt and Brough, *Mother R.*, 26.
37. Ted Morgan, *FDR: A Biography* (New York: Simon & Schuster, 1985), 768.
38. Fred W. Patterson, "Details Described by Fred Patterson," *American Funeral Director* (May 1945): 44.
39. Tom McGann, "Funerals of the Famous: Franklin Delano Roosevelt," *American Funeral Director* (August 1992): 67.
40. Patterson, "Details Described by Fred Patterson," 44.
41. Elliott Roosevelt and Brough, *Mother R.*, 26. According to Elliott's account, his mother was so shaken after seeing FDR's body down at Warm Springs that she ordered the coffin to be sealed "there and then." But it is probable that Elliott's memory is faulty concerning that detail, as Eleanor would request a final, private viewing of the remains up in Washington, and only after that occasion was the casket sealed for good.
42. Jonathan Daniels, *White House Witness: 1942–1945* (Garden City, NY: Doubleday & Company, 1975), 282.
43. "FDR Praised 10 Years After Death," *Washington Post*, April 12, 1955, 43.
44. M. Truman, *Harry S. Truman*, 223.
45. Doris Kearns Goodwin, *No Ordinary Time* (New York: Simon & Schuster, 1995), 615.
46. Eleanor Roosevelt, *This I Remember*, 346.
47. Elliott Roosevelt and Brough, *Mother R.*, 32.
48. Ibid., 43.
49. Ibid., 32.
50. Goodwin, *No Ordinary Time*, 79.
51. Joseph Gies, *Franklin D. Roosevelt: Portrait of a President* (Garden City, NY: Doubleday & Company, 1971), 14.
52. Robert H. Ferrell, *The Dying President* (Columbia: University of Missouri Press, 1998), 32.
53. Norman M. Littell, *My Roosevelt Years* (Seattle: University of Washington Press, 1987), 74.
54. Elliott Roosevelt and Brough, *Mother R.*, 33.
55. Ibid., 52.
56. "Val-Kill," in *The Great Estates Region of the Hudson Valley*, McKelden Smith, ed. (Tarrytown, NY: Historic Hudson Valley Press, 1998), 55.
57. "Springwood," in ibid., 53. According to the terms of the will, it had been FDR's desire for the estate to pass to the National Park Service inevitably—but Eleanor, the children, or any combination of them were, if they wished, entitled to live at the estate until the end of their lives. Elliott Roosevelt's memoirs make clear, however, that the obvious expense of such an arrangement quickly dissuaded his mother and siblings. It had, however, been wholly Eleanor's decision to cede the property to the Parks Department at the time she did.
58. Franklin D. Mares, *Springwood* (Little Compton, RI: Fort Church Publishers, 1993), 14.
59. Elliott Roosevelt and Brough, *Mother R.*, 52–53.
60. Ibid., 32
61. Ibid.
62. Ibid.
63. Joseph P. Lash, *A World of Love: Eleanor Roosevelt and Her Friends, 1943–62* (Garden City, NY: Doubleday & Co., 1984), 185.

64. Asbell, *When F.D.R. Died*, 185.
65. Edwin W. Pauley, "The Life and Times of Edwin W. Pauley," manuscript in the holdings of the Harry S. Truman Library and Museum, V-4. Independence, Missouri.
66. Bishop, *FDR's Last Year*, 663.
67. Ickes, personal diary entry of April 29, 1945, Collection of Franklin D. Roosevelt Presidential Library and Museum.
68. Ibid.
69. "Mr. Byrnes and Mr. Vinson," *Atlantic Monthly* (May 1945): 24.
70. Steve Neal, ed., *Eleanor and Harry* (New York: Scribner, 2002), 22.
71. Pauley, "Life and Times," V-4.
72. Bishop, *FDR's Last Year*, 661.
73. Henry Wallace, *Miscellaneous Recollections of the Interment Train* (Iowa City: Friends of the University of Iowa Libraries, 1974), 3.
74. Ibid., 5.
75. Asbell, *When F.D.R. Died*, 185.
76. Claude Wickard, personal papers, recollection of the death of F.D.R., 12, Collection of Franklin D. Roosevelt Presidential Library and Museum.
77. Wallace, *Miscellaneous Recollections*, 3.
78. Asbell, *When F.D.R. Died*, 185.
79. Wallace, *Miscellaneous Recollections*, 11.
80. "Washington-Hyde Park Schedule of President's Funeral Train," syndicated AP wire story, April 14, 1945.
81. "Throngs Here See Roosevelt Train," *Philadelphia Inquirer*, April 15, 1945, 1.
82. Ibid.
83. Ibid.
84. "FDR Praised 10 Years After Death," 43.
85. Harry S. Truman, *Memoirs by Harry S. Truman, Volume One: Year of Decisions* (Garden City, NY: Doubleday & Company, 1955), 28.
86. M. Truman, *Harry S. Truman*, 214.
87. Ibid., 223.
88. Harry S. Truman, *Off the Record: The Private Papers of Harry S. Truman*, ed. Robert H. Ferrell (New York: Harper & Row, 1980), 19.
89. "President's First Message Is Composed Aboard Train," *Washington Post*, April 16, 1945, 1.
90. George E. Allen, *Presidents Who Have Known Me* (New York: Simon & Schuster, 1960), 165.
91. "The Regular Guys," *Time* (August 12, 1946): 17.
92. "President's First Message Is Composed Aboard Train," 1.
93. Pauley, "Life and Times," V-5. One of the men who'd taken part in these talks was Fred M. Vinson, who in 1943 had taken over as FDR's director of economic stabilization after Byrnes left the post. Widely hailed for his economic acumen, Vinson—like Byrnes—had managed to save his political career by jumping ship from the Roosevelt to the Truman administration. Unlike Byrnes, however, Vinson accomplished it tactfully, without ruffling many feathers.
94. George E. Allen, Harry S. Truman Library "Oral History" series interview, May 15, 1969, www.trumanlibrary.org.
95. Pauley, "Life and Times," V-5.
96. "The Regular Guys," 17.
97. Ibid.
98. Pauley, "Life and Times," V-5.

99. Bishop, *FDR's Last Year*, 661.

100. Robert D. Graff and Robert Emmett Ginna, *FDR* (New York: Harper & Row, 1962), 234.

101. William D. Hassett, *Off the Record with F.D.R.* (New Brunswick, NJ: Rutgers University Press, 1958), 343.

102. "Hundreds Rise Early to View Funeral Train," *New York Herald Tribune*, April 16, 1945, 4.

103. Ibid.

104. Pennsylvania Railroad Office of the Chief Engineer, Track Layout, Pennsylvania Station, Plate No. 47910 (March 1944), author's collection.

105. "Trip of the President, Washington to Hyde Park, N.Y., and Return. April 14–15, 1945 (Corrected Itinerary)," Secret Service file, Franklin D. Roosevelt Presidential Library and Museum.

106. "Hundreds Rise Early to View Funeral Train," 4.

107. James MacGregor Burns, *Roosevelt: The Soldier of Freedom* (New York: Harcourt Brace Jovanovich, 1970), 610.

108. "Hundreds Rise Early to View Funeral Train," 4.

109. Joe Welsh, "All Aboard, Again!" *Railroads and World War II*, Special Edition No. 6 of *Classic Trains* magazine (2008): 13.

110. Lorraine B. Diehl, *The Late, Great Pennsylvania Station* (Lexington, MA: The Stephen Greene Press, 1985), 136.

111. Peter E. Lynch, *The New Haven Railroad* (St. Paul, MN: Motorbooks International, 2003), 58.

112. "Trip of the President, Washington to Hyde Park, N.Y., and Return. April 14–15, 1945. (Corrected Itinerary.)" Secret Service file, Franklin D. Roosevelt Presidential Library and Museum.

113. Alvin F. Staufer, *Thoroughbreds: New York Central's 4-6-4 Hudson* (Medina, OH: Author, 1974), 69, 332.

114. Freeman Hubbard, "Seven Coaches Painted Black," *Railroad* (December 1962): 26.

115. Asbell, *When F.D.R. Died*, 186.

116. Report of Michael F. Reilly, Supervising Agent, United States Secret Service, April 12, 1945, 2–3.

117. Bishop, *FDR's Last Year*, 662.

118. Ibid.

119. Asbell, *When F.D.R. Died*, 186.

120. Ibid.

121. Bishop, *FDR's Last Year*, 662.

122. Christine Sadler, "Roosevelt's Body Laid to Rest in Garden of His Birthplace," *Washington Post*, April 16, 1945, 1.

123. Wickard, personal papers, recollection of the death of F.D.R., 12.

124. Bishop, *FDR's Last Year*, 662.

125. Ibid., 663.

126. Ibid.

127. Roger J. Sandilands, *The Life and Political Economy of Lauchlin Currie* (Durham, NC: Duke University Press, 1990), 97.

128. Ibid., 96.

129. Ibid., 141.

130. Sherwood, *Roosevelt and Hopkins*, 208.

131. John Earl Haynes and Harvey Klehr, *Venona: Decoding Soviet Espionage in America* (New Haven, CT: Yale University Press, 1999), 146.

132. Technically, the KGB (*Komitet Gosudarstvennoi Bezopasnosti*, or Committee for State Security) did not acquire that name until 1954. The Soviet state security organization went by several acronyms prior to that year and, during the period of Currie's cooperation, was known as the NKGB. To avoid confusion, however, KGB is used to refer to the USSR's state security apparatus throughout this book.

133. John Earl Haynes, Harvey Klehr, and Alexander Vassiliev, *Spies: The Rise and Fall of the KGB in America* (New Haven, CT: Yale University Press, 2009), 262.

134. Haynes and Klehr, *Venona*, 129.

135. Sandilands, *The Life and Political Economy of Lauchlin Currie*, 149, 154–55.

136. Haynes, Klehr, and Vassiliev, *Spies*, 262.

137. Ibid. 265.

138. Ibid.

139. Ibid., 263.

140. Haynes and Klehr, *Venona*, 146–47.

141. Ibid.

142. Haynes, Klehr, and Vassiliev, *Spies*, 265.

143. Haynes and Klehr, *Venona*, 147.

144. Jay Walz, "Elizabeth Bentley Story: Career of a Star Witness," *New York Times*, November 22, 1953, E5.

145. NOVA Online, "Secrets, Lies and Atomic Spies: Elizabeth Bentley," original air-date February 5, 2002, Public Broadcasting Service, www.pbs.org.

146. Haynes and Klehr, *Venona*, 129–31.

147. "Secrets, Lies and Atomic Spies: Elizabeth Bentley."

148. Walz, "Elizabeth Bentley Story," E5.

149. Ibid.

150. "Break Seen Near in U.S. Spy Probe," *Washington Post*, November 20, 1954, 1.

151. Haynes and Klehr, *Venona*, 161.

152. Haynes, Klehr, and Vassiliev, *Spies*, 267.

153. Ibid.

154. "Currie, White Deny Aiding Red Spy Ring," *Washington Post*, August 1, 1948, M1.

155. Walz, "Elizabeth Bentley Story," E5.

156. "Currie Statement Before Committee," *Washington Post*, August 14, 1948, 3.

157. Haynes and Klehr, *Venona*, photo plates, 5.

158. Leo Smith, "How Red Agents Operated Inside the White House," *National Police Gazette* (March 1954): 6.

159. "Currie Loses Citizenship; Once an Aide to Roosevelt," *Washington Post*, March 28, 1956, 3.

160. "Lauchlin Currie, 91; New Deal Economist Was Roosevelt Aide," *New York Times*, December 30, 1993, B6.

161. Pavel Sudoplatov and Anatoli Sudoplatov, *Special Tasks: The Memoirs of an Unwanted Witness—a Soviet Spymaster* (Boston: Back Bay Books, 1994), 227–28. Pavel Sudoplatov confirmed the existence of Silvermaster's group in the body of his book, which he co-authored with his son, Anatoli. The authors mention Lauchlin Currie as a member of the Silvermaster ring in a footnote to that section.

162. Haynes and Klehr, *Venona*, 146.

163. Ibid., 31.

164. Ibid., 14–17, 35.

165. M. Truman, *Harry S. Truman*, 236.

SEVEN CAR NO. 3

1. "Platform in Garrison," *The New Yorker* (April 21, 1945): 20.
2. Ibid.
3. Ibid.
4. Ibid.
5. Ibid.
6. McCormick-Stillman Railroad Park, "The *Roald Amundsen*," www.therailroadpark.com.
7. Edwin W. Pauley, "The Life and Times of Edwin W. Pauley," manuscript in the holdings of the Harry S. Truman Library and Museum, V-3, Independence, Missouri.
8. Jonathan Daniels, *The Man of Independence* (Philadelphia: J. P. Lippincott Company, 1950), 267–68.
9. Harold Ickes, Personal Diary, Entry of April 28, 1945, Franklin D. Roosevelt Presidential Library and Museum, Hyde Park, New York.
10. Daniels, *The Man of Independence*, 266.
11. Bernard Asbell, *When F.D.R. Died* (New York: Holt, Rinehart and Winston, 1961), 185.
12. "The Regular Guys," *Time* (August 12, 1946): 17.
13. Joseph Gies, *Franklin D. Roosevelt: Portrait of a President* (Garden City, NY: Doubleday & Company, 1971), 2.
14. David McCullough, *Truman* (New York: Simon & Schuster, 1993), 365.
15. Ibid., 388.
16. Robert G. Nixon, Harry S. Truman Library "Oral History" series interview, October 19, 1970.
17. Edwin A. Locke, Harry S. Truman Library "Oral History" series interview, April 4, 1967.
18. Ibid.
19. Nixon, "Oral History" series interview.
20. "The Regular Guys," 17.
21. Daniels, *The Man of Independence*, 266–67.
22. Ibid., 306.
23. Gies, *Franklin D. Roosevelt: Portrait of a President*, 88.
24. Daniels, *The Man of Independence*, 306.
25. McCullough, *Truman*, 364.
26. "Reconversion" had been added to the war mobilizer's official title in October of 1944.
27. McCullough, *Truman*, 300.
28. Nixon, "Oral History" series interview.
29. McCullough, *Truman*, 138.
30. Richard Rhodes, *The Making of the Atomic Bomb* (New York: Simon & Schuster, 1986), 597.
31. Gordon Thomas and Max Morgan Witts, *Enola Gay* (New York: Stein and Day, 1977), 95.
32. Rhodes, *Making of the Atomic Bomb*, 597.
33. McCullough, *Truman*, 400.
34. Rhodes, *Making of the Atomic Bomb*, 596. Curtis LeMay would go on to publish an autobiography in 1965 titled *Mission With LeMay: My Story*.
35. Harry S. Truman, *Off the Record: The Private Papers of Harry S. Truman*, ed. Robert H. Ferrell (New York: Harper & Row, 1980), 47.

36. Peter Wyden, *Day One: Before Hiroshima and After* (New York: Simon & Schuster, 1984), 131.
37. James F. Byrnes, *All in One Lifetime* (New York: Harper & Brothers, 1958), 248.
38. James F. Byrnes, *Speaking Frankly* (New York: Harper & Brothers, 1947), 257.
39. David Robertson, *Sly and Able: A Political Biography of James F. Byrnes* (New York: W. W. Norton & Co., 1994), 391.
40. Wyden, *Day One*, 131.
41. Gordon and Witts, *Enola Gay*, 89.
42. Robertson, *Sly and Able*, 403.
43. Robert H. Ferrell, *Truman: A Centenary Remembrance* (New York: Viking Press, 1984), 146.
44. Ibid.
45. Robertson, *Sly and Able*, 391.
46. The account is rather confounding. On pages 247–48 of his 1952 book, *Mr. President*, author William Hillman asserts that Truman told him he first found out about Amercia's atomic ambitions two weeks after he became president: "The secret was disclosed to me as President by James F. Byrnes, who had been Director of War Mobilization under President Roosevelt, and Fred M. Vinson, who had succeeded Byrnes." Difficult as it is to fathom Truman being kept in the dark about the bomb for two weeks into his term, Vinson's role is also a mystery. According to Truman's own diary, Vinson's first appointment at the White House was not until May 17, and by all other accounts Byrnes was alone with Truman when he told the president about the nuclear weapon. Nonetheless, that Truman voiced this account at all suggests that Vinson at least had, at some point, been admitted into the circle of those who knew about the bomb prior to its being dropped on Japan.
47. James E. St. Clair and Linda C. Gugin, *Chief Justice Fred M. Vinson of Kentucky: A Political Biography* (Lexington: The University of Kentucky Press, 2002), 143–45.
48. During this period, Fred M. Vinson had acquired the nickname "Available Vinson" for his willingness to take on most any assignment in a pinch. Versatile though the longtime Kentucky Congressman was, however, his talents were widely acknowledged to be economic and judicial far more than military.
49. Fleet Admiral William D. Leahy, *I Was There* (New York: Whittlesey House, 1950), 440.
50. Harry S. Truman, *Memoirs by Harry S. Truman, Volume One: Year of Decisions* (Garden City, NY: Doubleday & Company, 1955), 11.
51. Leahy, *I Was There*, 429.
52. Gordon and Witts, *Enola Gay*, 171.
53. Byrnes, *Speaking Frankly*, 257.
54. H. S. Truman, *Off the Record*, 53.
55. Ibid., 54.
56. Ibid., 55.
57. William D. Leahy, personal diaries, April 12–19, 1945, Collection of the Wisconsin Historical Society, Madison, Wisconsin.
58. Michael Kohl, Head of Special Collections, Clemson University Libraries, communication with author, July 16, 2008.
59. Byrnes, *Speaking Frankly*, 49.
60. "The Frederick Moore Vinson Collection, 1907–1953," catalog finding aid, University of Kentucky Libraries, Special Collections and Digital Programs, Lexington, Kentucky.
61. Matthew A. Harris, Research and Reference Coordinator, Special Collections Library of the University of Kentucky, electronic correspondence with author, October 6, 2009.

62. H. S. Truman, *Off the Record*, 19.
63. Francis Biddle, *In Brief Authority* (New York: Doubleday & Company, 1962), 363.
64. Elliott Roosevelt and James Brough, *Mother R.* (New York: G. P. Putnam's Sons, 1977), 34.
65. Pauley, "Life and Times," V-5.
66. "Trip of the President, Washington to Hyde Park, N.Y., and Return. April 14–15, 1945 (Corrected Itinerary)," Secret Service file, Franklin D. Roosevelt Presidential Library and Museum, Hyde Park, New York.
67. Pauley, "Life and Times," V-6.
68. Ibid., V-7.
69. Freeman Hubbard, "Seven Coaches Painted Black," *Railroad* (December 1962): 27.
70. Jim Bishop, *FDR's Last Year* (New York: William Morrow & Co., 1974), 661.
71. "Maragon Is Guilty of Lying to Senate," *New York Times*, April 27, 1950, 1.
72. "Little Helper," *Time* (August 15, 1949): 14.
73. "House Job 'Bumping' Denied by Maragon," *New York Times*, April 6, 1956, 46.
74. Drew Pearson, "Maragon Probe Worries Greeks," *Washington Post*, August 8, 1949, B15.
75. "Friendship & Nothing More," *Time* (September 12, 1949): 18.
76. "Little Helper," 14.
77. Nixon, "Oral History" series interview.
78. McCullough, *Truman*, 365.
79. Drew Pearson, "Washington Merry-Go-Round," *Washington Post*, March 18, 1947, 4.
80. "Friendship & Nothing More," 18.
81. Pearson, "Washington Merry-Go-Round," 4.
82. Frank S. W. Burke, Assistant Superintendent, Commanding Detective Bureau, letter dated May 3, 1933. Burke reviewed John Maragon's file for an unidentified requestor identified only as "the Major and Superintendent." The allegations against Maragon were undated but appeared "on official Police Department paper," according to Burke. Burke's report of May 3, 1933—part of the Harry H. Vaughan files currently in the Truman Presidential Library—was accompanied by a letter to Maragon from Burke dated two days later. That letter informs Maragon that his entire file, which presumably included the documents Burke referenced earlier, had been removed and destroyed.
83. Wm. H. Neblett, letter to Major General Harry H. Vaughan, April 3, 1947, Papers of Harry H. Vaughan, Harry S. Truman Library and Museum.
84. Pearson, "Maragon Probe Worries Greeks," B15.
85. Burke letter.
86. "John Maragon Refuses to Be Fingerprinted," *Washington Post*, December 8, 1929, M1.
87. Superintendent Burke's review of Maragon's police file on or about May 3, 1933, revealed an envelope marked: "Maragon, John F. Wanted 10-15-26." Inside was a memorandum indicating that Maragon was "wanted by DB for Investigation Suspicion of Murder, 10-15-26." At the time of Scriviner's murder, according to a report prepared by William H. Neblett for Colonel Vaughan on April 3, 1947, Maragon was surprised to read in the *Washington Post* that he was wanted for questioning in the case. On October 17, 1926, Maragon sent a telegram from a hotel in Miami to Henry Pratt, Washington, D.C., Chief of Detectives, asking if the department was "looking for me." Chief Pratt responded the same day with a telegram that read: "You are not wanted by this department." Maragon's presence in Miami at the time of a murder in Washington is what persuaded the authorities to take their investigation elsewhere.

88. "John Maragon Refuses to Be Fingerprinted," M1.

89. Pearson, "Maragon Probe Worries Greeks," B15.

90. "Little Helper," 14.

91. Pearson, "Washington Merry-Go-Round," 4.

92. "Little Helper," 14.

93. Daniels, *The Man of Independence*, 267.

94. Pearson, "Washington Merry-Go-Round," 4.

95. Daniels, *The Man of Independence*, 267.

96. Pearson, "Washington Merry-Go-Round," 4.

97. Harry H. Vaughan, Memorandum to Ruth Shipley, U.S. Passport Bureau, August 3, 1945.

98. H. Walton Cloke, "Truman Name Used by Vaughan to Get Maragon Passport," *New York Times*, August 26, 1949, 1.

99. Ibid.

100. J. W. Roberts, Supervising Customs Agent, Report of Seizure No. 11554, August 17, 1945, 1, Papers of Edward Foley, Jr., Harry S. Truman Library and Museum.

101. Ibid.

102. Ibid.

103. Cloke, "Truman Name Used by Vaughan to Get Maragon Passport," 1.

104. Ibid.

105. "Little Helper," 14.

106. Nixon, "Oral History" series interview.

107. "Little Helper," 14.

108. Ibid.

109. "Old Truman Friend '5%' Case Witness," *New York Times*, July 29, 1949, 10.

110. Robert J. Donovan, *Tumultuous Years: The Presidency of Harry S. Truman 1949–1953* (New York: W. W. Norton, 1982), 117–18.

111. Ibid., 115–16.

112. Ibid., 116–17.

113. H. Walton Cloke, "Senator Asks Data in Maragon Escape from Prosecution," *New York Times*, August 20, 1949, 1.

114. "Old Truman Friend '5%' Case Witness," 10.

115. "Friendship & Nothing More," 18.

116. H. Walton Cloke, "Army Flew Perfume Oil In, 5 Percenter Inquiry Hears," *New York Times*, August 23, 1949, 1.

117. Cloke, "Truman Name Used by Vaughan to Get Maragon Passport," 1.

118. Ibid.

119. "Maragon Is Guilty of Lying to Senate," 1.

120. "House Job 'Bumping' Denied by Maragon," 46.

121. Pearson, "Washington Merry-Go-Round," 4.

122. Bishop, *FDR's Last Year*, 663.

123. "Hundreds Rise Early to View Funeral Train," *New York Herald Tribune*, April 16, 1945, 4.

124. R. E. Dougherty, District Engineer of the New York Central Railroad, letter to Roosevelt attorney John M. Hackett, July 14, 1916, Franklin D. Roosevelt Presidential Library and Museum.

125. Olin Dows, *Franklin Roosevelt at Hyde Park* (New York: American Artists Group, 1949), 130.

126. Claude Wickard, personal papers, recollection of the death of F.D.R., 12, Collection of Franklin D. Roosevelt Presidential Library and Museum.

EIGHT "WHERE THE SUNDIAL STANDS"

1. "Hyde Park, Draped in Black, Awaits Arrival of Roosevelt's Body for the Burial Today," *New York Times*, April 15, 1945, 3.
2. A. J. McGehee, "Bringing the President Home," *American Heritage* (April 1995): 40.
3. Jonathan Daniels, *White House Witness, 1942–1945* (Garden City, NY: Doubleday & Company, 1975), 282.
4. A number of accounts later said that a horse-drawn caisson took the casket along the narrow dirt road that wound its way up through the woods from the railroad tracks below. This was not true. No team of horses could have pulled a 760-pound casket balanced atop an artillery caisson up a steep path furrowed with mud and tree roots.
5. Michael F. Reilly, Supervising Agent, United States Secret Service, Report of April 12, 1945, 2–3.
6. McGehee, "Bringing the President Home," 40.
7. Ibid.
8. Ibid.
9. Cadet Luther C. Campbell, Jr., letter to his mother, April 15, 1945, Franklin D. Roosevelt Presidential Library and Museum, Hyde Park, New York.
10. McGehee, "Bringing the President Home," 40.
11. Campbell, letter to his mother.
12. Letter of unidentified West Point Cadet ("Grover") to his father, April 16, 1945.
13. Ibid.
14. Campbell, Luther C., Jr., letter to his mother.
15. Robert S. Bird, "Roosevelt Is Buried in Hyde Park Garden," *New York Herald Tribune*, April 16, 1945, 1.
16. Ibid.
17. John G. Rogers, "At a Grave in a Rose Garden: The Nation Buries Its President," *New York Herald Tribune*, April 16, 1945, 1.
18. McGehee, "Bringing the President Home," 40.
19. William D. Hassett, *Off the Record with F.D.R.* (New Brunswick, NJ: Rutgers University Press, 1958), 343.
20. Robert G. Nixon, Harry S. Truman Library "Oral History" series interview, October 19, 1970, Harry S. Truman Library and Museum, Independence, Missouri.
21. Bird, "Roosevelt Is Buried in Hyde Park Garden," 1.
22. Ibid.
23. Tom McGann, "Funerals of the Famous: Franklin Delano Roosevelt—Part II," *American Funeral Director* (September 1992): 54.
24. Bernard Asbell, *When F.D.R. Died* (New York: Holt, Rinehart and Winston, 1961), 197.
25. "State Approves Burial on Estate," *Poughkeepsie New Yorker*, April 14, 1945.
26. Hassett, *Off the Record with F.D.R.*, 343.
27. Frank L. Kluckhohn, "Roosevelt Is Buried with Solemn Rites," *New York Times*, April 16, 1945, 1.
28. Hassett, *Off the Record with F.D.R.*, 344.
29. Note on Treasury Department letterhead regarding arrival of Prime Minister Mackenzie King dated April 15, 1945, Secret Service file, Franklin D. Roosevelt Presidential Library and Museum.

30. "Mackenzie King Attends Rites at Hyde Park," International News Service wire story, April 15, 1945.

31. Hassett, *Off the Record with F.D.R.*, 344.

32. Christine Sadler, "Roosevelt's Body Laid to Rest in Garden of His Birthplace," *Washington Post*, April 16, 1945, 1.

33. "Don't Drape Buildings, WPB Asks of Cities," *Washington Post*, April 14, 1945, 4.

34. Rogers, "At a Grave in a Rose Garden," 1.

35. Alonzo Fields, *My 21 Years in the White House* (New York: Coward-McCann, 1961), 116–117.

36. "President's Cousin Takes Fala to Burial Service," *New York Herald Tribune*, April 16, 1945, 4.

37. Ted Morgan, *FDR: A Biography* (New York: Simon & Schuster, 1985), 770.

38. Bird, "Roosevelt Is Buried in Hyde Park Garden," 1.

39. McGehee, "Bringing the President Home," 40.

40. Hassett, *Off the Record with F.D.R.*, 344.

41. Kluckhohn, "Roosevelt Is Buried with Solemn Rites," 1.

42. Jim Bishop, *FDR's Last Year* (New York: William Morrow & Co., 1974), 667.

43. Elliott Roosevelt and James Brough, *Mother R.* (New York: G. P. Putnam's Sons, 1977), 35.

44. Hassett, *Off the Record with F.D.R.*, 345.

45. Kluckhohn, "Roosevelt Is Buried with Solemn Rites," 1.

46. "Fala Present at Burial of Master at Hyde Park," *Baltimore Sun*, April 16, 1945, 5.

47. Margaret Suckley, *Closest Companion: The Unknown Story of the Intimate Relationship Between Franklin Roosevelt and Margaret Suckley*, ed. Geoffrey C. Ward (Boston: Houghton Mifflin, 1995), 422.

NINE   HOMEWARD

1. "Trip of the President, Washington to Hyde Park, N.Y., and Return. April 14–15, 1945. (Corrected Itinerary.)" Secret Service file, Franklin D. Roosevelt Presidential Library and Museum.

2. James V. Forrestal, Personal Diary, Entry of April 15, 1945. The Seeley G. Mudd Manuscript Library, Princeton University, Princeton, New Jersey.

3. Frank L. Kluckhohn, "Roosevelt Is Buried with Solemn Rites," *New York Times*, April 16, 1945, 1.

4. Robert G. Nixon, Harry S. Truman Library "Oral History" series interview, October 19, 1970, Harry S. Truman Library and Museum, Independence, Missouri.

5. Ibid.

6. Jim Bishop, *FDR's Last Year* (New York: William Morrow & Company, 1974), 669.

7. "Springwood," in *The Great Estates Region of the Hudson Valley*, ed. McKelden Smith (Tarrytown, NY: Historic Hudson Valley Press, 1998), 53.

8. Kluckhohn, "Roosevelt Is Buried with Solemn Rites," 1.

9. William C. Murphy, Jr., "Roosevelt Is Buried in Garden at Hyde Park," *Philadelphia Inquirer*, April 16, 1945, 1.

10. Ibid. The report of Secret Service agent Mike Reilly also makes clear that while the coffin had been offloaded at the foot of the estate, the funeral train departed from the depot at Hyde Park. William Hassett's journal confirms this arrangement as well.

11. Harry S. Truman, *Off the Record: The Private Papers of Harry S. Truman*, ed. Robert H. Ferrell (New York: Harper & Row, 1980), 19.

12. Harry S. Truman, *Memoirs by Harry S. Truman, Volume One: Year of Decisions* (Garden City, NY: Doubleday & Company, 1955), 19.

13. Murphy, "Roosevelt Is Buried in Garden at Hyde Park," 1.

14. Elliott Roosevelt and James Brough, *Mother R.* (New York: G. P. Putnam's Sons, 1977), 36.

15. Doris Kearns Goodwin, *No Ordinary Time* (New York: Simon & Schuster, 1994), 209.

16. "First Kids," The White House Historical Association, www.whitehousehistory. org.

17. Goodwin, *No Ordinary Time*, 617.

18. Ibid.

19. John Whitcomb and Claire Whitcomb, Real Life at the White House (New York: Routledge, 2000), 322.

20. The rats were, if anything, a harbinger of far worse problems with the White House, whose original wooden beams had been mercilessly heaped upon by 150 years' worth of renovations and additions. After the leg of Margaret Truman's grand piano punched through the parquet and the president's own bathroom floor began to sink while he was in the tub, Truman ordered a thorough investigation of the mansion's structural integrity. The report came back that the White House was in imminent danger of collapse. The Trumans moved back to Blair House in late 1948 while the White House was thoroughly gutted and rebuilt from within.

21. Elliott Roosevelt and Brough, *Mother R.*, 35–36.

22. William D. Hassett, *Off the Record with F.D.R.* (New Brunswick, NJ: Rutgers University Press, 1958), 346.

23. A possibility also exists that the *Conneaut* was left behind entirely. On the route up to Hyde Park, the funeral train had numbered eighteen cars. A page-three story in *The New York Times* of April 16 noted that the funeral train, as it pulled into Penn Station on its return to Washington, consisted of only seventeen cars. Assuming the reporter counted correctly, the missing car might well have been the *Conneaut*.

24. Henry Morgenthau, Personal Diary, Entry of April 16, 1945, The New York Public Library, New York, New York.

25. Report of Michael F. Reilly, Supervising Agent, United States Secret Service, April 12, 1945, 2–3.

26. Francis Biddle, *In Brief Authority* (Garden City, NY: Doubleday & Company, 1962), 363.

27. Ibid.

28. Roy Jenkins. *Franklin Delano Roosevelt* (New York: Times Books, 2003), 33.

29. "Josephus Daniels," *Encyclopedia of the State Library of North Carolina*, http:// statelibrary.ncdcr.gov.

30. Biddle, *In Brief Authority*, 364.

31. Ibid.

32. Henry Wallace, *Miscellaneous Recollections of the Interment Train* (Iowa City: Friends of the University of Iowa Libraries, 1974), 13.

33. James E. St. Clair and Linda C. Gugin, *Chief Justice Fred M. Vinson of Kentucky: A Political Biography* (Lexington: University of Kentucky Press, 2002), 128.

34. Claude Wickard, personal papers, recollection of the death of F.D.R., 14, Collection of Franklin D. Roosevelt Presidential Library and Museum.

35. William D. Leahy, *I Was There* (New York: Whittlesey House, 1950), 345.
36. Ibid., 346.
37. Ibid., 344.
38. Morgenthau, Personal Diary, entry of April 16, 1945.
39. Ibid.
40. Jonathan Daniels, *The Man of Independence* (Philadelphia: J. P. Lippincott Company, 1950), 305.
41. Harold Ickes, Personal Diary, entry of April 29, 1945, Collection of the Franklin D. Roosevelt Presidential Library and Museum.
42. Claude Wickard, personal papers, Recollection of the Death of F.D.R., 15.
43. "President's First Message Is Composed Aboard Train," *Washington Post*, April 16, 1945, 1.
44. Ibid.
45. Steve Neal, ed., *Eleanor and Harry* (New York: Scribner, 2002), 15.
46. Ibid., 17.
47. "Eleanor Roosevelt and Civil Rights," The Eleanor Roosevelt National Historic Site, www.nps.gov/elro.
48. Harry S. Truman, *Memoirs by Harry S. Truman, Volume One: Year of Decisions* (Garden City, NY: Doubleday & Company, 1955), 36.
49. Elliott Roosevelt and Brough, *Mother R.*, 39.
50. Ibid.
51. Julia Solis, *New York Underground: The Anatomy of a City* (New York: Routledge, 2005), 114. The catalyst for the banning of steam locomotives in Manhattan was a January 1902 rear-end collision between two trains in the New York Central Railroad's Park Avenue Tunnel. The culprit was accumulated locomotive exhaust that had obscured the engineer's view of the signals. Seventeen died, and many more suffered smoke inhalation. Pennsylvania Railroad president Alexander Cassatt had, however, been committed to electrifying the tracks leading in and out of his new Pennsylvania Station long before the 1908 law appeared on the books. The river tunnels to the west and east of Penn Station that the FDR funeral train would use had been equipped with electric traction since their opening in 1910.
52. "Many Wait to See Truman in N.Y.," *Baltimore Sun*, April 16, 1945, 8.
53. Wallace, *Miscellaneous Recollections*, 15.
54. Morgenthau, Personal Diary, entry of April 16, 1945.
55. Ibid.
56. Whitcomb, *Real Life at the White House*, 303.
57. Goodwin, *No Ordinary Time*, 175.
58. Morgenthau, Personal Diary, entry of April 16, 1945.
59. Ibid.
60. Ibid.
61. Elliott Roosevelt and Brough, *Mother R.*, 54.
62. Ibid., 54–55.
63. Morgenthau, Personal Diary, entry of April 16, 1945.
64. Ickes, Personal Diary, entry of April 29, 1945.
65. Joseph P. Lash, *A World of Love: Eleanor Roosevelt and Her Friends, 1943–1962* (Garden City, NY: Doubleday & Company, 1984), 184–85.
66. Lansing Warren, "Truman Drafts Speech for Today," *New York Times*, April 16, 1945, 1.
67. Biddle, *In Brief Authority*, 364.

68. Margaret Truman, *Harry S. Truman* (New York: William Morrow & Company, 1973), 213.
69. Robert H. Jackson, *That Man: An Insider's Portrait of Franklin D. Roosevelt* (New York: Oxford University Press, 2003), 167.
70. M. Truman, *Harry S. Truman*, 224.
71. Wallace, *Miscellaneous Recollections*, 17.
72. Edwin W. Pauley, "The Life and Times of Edwin W. Pauley," manuscript in the holdings of the Harry S. Truman Library and Museum, V-9, Independence, Missouri.
73. Ickes, Personal Diary, entry of April 29, 1945.
74. Anthony Leviero, "Pauley Oil Offer 'Rawest' Ever Put to Him, Ickes Says," *New York Times*, February 6, 1946, 1.
75. Wolfgang Saxon, "Edwin Wendell Pauley Sr., 78," *New York Times*, July 29, 1981, A19.
76. Daniels, *Man of Independence*, 304–5.
77. Ickes, Personal Diary, entry of April 29, 1945.
78. Leviero, "Pauley Oil Offer 'Rawest' Ever Put to Him, Ickes Says," 1.
79. Ickes, Personal Diary, entry of April 29, 1945.
80. "James Roosevelt Delayed in Flight," *New York Times*, April 16, 1945, 3.
81. Arthur Halliburton, "James Roosevelt Loses Race to Attend Funeral," *New York Herald Tribune*, April 16, 1945, 1.
82. James Roosevelt and Sidney Shalett, *Affectionately, F.D.R.: A Son's Story of a Lonely Man* (New York: Harcourt, Brace & Co., 1959), 366.
83. Ibid.
84. Ibid.
85. Halliburton, "James Roosevelt Loses Race to Attend Funeral," 1.
86. "James Roosevelt Delayed in Flight," 3.
87. The newspapers reported that the train was fifty minutes late. It was not. The reporters had probably been using an earlier schedule. The latest revision plainly slated the train to arrive at 4:11—making POTUS, in fact, early. It would leave on time, too, at 4:26 P.M.
88. Wickard, personal papers, recollection of the death of F.D.R., 16.
89. Pauley, "Life and Times," V-10.
90. H. S. Truman, *Memoirs by Harry S. Truman, Volume One: Year of Decisions*, 36.
91. "President's First Message Is Composed Aboard Train," 1.
92. Ibid.
93. Warren, "Truman Drafts Speech for Today," 1.
94. It's anyone's guess what Allen might have said about Pauley's subsequent claim—in memoirs that were never published—that he had been responsible for much of the speech. In Chapter 5, p. 7, of his memoirs, the oil baron would humbly pronounce that "I certainly don't claim the speech as any masterpiece."
95. George E. Allen, *Presidents Who Have Known Me* (New York: Simon & Schuster, 1960), 165.
96. Allen placed this incident at "one of the stops en route from Hyde Park to Washington" (p. 165), although it's overwhelmingly likely that that stop was New York City. Penn Station was the only stop that afforded a sufficient amount of time for passengers to take a leisurely break on the platform. The only other stop of considerable length was for the engine change at Mott Haven in the Bronx—where there was no platform and, in all likelihood, passengers were not even permitted off the train.
97. Allen, *Presidents Who Have Known Me*, 165.

98. Halliburton, "James Roosevelt Loses Race to Attend Funeral," 1.
99. James Roosevelt and Shalett, *Affectionately, F.D.R.*, 366.
100. Ibid.
101. Ibid., 366–67.
102. Ibid., 367.
103. In her memoirs, Grace Tully recalled only that FDR's funeral memorandum "was found" in his bedroom safe, but not by whom. Similarly, biographer Bernard Asbell notes on p. 197 of *When FDR Died* that the four-page document "was found in the safe in his bedroom"—again, the discoverer is not revealed.
104. Franklin D. Roosevelt, "In the event of my death . . .," Transcription of FDR's handwritten final wishes, December 26, 1937, The Franklin D. Roosevelt Presidential Library and Museum.
105. Ibid.
106. Hassett, *Off the Record with F.D.R.*, 346.
107. Leahy, *I Was There*, 346.
108. Lash, *A World of Love*, 186.
109. Elliott Roosevelt and Brough, *Mother R.*, 35.
110. "A Still Smiling Mrs. Roosevelt," Press Association (U.K.) photograph caption, April 15, 1945, author's collection.
111. "U.S. at War: Bugler: Sound Taps," *Time* (April 23, 1945): 19.
112. "President's First Message Is Composed Aboard Train," 1.

TEN   "WE DO NOT FEAR THE FUTURE"

1. Margaret Truman, *Harry S. Truman* (New York: William Morrow & Company, 1973), 220, 225.
2. Edwin W. Pauley, "The Life and Times of Edwin W. Pauley," The Harry S. Truman Library and Museum, V-10, Independence, Missouri.
3. Bert Andrews, "Truman Firm on Unconditional Surrender," *New York Herald Tribune*, April 17, 1945, 16.
4. Ibid.
5. Frank L. Kluckhohn, "Truman Asks World Unity to Keep Peace," *New York Times*, April 17, 1945, 12.
6. "Address Heard by 16,850,000," *Los Angeles Times*, April 17, 1945, 9.
7. Robert H. Ferrell, *Truman: A Centenary Remembrance* (New York: The Viking Press, 1984), 161.
8. Kluckhohn, "Truman Asks World Unity to Keep Peace," 12.
9. Ibid.
10. M. Truman, *Harry S. Truman*, 224.
11. "Truman Starts Speech Before He's Introduced," *New York Herald Tribune*, April 17, 1945, 16.
12. "President Truman's Address Before a Joint Session of the Congress," April 16, 1945, transcript, Harry S. Truman Library, http://www.trumanlibrary.org/ww2/stofunio.htm. All quotes herein taken from Truman's address are drawn from this document.
13. Andrews, "Truman Firm on Unconditional Surrender," 16.
14. Ibid.
15. David McCullough, *Truman* (New York: Simon & Schuster, 1993), 360.
16. Kluckhohn, "Truman Asks World Unity to Keep Peace," 12.

17. "Mrs. Truman in Tears," *New York Times*, April 17, 1945, 13.
18. "Congress Acclaim Won by Truman," *New York Times*, April 17, 1945, 17.
19. "Truman Speech Evokes General Commendation," *New York Herald Tribune*, April 17, 1945, 16.
20. "Congress Acclaim Won by Truman," 17.
21. Ibid.
22. Ibid.
23. "Truman Speech Evokes General Commendation," 16.
24. "The President's Address," *New York Times*, April 17, 1945, 22.
25. "We Do Not Fear the Future," *Time* (April 23, 1945): 17.
26. "The President's Address," 22.
27. "First Speech," *Washington Post*, April 17, 1945, 8.
28. "President Truman's Good Start," *Los Angeles Times*, April 17, 1945, A4.
29. "The Faith," *Newsweek* (April 23, 1945): 27.
30. "Truman's Mother, 92, Hears Speech," *New York Times*, April 17, 1945, 13.
31. "The Buck Stops Here Desk Sign," Harry S. Truman Library and Museum, www.trumanlibrary.org/buckstop.htm.
32. Jonathan Daniels, *The Man of Independence* (Philadelphia: J. B. Lippincott Company, 1950), 268.
33. Harry S. Truman, *Memoirs by Harry S. Truman, Volume One: Year of Decisions* (Garden City, NY: Doubleday & Company, 1955), 422.
34. Gordon Thomas and Max Morgan Witts, *Enola Gay* (New York: Stein and Day, 1977), 133.
35. Ibid.
36. Peter Wyden, *Day One: Before Hiroshima and After* (New York: Simon and Schuster, 1984), 294.
37. H. S. Truman, *Memoirs by Harry S. Truman, Volume One: Year of Decisions*, 419.
38. Ibid.
39. Harry S. Truman, *Off the Record: The Private Papers of Harry S. Truman*, ed. Robert H. Ferrell (New York: Harper & Row, 1980), 304.
40. Miller Center of Public Affairs, University of Virginia, "Harry S. Truman (1884–1972), Domestic Affairs," The American President: An Online Reference Resource, http://millercenter.org.
41. Ferrell, *Truman: A Centenary Remembrance*, 173.
42. "Inaugural Address of the President," Washington, D.C., March 4, 1933. National Archives and Records Administration, www.archives.gov.

EPILOGUE

1. "Mrs. Roosevelt Dies at 78 After Illness of Six Weeks," *New York Times*, November 8, 1962, 1.
2. Drummond Ayres, Jr., "Truman 33D President, is Dead," *New York Times*, December 27, 1972, 1.
3. Albin Krebs, "Anna Roosevelt Halsted, President's Daughter, Dies," *New York Times*, December 2, 1975, 42.
4. Martin Weil, "Elliott Roosevelt, 80, Writer," *Washington Post*, October 28, 1990, B7.
5. Robert D. McFadden, "John A. Roosevelt, Youngest Son of Late President, is Dead at 65," *New York Times*, April 28, 1981, B18.

6. Lawrence Van Gelder, "Margaret Truman Daniel, President's Daughter and Popular Author, Dies at 83," *New York Times*, January 30, 2008, B6.

7. Glenn Fowler, "Margaret Suckley, 99, Archivist and Aide to Franklin Roosevelt," *New York Times*, July 2, 1991, D18.

8. Tom McGann, "Funerals of the Famous: Franklin Delano Roosevelt—Part II," *American Funeral Director* (September 1992): 63.

9. "Laura F. Delano Is Dead; Dog Show Judge was 86," *New York Times*, January 28, 1972, 40.

10. Wolfgang Saxon, "Elizabeth Shoumatoff, 92, Dead; Painted Portraits of 2 Presidents," *New York Times*, December 1, 1980, D13.

11. "Mrs. W. Rurtherfurd," *New York Times*, August 1, 1948, 56.

12. Joseph D. Whitaker, "Grace Tully, Secretary, Confidante of FDR, Dies," *Washington Post*, June 16, 1984, B4.

13. "A. S. Prettyman Dies," *New York Times*, February 5, 1957, 23.

14. Crispin Y. Campbell, "Memoirs of a Porter Aboard the Presidential Pullman," *Washington Post*, March 3, 1983, D.C.3.

15. Edward T. Folliard, "W. D. Hassett, Aide to FDR, Truman," *Washington Post*, August 31, 1965, B4.

16. "Jonathan Daniels Dies; Editor, Press Secretary to Roosevelt," *Washington Post*, November 7, 1981, B6.

17. "Josephus Daniels," *Encyclopedia of the State Library of North Carolina*, http://statelibrary.ncdcr.gov. (See also www.ussjosephusdaniels.com.)

18. Norimitsu Onishi, "Howard Bruenn, 90, Roosevelt's Doctor in Last Year of Life," *New York Times*, August 2, 1995, D20.

19. "McIntire Terms FDR 'Strong Man' at Yalta," *Washington Post and Times Herald*, March 24, 1955, 4.

20. "Admiral M'Intire Dead in Chicago," *New York Times*, December 9, 1959, 45.

21. "Dr. James Paullin of Atlanta, Was 69," *New York Times*, August 15, 1951, 24.

22. Jack Allen, grandson of Fred Patterson, e-mail correspondence with author, July 14, 2009.

23. Jonathan Daniels, *The Man of Independence* (Philadelphia: J. B. Lippincott Company, 1950), 309–10.

24. "James Byrnes Dies at 92; Was 'Assistant President,'" *New York Times*, April 10, 1972, 1.

25. Anthony Leviero, "Pauley Oil Offer 'Rawest' Ever Put to Him, Ickes Says," *New York Times*, February 6, 1946, 1.

26. Daniels, *The Man of Independence*, 304.

27. Wolfgang Saxon, "Edwin Wendell Pauley Sr., 78," *New York Times*, July 29, 1981, A19.

28. "Harold L. Ickes Dead at 77; Colorful Figure in New Deal," *New York Times*, February 4, 1952, 1.

29. "Henry Agard Wallace, 33rd Vice President (1941–1945)," The United States Senate, www.senate.gov.

30. "Henry A. Wallace Is Dead at 77; Ex-Vice President, Plant Expert," *New York Times*, November 19, 1965, 1.

31. "Claude Wickard Killed in Crash," *New York Times*, April 30, 1967, 87.

32. "Henry Morgenthau Jr., 75, Dies; Secretary of Treasury, 1934–45," *New York Times*, February 7, 1967, 1.

33. "Fleet Admiral Leahy Dies at 84; Presidents' Chief of Staff in War," *New York Times*, July 21, 1959, 1.

34. "Robert Hannegan Dies in Home at 46," *New York Times*, October 7, 1949, 27.
35. "George Allen, Presidents' Crony, Dies," *New York Times*, April 24, 1973, 44.
36. "Merriman Smith Is Dead at 57, an Apparent Suicide," *New York Times*, April 14, 1970, 47.
37. "Lauchlin Currie, 91; New Deal Economist Was Roosevelt Aide," *New York Times*, December 30, 1993, B6.
38. "John Maragon Is Ousted as Employe [*sic*] of House," *New York Times*, April 1, 1959, 12.
39. *The Complete Roster of Heavyweight Pullman Cars* (New York: Wayner Publications, 1985), 148–52.
40. Ibid., 129.
41. Ibid., 96.
42. Ibid., 97.
43. Fred Heatley, "461. Strates Show, FDR Funeral Car," posted message of March 4, 2005, www.circushistory.org.
44. American Society of Mechanical Engineers, *Pullman Sleeping Car Glengyle: A National Historic Mechanical Engineering Landmark* (Dallas: Author, 1987), 8.
45. National Museum of American History, "Steam Locomotive, Southern Railway No. 1401," Smithsonian Institution, http://americanhistory.si.edu.
46. Bob Adler, McCormick-Stillman Railroad Park, e-mail message to author, October 14, 2008. See also www.therailroadpark.com.
47. United States Department of the Interior, National Park Service, "National Historic Landmark Nomination: U.S. Car #1/Ferdinand Magellan," Washington, D.C., June 18, 1984, 8.
48. "Presidential Rail Car U.S. No. 1," Gold Coast Railroad Museum, http://gcrm.org/magellan.aspx.

INDEX

244 INDEX